The Emotional Side of Organizations

Applications of Bowen Theory

Georgetown Family Center

Washington, DC

The papers in this publication were originally presented at the Conference on Organizations sponsored by the Georgetown Family Center April 22-23, 1995.

Conference Organizers: Patricia A. Comella, Joyce Bader,
Judith S. Ball, and Kathleen K. Wiseman

The Emotional Side of Organizations is published by the Georgetown Family Center

Managing Editor: Ruth Riley Sagar
Design and Production: Elizabeth M. Utschig

Reprinted March 1999

ISBN 0-9658540-1-9

Printed in the United States of America

The Emotional Side of Organizations

Applications of Bowen Theory

Papers Presented at the Georgetown Family Center's Conference on Organizations, April 22-23, 1995

Edited by Patricia A. Comella, Joyce Bader, Judith S. Ball, Kathleen K. Wiseman and Ruth Riley Sagar

ACKNOWLEDGEMENTS

In 1981 the Georgetown Family Center convened a meeting where eight presenters shared their thinking and experience about the application of Bowen family systems theory to the workplace. Organizational consultants, chief executive officers, managers, and faculty from the Georgetown Family Center presented papers. These papers, along with several that had been presented at a conference on organizations in 1978, were edited by Ruth Sagar and me. This collection of papers became known as the "little red book" or more formally, *Understanding Organizations*. This publication was an effort at the Georgetown Family Center to commit to writing the thinking about human functioning in the workplace. Since that time, others have thought about and written about the workplace and the application of Bowen theory. In April 1995, twenty-eight people presented their thinking at the third conference on organizations. I believe this ongoing inquiry about human functioning at the workplace will lead to greater effectiveness for those of us who consult to work systems and improved productivity for those who work in organizations.

The effort to organize the 1995 conference, to write the papers and to edit and publish the proceedings was itself a demonstration of productivity and effectiveness. For each of the participants in the conference, this effort was an extra responsibility added to the demands of an already complex work life. A special thank you—to all the conference presenters who made and continue to make the effort to apply theory in the real world, to the three co-organizers who demonstrated that togetherness does not have to adversely affect individual productivity, to Dr. Michael Kerr and the faculty of the Family Center who have supported this ongoing effort, to Ruth Riley Sagar who managed the editing of this publication, to Elizabeth M. Utschig whose book design, diligence, and attention to detail made this publication possible, to my own family whose presence makes it all worthwhile and, of course, to Murray Bowen, MD, whose vision and intellectual rigor described a theory that continually challenges us all.

Kathleen K. Wiseman

March 12, 1996
Washington, DC

FOREWORD

Murray Bowen developed *family systems theory* from research he conducted between the late 1940s and early 1960s. He published the theory in 1966, and continued to amplify and extend it until his death in 1990. Bowen studied families with the full range of human problems, well-functioning families, and various types of nonfamily groups. He also read extensively in many disciplines, especially the natural sciences. These family studies and background reading are the basis of the theory.

Bowen theory is distinct from psychoanalytic theory. Freud's basic ideas have dominated thinking about human behavior through most of this century. They have infiltrated the popular culture to the point most people are unaware of their origin. A basic tenet of the psychoanalytic model is that an individual's psychopathology is what causes the various psychiatric disorders. The psychopathology is a product of traumatic or otherwise disturbed childhood experiences. Treatment aims at bringing unconscious conflicts and their associated feelings into awareness, thus allowing expression of the feelings and resolution of the conflicts. Freud studied individual patients, and not families or other groups, but many efforts have been made to extend his ideas to explain how family and nonfamily groups function.

Bowen theory makes two quantum leaps beyond psychoanalytic theory. One leap is to expand the observing lens from the individual to the "emotional unit." Families function as emotional units in that the relationship system governs individual functioning as much as forces within individuals govern their functioning. For example, one family member's clinical symptoms reflect something about how the whole family is functioning, not just how the "patient" is functioning. A second leap is to broaden concepts about emotionality to include man's relationship to all life. In other words, because of a common evolutionary heritage, the "dance of life" in the human species is far more similar to the "dance of life" in other species than is generally recognized. Man's large brain notwithstanding, human relationship systems follow the laws of all natural systems.

Bowen saw early in his research that the "patterns of emotional functioning" present in human families existed in nonfamily groups as well. For example, staff and patients on a psychiatric ward can function as an emotional unit, with conflicts between staff members manifesting in increased symptoms in the patients; families treated in a mental health center can get worse in response to anxiety in the center's staff; tensions within a department of a medical school can fuel the "scapegoating" of a faculty or staff member to the point of seriously undermining his functioning. Eventually, Bowen and others knowledgeable about his theory observed that emotional processes can affect the functioning of large organizations, even whole societies.

Probably more is known about the application of family systems theory to families than to nonfamily groups, especially large groups. This discrepancy in knowledge is a product of legions of therapists having applied the theory to clinical work, but, to date, fewer people have applied it to organizational consulting or societal issues. This is changing as more people are recognizing that Bowen theory applies to more than human families.

Over the years, the Georgetown Family Center has sponsored a number of meetings on applying Bowen theory to organizations, but the conference spawning this proceedings was the most ambitious thus far. Bowen characterized the early years of the family movement as a "healthy unstructured state of chaos." People were going in many new directions, some of which would prove to be productive and others not, but the overall thrust would be constructive. Such a characterization may fit the current period of extending the theory to organizations. The application of natural systems thinking to human behavior could eventually be recognized as a critical turning point in man's understanding of himself, a shift in paradigms with enormous practical implications.

Michael E. Kerr

March 10, 1996
Washington, DC

PREFACE

In 1982, the Georgetown University Family Center published *Understanding Organizations: Applications of Bowen Family Systems Theory*. The publication developed from two conferences which the Family Center sponsored on the application of the theory to organizations, one in December 1978 and the other in December 1981. It also represented long-standing interest in developing and applying family systems theory in the workplace.

This interest continued when the Family Center became administratively separate from the Georgetown University Medical School, incorporating in the District of Columbia as the Georgetown Family Center in 1990, an independent, non-profit educational institution. In 1993, Dr. Michael Kerr, Director of the Family Center, invited individuals interested in the application of Bowen family systems theory to organizations to participate in periodic meetings at the Family Center devoted exclusively to this application. Meetings began in June 1993. By March 1994, there had been nine meetings covering wide ranging questions about the emotional side of organizations. The meetings provided an opportunity to review and think about current trends in the workplace and to hear case presentations about a variety of organizations. Themes began to emerge from these meetings and discussions which suggested areas for fruitful activity and development.

Four of the participants in the meetings (Joyce Bader, Judith S. Ball, Patricia A. Comella and Kathleen K. Wiseman) began to hold meetings to consider the implications of the themes for future directions. They came to propose to Dr. Kerr a conference and proceedings on the application of Bowen family systems theory to organizations and other social systems. The conference and proceedings, if approved, would be a step along the way to fuller development of the application of Bowen family systems theory to social systems other than the human family. They would reflect work in progress.

The faculty of the Family Center approved the proposal, and planning of the conference proceeded. The four sponsors of the proposal became the co-organizers of the conference and, along with Ruth Riley Sagar of the Georgetown Family Center, co-editors of the proceedings.

Twenty-seven papers comprise the proceedings. They are organized into seven sections, entitled:

- "Theoretical Considerations"
- "The Organization as an Emotional System"
- "Human Social Systems"
- "Defining a Self within Social Systems"
- "Case Studies"
- "Practitioners"
- "Nonhuman Social Systems."

For each section there is an introduction which places the papers into context and offers a theoretical perspective on the general theme of the section. Excerpts from an interview between Dr. Bowen and Kathleen Wiseman complete the introduction.

The papers and the introductory pieces to the sections are viewed as works in progress. Indeed, the conference organizers and editors of this proceedings believe that any application of Bowen family systems theory is likely to be a work in progress. Consistent with this view, the conference organizers and editors expect the application of the theory to continue to evolve, and to provide continuing opportunities for those with a natural systems perspective to contribute.

What is a work in progress? An application of Bowen family systems theory to the understanding of human social systems is a work in progress. So is an application of Bowen family systems theory to use the new part of the brain—the intellect—to see and understand the old, automatic part of the brain as it makes its decisions. So is an application of the theory to the task of becoming a more responsible self in the social systems of which one is a part. Each advance in understanding a social system, or in observing and understanding the automatic side of functioning, or in apprehending one's own contribution to system functioning has the potential to offer new possibilities to the individual: new vistas where more choices come into view, where there is more flexibility to choose, and where increased cooperation and coordination in functioning as a responsible member of a social system become possible. The incremental changes, minor though they may be when viewed in isolation, are cumulative in effect. These cumulative effects may stimulate the individual to continue to seek new vistas; hence, the term "work in progress"—and the promise of applying a natural systems theory to understanding the human species as part of life on Earth.

Another term for "work in progress" might be "odyssey." Dr. Bowen (1913-1990) spent over forty years of his life working to understand how the human species is part of life on Earth. His theory —a natural systems theory of the human individual, the human family, and human social systems—came out of those efforts. The theory had and still has a primary application in therapy and, indeed, the therapeutic setting contributed much to development of the theory. Dr. Bowen believed that if a theory about the human was worth applying to other humans, it was worth applying to himself. In the "Epilogue" to *Family Evaluation: An Approach Based on Bowen Theory* Dr. Bowen stated:

> [The integration of theory and therapy] was part of the odyssey. There was theoretical evidence that theory might someday become a real science. Therapists could help if they could find a way to govern their thinking in a scientific direction. . . . *The theory was always first.* It governed everything that occurred. When something occurred in the therapy that had not been predicted by the theory, the error was either in the theory or in the therapist. If the error was in the theory, it was extended or modified. If the therapist was in error, it could be corrected by the precision of the theory. Considerable effort went into the integration of theory and therapy. It helped confirm the background notion that *a therapist is what his THEORY TELLS HIM TO BE.* When a therapist pays primary attention to theory, there is automatic attention to the therapist's own level of maturity. The theory and therapy then proceed in tandem, and the therapy proceeds with more sureness. (365-366)

Dr. Bowen also believed in making the theory accessible to others, but never in forcing it upon others. Videotaped and audiotaped interviews were important media for presentations about theory and its applications. In the latter part of the 1980s, Kathleen Wiseman interviewed Dr. Bowen concerning theory and family businesses. The editors have included excerpts from the interview in the introductions to the sections to illustrate points of theory or its application to the human as part of life on Earth.

Patricia A. Comella

January 4, 1996
Marshall, VA

CONTENTS

1

THEORETICAL CONSIDERATIONS

THEORETICAL CONSIDERATIONS

Introduction

Bowen family systems theory is a natural systems theory about the human family and, by extension, about the larger social systems of which human families and their members are a part. It is a theory grounded in facts. Presently, the theory has eight concepts, each of which Dr. Bowen added after determining the soundness of its factual base.

With one exception each paper presented at the Conference on Organizations and included in this proceedings is an application of Bowen family systems theory to understanding the functioning of social systems. Each of the presenters has in some way and at some level taken on the challenge of learning and thinking about and applying the theory. Some have labored for many years; some for a few years. Some have chosen to try to bring a systems perspective to thinking about the functioning of social systems; others have taken an eclectic approach, drawing upon a number of theories and models about functioning as they try to think about and interpret what they see concerning emotional process in the human species. The common denominator among the presenters is an effort to learn about systems and to make use of Bowen theory in their work.

A systems theory about the emotional side of functioning is not an easy theory to grasp or apply. In contrast to a relatively straightforward model of individual theory, a systems theory, such as Bowen theory, has a number of interrelated variables which reflect mutually influencing relationships among the system's members. Grasping and applying a systems theory of emotional functioning in its entirety often begins with a focus on one or two elements of the theory. The effort to move to a systems view of the functioning of members of a social system is particularly challenging when the move is from a useful model of individual behavior, such as Freudian theory.

Dr. Bowen, in his interview with Kathleen Wiseman, discussed these challenges:

> Now to the way people hear it, a systems theory of emotional functioning, there's a very small percentage that can hear it in a matter of months or years. It takes that long. Then there's a group, a big group of them every year [trainees at the Georgetown Family Center enrolled in various postgraduate courses concerning the theory] who work with one or two ideas within the theory.... But their comments give me evidence that they're still thinking Freudian theory.... Then there's a fair group who never appear to understand and this is average throughout our society....
>
> But operating with one or two points is a beginning. I would say that the lag

> time for civilization has gone from fifteen to twenty centuries to maybe one or two. But I do think it takes maybe two centuries for people to hear a way of thinking.

With the foregoing in mind, the editors decided to include three papers in the first section of the proceedings, entitled, "Theoretical Considerations." The three papers present perspectives on Bowen family systems theory. The goal of the section is to introduce aspects of the theory to the reader, particularly readers who may be encountering the theory for the first time.

The first paper, "A Brief Summary of Bowen Family Systems Theory," was written by Patricia A. Comella, one of the conference organizers and editors of the proceedings and a member of the faculties of the Georgetown and Princeton family centers. Originally published in *Family Center Report* (Spring 1994) it is intended to provide readers new to Bowen theory with a succinct description of the eight concepts of the theory. Many of the papers reference the concepts and the brief summary will provide a convenient guide.

The second paper is by Dr. Michael E. Kerr, Director of the Georgetown Family Center and author with Dr. Bowen of the book, *Family Evaluation, an Approach Based on Bowen Theory* (1988: W. W. Norton & Co.), as well as numerous articles concerning the theory. In his paper, entitled, "The Extension of Bowen Theory to Nonfamily Groups," Dr. Kerr places human functioning in a broad evolutionary context and reminds the reader of the emotional side of behavior and functioning in social groups.

In the third paper, Joyce Bader, another of the organizers and editors and an independent consultant to organizations, compares Bowen family systems theory to two classical theories of organizational behavior and functioning, Frederick Taylor's Scientific Management and Kurt Lewin's Action Research. The paper compares the three theories along various dimensions of a consultant's practice and discusses how Bowen theory may assist in resolving problematic aspects of a traditional consultancy.

A Note on the Interview

In the late 1980s, Kathleen Wiseman asked Dr. Bowen to discuss a series of questions she was developing on the application of theory to administrative systems, specifically family businesses. She suggested an interview format which she would audiotape for further review. At the time she was particularly interested in family businesses as the most dramatic example of family process in the workplace, but she subsequently broadened the lens to consider Dr. Bowen's comments in light of all organizational systems. Dr. Bowen encouraged her and others to make their own applications but his emphasis was always on explaining theory.

The transcript of the interview contains many statements that, had Dr. Bowen edited them, would have been explained in much more detail. Although the language and transitions are not always smooth the editors of this proceedings thought the content of the interview had such value for connecting the ideas of the various speakers, they decided to publish it.

—RRS

A BRIEF SUMMARY OF BOWEN FAMILY SYSTEMS THEORY

Patricia A. Comella, JD

Bowen family systems theory is about the emotional functioning of the human species. The theory is grounded in known facts about human functioning and about the human species as part of life on Earth.

To date, major expositions of Bowen family systems theory have inextricably bound together the presentation of the theory in the therapeutic setting. This is natural as psychotherapy provided both the context and the laboratory in which Dr. Bowen developed the concepts of family systems theory.

As more becomes known about functioning and emotional process in the human and other species, however, it is clear that the theory has and will have applications other than the psychotherapeutic. For example, the theory is being applied to understanding the role of the emotions in the course of physical diseases such as cancer and psoriasis. It is being used to understand organizational behavior and functioning. It is likely to offer insights into the behavior of other species, and it had the potential for wide application in understanding the complex societal and institutional issues of our day.

Such applications involve disciplines other than those traditionally associated with psychotherapy. It becomes desirable, therefore, to develop a statement of Bowen family systems theory which is independent of a particular application. The summary which follows is an effort to develop such a statement. Depending on the application, the statement may be amplified and illustrated with examples and discussion appropriate to the application and the audiences to whom the discussion is directed.

Presently, Bowen family systems theory is comprised of eight concepts. Each concept has been added only after its factual basis has been established. The theory postulated that the human family is a multigenerational, natural, living system and that the emotional functioning of each member of the system affects the functioning of the other members in predictable ways.

An *emotion* is the automatic response of an organism to its environment, including others with whom the organism is in relationship. A natural, living system is one that is shaped by the selective forces of nature which affect whether and how the system survives from generation to generation. Each member of a natural, living system responds to these selective forces in basic, fundamental ways; that is, in emotional ways. Emotions may be transmitted between and among individuals who are members of the system and it is through this *emotional process* that each member of a natural living system may affect the functioning of other members of the system.

Emotions organize an individual's biology. One class of emotions is captured by the term *anxiety*. *Anxiety* is the response of an organism to a threat. The threat may be imminent, in which case the response is one of *acute anxiety*. The threat may be remote and may never even occur, in which case the response is one of *chronic anxiety*, extending over an indeterminate period of time. Anxiety, including chronic anxiety, constrains the range of responsive options available and in this manner limits functioning across the full range of responses.

Sometimes an emotion, especially anxiety, is so intense and sustained that it becomes impossible to contain it within the organism or within a two-person relationship. A third person is then brought into the relationship through the operation of emotional process. This process is described in the theory by the concept of *triangles*. The process may occur repeatedly through *interlocking triangles*.

The primary triangle of an individual is with the primary caretakers, usually the parents. The individual's basic patterns of emotional response are shaped in this triangle. There is a primary triangle between the parents and each of the offspring, as well as interlocking triangles among the members of this *nuclear family emotional system*.

The variation among individuals in their basic patterns of response is described by the concept of the *scale of differentiation*. Basic patterns of response within a nuclear family emotional system will show little variation among family members. The basic level of differentiation of the offspring will be largely shaped by the basic level of differentiation of the parents. The intensity of the basic responses is a function of the unresolved emotional attachment of each of the parents to their own families of origin. This concept is described by the concept of the multigenerational emotional process. One implication of the multigenerational emotional process is that between any two generations, little variation in basic levels of differentiation is to be expected without unusual and unpredictable life circumstances.

Between the spouses, the unresolved emotional attachment will exhibit itself as emotional distance between the spouses, marital conflict, or underfunctioning in one spouse compensated by overfunctioning in the other spouse. These patterns of functioning are encompassed by the concept of the *nuclear family emotional system.*

The unresolved emotional attachment to the past generation may also take the form of transmission of the problem arising out of the unresolved attachment to the next generation. The family in which this occurs is said to be a child-focused family. When this occurs, the child who is the focus of the parent's anxiety will be less free of the multigenerational emotional process than his or her siblings. The concept, *family projection process*, describes this aspect of the nuclear family emotional process.

Siblings in a nuclear family emotional system occupy different functioning positions in the family according to their sex and birth order and according to the sex of the siblings who precede or follow them. The functioning position of the only child has unique aspects. These differences among siblings are encompassed by the concept of *sibling position.*

Individuals vary in their ability to separate themselves from the family of origin to begin their lives in the present generation and to begin the nuclear family out of which will come the next generation. The variation of ability to separate is related to the degree of unresolved emotional attachment to each of the parents in the family of origin. For example, some individuals may never leave their family of origin. Some individuals may break off contact with the families of origin altogether or maintain only superficial or sporadic contact. Others have the ability to remain in emotional contact with the family of origin while living out their lives in the present generation and rearing the next generation. The variation among individuals in accomplishing separation is encompassed by the concept of *emotional cutoff.*

Emotional process between and among individuals operates in all significant relationships. Thus, emotional process is not a phenomenon of the family alone, but a phenomenon of the larger society of which the family is a part. At different times and under different circumstances, emotional process at the societal level may be more or less intense and there may be periods of time during which societal emotional functioning is decreasing or increasing overall. These variations are described by the concept *societal emotional process.*

These eight concepts make up the theory today. As more facts about emotional process in the human species and about the human species as part of life on earth become known, the theory may change. Perhaps one day it even will be replaced by a new theory which is more accurate than the present theory.

Only when the automatic process is interrupted in some manner will the automatic outcome be changed. Out of this last implication come applications of the theory to achieve change.

THE EXTENSION OF BOWEN THEORY TO NONFAMILY GROUPS

Michael E. Kerr, MD

Mammalian families probably evolved from the protective relationship a mother provides for her young. Forming long-lasting family units seems to help the mother do a better job of protecting and feeding her offspring until they are able to provide for themselves. The mother can do a better job because she gets help, sometimes direct help with the care of the young and sometimes help because others worry about and do tasks the mother would have to do if others did not do them. This includes such things as gathering food, building and maintaining a nest, and watching out for as well as fighting predators. The young depend on the mother, the mother depends on others to help her, and others depend on the mother to hold up her end of the "bargain." This "bargain" is a contract of sorts, written in the language of evolution.

When the young grow up, pair off (those that do), mate, and have young of their own, these new units sometimes cooperate with other units in a way that enhances the survival and child rearing success of all concerned. These are usually multigenerational family units as happens with elephants, baboons, and human beings. The family's mission is clear, and cooperation is critical to meeting the objectives of survival, successful reproduction, and successful child rearing.

The creativity and initiatives taken by members of these family units are very important too. Often individuals are capable of developing a more efficient and effective way of accomplishing tasks, not just doing it the way everyone else has always done it. It can contribute much to the group, but others, of course, must decide if a novel approach to something is worth preserving or discarding. Some resistance to change is essential. Some will recall the young female monkey who was the first to wash off her sweet potatoes in salt water. Other young males and females copied her, the children taught it to their mothers, and the mothers taught it to their other children. Most adult males went to their graves without trying it. It seems the males were "wrong" on this one, but they have probably been "right" to resist change on other occasions.

Murray Bowen (1978) noted many years ago that some families seem to get the mission accomplished rather efficiently and effectively, and they seem to have a good time doing it. Other families manage to get it done, but they lose their sense of humor along the way. There is more than a modicum of weeping and gnashing of teeth and a number of the participants come up limping in one form or another. Then there are other families that are barely effective, remarkably inefficient, and accomplish little if any of the mission. He described many gradations of difference among families rather than "types" of families, or "normal" and "abnormal" families.

Organizations or institutions in human society can be thought of as extensions of families. Families spawn the people that work in them, and the organizations usually exist to support the survival and well-being of people and their families. Some organizations make diapers, which enhance the survival of the child; some make cars, which enhance the ability to procure needed resources; some make laws, which help preserve an orderly society for people to survive and rear their young in; some organizations just promote people having a good time, which obviously helps too.

Every organization or institution in society exists for one purpose or another, and each depends on people to carry out the necessary tasks. Some organizations seem to get the mission accomplished rather efficiently and effectively, and their members seem to have a good time doing it—they are "happy ships" much of the time. Other organizations manage to get their goals accomplished, more or less, but they lose their sense of humor along the way. There is more than a modicum of weeping and gnashing of teeth, and a number of the participants come up limping in one form or another (just like in families, the ones that are limping are often used to explain why the organization is not more efficient and effective). Then there are other organizations that are barely effective, remarkably inefficient, and accomplish little if any of the mission. They go out of business sooner rather than later.

Like species, some businesses extinct largely out of bad luck. There are some things an evolving species cannot anticipate, like an asteroid colliding with the earth. The cockroaches did not mind; they survived the asteroid. The dinosaurs had a good time while it lasted, but they did not survive the asteroid. On the other hand, some businesses extinct not out of bad luck, but based on the people who are the business. Many people have many ideas about what this people problem is all about. *Bowen theory anchors the explanation in emotional process.* This is not an easy idea to grasp. People may entertain the idea of emotional process on an intellectual level—talk about parallels between chimpanzees and human beings, for example,—but not *act* consistently with what they say they believe.

To think about emotional process, it may be useful to talk about some of the largest family businesses in existence, honeybee and ant colonies. Social insect colonies consist of individuals that perform different functions: the queen lays eggs and tends them, the workers gather food, work on the nest, and help with the brood, and the soldiers defend the nest. The individuals in different "castes," as they are known, often differ dramatically in structure as well as function. The system has requirements of individuals so it can accomplish its mission, but the system also allows individuals some leeway to pursue their particular interests.

E. O. Wilson (1975), in *Sociobiology: The New Synthesis*, describes some of the leeway the system allows members of the worker caste in these insect colonies, but the leeway they are granted must always be balanced by what must be accomplished for the organization to survive. Everyone depends on everyone else in an insect colony, yet flexibility and innovation are also possible. Wilson writes:

> In honeybees and in ants of the genera *Formica* and *Pogonomyrmex*, "personality" differences are strongly marked even within single castes. Some individuals, referred to by entomologists as the elites, are unusually active, perform more than their share of lifetime work, and incite others to work through facilitation. Other colony members are consistently sluggish. Although they are seemingly healthy and live long lives, their per-individual output is only a small fraction of that of the elites. Specialization also occurs. Certain individuals remain with the brood as nurses far longer than the average, while others concentrate on nest building or foraging. Yet somehow the total pattern of behavior in the colony converges on the species average. When one colony with its hundreds or thousands of members is compared with another of the same species, the statistical patterns of activity are about the same. We know that some of this consistency is due to negative feedback. As one requirement such as brood care or nest repair intensifies, workers shift their activities to compensate until the need is met, then change back again. Experiments have shown that disruption of the feedback loops, and thence deviation by the colony from the statistical norms, can be disastrous. It is therefore not surprising to find that the loops are both precise and powerful. (1975, 549)

Bowen theory refers to what Wilson is describing in insect colonies as an emotional process. One of the most obvious features of emotional process is reciprocal functioning. It is fascinating to think of a bee being temporarily diverted from what it most likes to do in order to do what must be done for the good of the group. All through nature this balance exists between individual interests and obligations to the "team." Bees and ants generally have chemical discussions about these matters rather than the verbal exchanges that characterize such discussions among human beings.

Leaving the insects, but before returning to the mammals and human beings, it may be useful to spend a little time with a fairly close group of relatives, the birds. Jonathan Weiner (1994) has written a book entitled, *The Beak of the Finch*. In it he describes research done primarily by Peter and Rosemary Grant over the past two decades. Their research has also been greatly aided by the work of graduate students over this period. The book is superb in its description of one species' emotional response to an environmental crisis, and its emotional response to times of plenty. It is much easier to be neutral about the process in birds than about what may be a similar process in our own species. Many people believe society is in a highly anxious state these days. Furthermore, what is happening in society is significantly affecting not only families, but how people are interacting in all of society's organizations and institutions.

A useful question to ask is: How much does the background anxiety of a society affect the decision-making of the society's organizations and institutions? Weiner's book describes the impact of shifts in the environment on bird families. However, family structure is such an integral part of the fabric of bird societies that changes in family structure can be expected to affect the institutions of bird society. If the family changes, the institutions change, which in turn affects the families. What is an institution in a bird society? The term is used broadly in this presentation to describe how birds manage land, how "rights" to the land are passed from one generation to the next, and, more generally, how individuals are affected by the practices of those in the larger society.

The Grants have been studying several species of finches on one of the Galapagos Islands. A long drought occurred on the island not long after the Grants began their studies. They and their co-workers carefully studied how the birds functioned during this difficult period.[1]

The species of finch in these examples is *Geospiza fortis*, which is a medium ground finch. For the most part, it makes its living by cracking open and eating seeds it finds on the ground. A key part of the Grants' research proves that evolutionary change does occur based on natural selection, which supports, of course, Darwin's theory. Darwin never saw evolution occur. He carefully documented the results of evolution, the vast spectrum of species and each one's unique adaptations, and then assumed what must have occurred to lead to those adaptations. The Grants' efforts involved making very careful measurements of the birds' beaks and of the seeds their beak size enabled them to eat.

Normally, it begins to rain in January out on the Grants' island. After it has been raining for a time, the *fortis* finches will pair up, copulate, lay eggs, and then nurture their nestlings. In the year of the long drought, however, it began to rain on schedule in January, but then it quickly stopped. Without the rain, the finches did not pair up. They responded to the unfavorable situation by focusing on staying alive.

Over the next year and a half or so, the supply of seeds on the island gradually dropped, and many birds died. Weiner describes how the birds tried fascinating new ways to open types of seeds they could previously ignore. They were down to few resources and had to improvise. The Grants were later able to show how birds with certain sized beaks were able to survive the drought, and that this change was passed with fidelity to their offspring. During this time, the birds did not bother each other very much. Occasional fights occurred over a contested seed, but they were more interested in looking for seeds and finding ways to eat them than they were interested in other birds.

As the drought continued, the population of *fortis* dropped from about 1200 to about 300. During this entire period no reproduction occurred. Due to having smaller beaks (thus access to fewer seeds), the females died much faster than the males. Consequently, near the end of the drought a 6:1 male to female ratio existed. When it finally did begin to rain, the birds began to pair up. It was very definitely a "buyer's market" for the females. Weiner writes:

> The males built nests in the cactus and sang for days on end from the highest cactus top they owned. The females hopped from territory to territory, inspecting the nests and presumably the singers. Of course, the skewed sex ratio put a spin on that breeding season. Among *fortis* there were now six males

---

[1]As an aside, the droughts and the flush times in the Galapagos apparently are closely related to the cycles of El Niño. This was not known until some years after the Grants began their study.

> for every female. Each female could choose among many males, but only one male in every six could win a female. The males flew after the females that visited their territories in what the finch watchers called the "sex chase." The females hopped around and flew around to visit nest after nest, and took part in chase after chase, before one by one they each settled down with a single male.
>
> Again the finch watchers watched and measured. They found that the males the females had picked were not a random sample, any more than the ones the drought had spared were a random sample. The successful males tended to be the largest of the large. They were the males with the very blackest, most mature plumage and the ones with the deepest beaks. (1994, 80)

The males that the females selected also tended to have the biggest territories. Thus, the pairing up process was orderly and precise. The males worked to represent their strengths, and the females made their decisions carefully about a male.

In January 1983, after about a year of drought, it began to rain, and rain, and rain, and rain. It was an unbelievable amount of rain. Soon, plants on the island were lush and seeds were everywhere. The mass of seeds after six months of rain was almost a dozen times greater than the year before. "There were also more than five times as many caterpillars to eat, and every one of them about four times normal size." (Weiner 1994, 101) It was rags to riches for the ground finches. Weiner quotes one of the graduate students, Lisle Gibbs, describing the birds during that time, and then Weiner amplifies those comments:

> "The birds went crazy," Gibbs says. The year before there had been no breeding at all. Now they bred like hell." On [the island], females produced up to forty eggs and fledged twenty-five young. . . . In the steamy rains more and more birds were turning bigamous or polygamous . . . one female finch went through four males, one after the other.
>
> The longer the copulatory frenzy lasted, the more finch fledglings were hopping on the wet lava . . . By June there were more than two thousand finches on [the island].
>
> Most finches do not breed until they are two years old, and by then the finch watchers have gotten personally acquainted with each one of them. But in the middle of the breeding season, Gibbs and his assistant started to see banded birds they could not recognize. "Finally, we realized they were kids—three months old," Gibbs says. The young birds they had banded in their first weeks on the island were pairing off and mating in the cactus bushes. No one on earth had ever reported anything like this: passerine birds are not supposed to breed in the same season they are born. But as the rains kept falling, almost every finch on the island was caught up in the breeding rush, like a gold rush. (1994, 101-102)

When Murray Bowen first wrote about societal emotional process, he suggested it had more to do with man's relationship to the natural world than with man's relationship with his fellow man. This research seems consistent with that idea. If these were human beings rather than birds, it would be tempting to label the breakdown in monogamy as evidence of psychopathology, and to get judgmental about it. With the birds, it seems easier to concentrate on how dependent their behavior is on the conditions in which they exist.

The birds' response to the time of plenty was not especially adaptive in that death was everywhere when the next dry period came. Perhaps some bright bird could have studied this process as it was unfolding, and attempted to inform the other birds about the importance of cooling their sex drives because trouble lay ahead. However, it seems unlikely most of the others would have listened, at least not until the seed number began to decline significantly. As an aside, Weiner did not describe anything the Grants and their co-workers might have observed about individual variation in the behavior of the birds during this period. Whatever emotional forces drove these birds to a "copulatory frenzy," whatever emotional forces drove the equivalent of a rapid rise in teenage pregnancy, they did not report whether those forces governed all the birds to the same degree. Was every bird's functioning equally vulnerable to the decline in social institutions?

It is difficult for most people to think this way about their own behavior, to think about human behavior with the same detachment and objectivity the Grants brought to their finch studies. The human tends to be preoccupied with attitudes and feelings. The tendency is to equate emotions with feelings.

Feelings are the proverbial slippery slope. When people get focused on feelings, it is very easy to lose track of what is going on between people, to lose sight of the importance of watching the interaction. When people get focused on feelings, it is tempting to believe that if people could just express their feelings, things would improve. The more people focus on feelings, the more they tend to explain *why* they do what they do based on how they feel. "You treat me the way you do because you are an angry person," is one example. Another example is, "I act the way I do because I feel guilty." Still another example is the following exchange: the husband says, "You are cold to me, and I hate you for it." The wife responds, "You constantly criticize me." The husband counters, "I'm just telling you how I feel." They have had this exchange hundreds of times.

The statements in the examples are accurate within narrow limits, but feelings are linked to a more fundamental dance of life. Perhaps the elite bees E. O. Wilson describes (if they could feel) might feel angry about and overwhelmed by the amount of work they are doing. The sluggish bees might feel guilty as they watch others do so much work. It is unlikely social insects feel anything equivalent to what human beings feel, but they are emotional creatures. Their emotionality seems to dictate that they act similarly to how human beings often act.

Feelings can be used as a sign of how "stuck" people are in a relationship system, as a sign of how much the system dictates their functioning. Feelings are part of a relationship process. They both reflect what transpires in a relationship system and reinforce what transpires. In other words, an individual's guilty feelings arise in the context of a relationship, the guilt plays a part in how the individual behaves in the relationship, and others in the system behave in ways that reinforce the guilt. Perhaps the others feel entitled to special treatment. Feelings are an important part of the process, but the overall relationship is anchored in an emotional process (one example of which is reciprocal functioning) that is deeper or older in an evolutionary sense than feelings. What are the forces a female finch responds to when she loses interest in yet another mate? Is it because she feels he has become less interesting? Alternatively, are both the male and female caught in a web of forces that are deeper than feelings? Thus, guilt is not the "cause" of behavior, but part of a larger system process.

A group has been meeting at the Georgetown Family Center about once a month for nearly two years. This group has focused specifically on the extension of Bowen family systems theory to organizations. A principal conclusion of the group is that a contribution of Bowen theory is its focus on emotional process to explain the different levels of functioning of organizations and institutions in society. An organization is an emotional system, and emotional forces can support or undercut sound administrative practices. As has hopefully been evident from the discussion thus far, emotional process is observed by watching what people do in relationship to one another, and not by listening to what they say they do. For example, a person might say he has tried to be "helpful" to others, yet his actions can be observed to undercut the initiative of others.

How can people become better observers of emotional process? There is probably no limit on people being able to become better at this. Society, at least its more vocal segments, acts as if it wants to bury the notion that relationships are central to human problems. One form of this is to blame others, such as one's parents, for having "caused" one's problems. This, of course, denies the part that person played and plays in the nature of the relationships with one's parents. Another form is to assume self has nothing to do with the problems in the other. This author's position is that human problems are linked to the human emotional process. If people could get past focusing on attitudes and feelings to explain behavior, the role of relationships in human problems would be easier to observe and thus easier to accept. All people are part of this web of emotional process. Bowen theory is not about "abnormal" or "pathological" people and families; it is about *all* people and *all* families. The concept of an emotional system that governs individual and relationship functioning is one of the basic ideas of Bowen theory. The theory also contains two central variables: *differentiation* and *chronic anxiety*. Both of these variables apply to nonfamily groups such as organizations.

Some type of anxiety system may exist in species throughout the phylogenetic tree. Anxiety has been studied extensively in a small multicellular marine snail (Kandel 1983). The mechanisms that mediate anxiety in this creature are less complex than the human mechanisms, but the basic elements of the anxiety process appear to be identical in man and the marine snail.

Interconnected biochemical, physiological, psychological, and relationship components of chronic anxiety exist in human beings. Much of the psychological component of anxiety seems to consist of *anticipating something might happen that one will not be able to manage.* In other words, an individual's anxiety gets fueled by a lack of confidence he can deal with what might come along, particularly in relationships. Attitudes and feelings such as feeling sorry for others, feeling responsible for others, or feeling dependent on others are part of this process. Such attitudes and feelings drive people to function in reaction to others. Thus, a chronic anxiety develops related to the inevitable uncertainty about the acceptance, approval, needs, expectations, and moods of important others.

Marine snails get chronically anxious if they don't know when they are going to receive an electric shock. If the snails consistently get a warning just before a shock is about to occur, they are able to calm down between shocks. However, if they receive no warning, they become chronically anxious. In essence, they are in a constant state of physiological preparedness for a shock. It is very similar to a human being continually worrying about when something might go wrong.

People can reduce their chronic anxiety. The process involves an individual developing more confidence he can deal with what might happen, particularly in important relationships. There is more to the process than trying to be less reactive or less anxious. People closely involved with each other know each other's vulnerabilities. One person might try to stay calm, try not to react to the words and actions of others, but others know what "buttons" to push.

The process of reducing chronic anxiety is a long-term one. It involves increasing one's level of differentiation of self. A successful effort towards more differentiation depends primarily on developing a systems view of human behavior and on being able to act consistent with that view. A systems view includes the part self plays in a relationship system and the part others play. It is reflected in the ability to get beyond blame and self-blame, to get beyond regarding oneself as a victim of, or a burden to, the system. A key component of learning to think systems about human behavior is engaging emotionally difficult situations over and over. By doing this, people learn more about how they react to others and about what they are sensitive to in others. If people avoid intense emotional arenas such as their families, or if they keep contacts brief and superficial, they cannot learn anything. The ideal learning situation is being able to move into and out of the system over time. People usually need some physical distance from a relationship system to think clearly about it.

The basic effort is to get a more factual view of the system. It takes a clear perspective on how a system operates for an individual to gain some control over what he typically does when he is anxious. People are vulnerable to acting on their anxiety unless they can truly convince themselves this creates more problems than it solves. In other words, it is necessary to recognize the impact of one's anxiety-driven behaviors on the system and to recognize how the system triggers one's anxiety-driven behaviors. It takes time to observe enough facts about a system to develop real conviction about how the system operates. It takes conviction to act on a systems view because both one's internal reactions and the reactions of others automatically oppose behavior that is out of step with the previous emotional flow of a system. Theory is a lens for looking at a system, but people must convince themselves that the theory describes the system accurately. It is constructive for people to make this type of effort in all important relationship systems, not just in their families.

A problem in emphasizing the control of reactivity over trying to get a more theoretical or factual view of the system is that it is easy to slip, often imperceptibly, into using physical or emotional distance to get less reactive. Distance can reduce one's own anxiety, but raise the level of anxiety in the system. An emphasis on controlling reactivity also makes it easy to slip into altering one's thoughts, feelings, and behavior to keep others calm. Excessive accommodating to keep the system harmonious can make it easier to control aspects of one's reactivity, but at the cost of giving up self to the system.

Paradoxically, it is the ability to tolerate periods of anxiety and reactivity in oneself that is critical to the process of differentiation and the reduction of chronic anxiety. Knowing how a system operates allows an individual to tolerate the anxiety of the moment, the anxiety that pushes for the immediate relief of distressing conditions. Knowing how an emotional system works means the person knows that acting to relieve the anxiety of the moment "fixes" problems in the short-run, but compounds them in the long-run.

If a person acts to relieve the anxiety of the moment, he is not functioning as a "self" in the system. He is acting based on his anxiety about the situation. He is like the snail that is always waiting for the next shock. His internal equilibrium depends on the stability of his emotional environment. In contrast, if a person has a fairly factual view of the system, if he has conviction about the long-term value of not acting to relieve immediate anxiety, he can better maintain a "self" in the system. He can stick with what he thinks, rather than be pushed and pulled by the anxiety-driven needs and expectations of himself and others. Thus, he does not have to worry about when the next shock might be coming. He knows he can deal with it.

If one person in a family or work system can better manage his anxiety, it can have a significant impact on the level of anxiety in the entire system. The more important the person's functioning is to the system, the more impact he or she can have on it. People can get interested in watching how anxiety affects their systems. As anxiety builds, gossip increases, paranoia increases, polarized discussions are more frequent, people feel overused and underappreciated, and the "elites" start complaining about the "sluggish" ones. This can be an interesting process to watch provided one sees it as a phenomenon rather than getting embroiled in the content of all the issues. One person's ability to watch, and to have that objectivity reflected in his actions, is extraordinarily useful to others. It is counterproductive to tell others they are anxious or to try to calm them down; it is productive to get oneself under better control.

This presentation will conclude with a few comments about *triangles*. Bowen theory describes the functioning of multiperson systems. The "molecule" of a multiperson system is the triangle, which is a three-person system. Triangles connect in interlocking fashion. The concept describes how a continual relationship problem that appears to involve only two people actually includes a third person who has taken sides. For example, a mother lamenting the sibling conflict of her children does not see how her effort to prevent or resolve the conflict perpetuates it; a son lamenting his distant relationship with his father and extolling the close relationship with his mother has usually taken sides on issues between his parents; and a manager lamenting conflict between two of his supervisees is often in a position similar to the mother and her two warring children. An important point about triangles is that conflicts between two people will resolve if a third person who is important to the warring parties stays *in contact* with them and remains *neutral*.

Dr. Bowen used to say that if there is a problem anywhere in his organization, he is playing a part in it. His effort was to stop focusing on others and start focusing on his own functioning. This is a powerful idea. Perhaps there are some exceptions, but they are rare. No matter how "pathological" or "inept" some employees may appear to be, their impaired functioning is usually linked to triangles. This does not imply it is never indicated to fire someone, but it is important to recognize that probably more people get fired because of triangles than because they are not right for the job.

REFERENCES

Bowen, Murray. 1978. *Family Therapy in Clinical Practice*. New York: Jason Aronson.

Kandel, Eric R. 1983. "From Metapsychology to Molecular Biology: Explorations into the Nature of Anxiety." *American Journal of Psychiatry*, XX:1277-1293.

Weiner, Jonathan. 1994. *The Beak of the Finch*. New York: Alfred A. Knopf.

Wilson, Edward O. 1975. *Sociobiology: The New Synthesis*. Cambridge, Massachusetts: The Belknap Press of Harvard University Press.

RETHINKING THE CONSULTANT'S ROLE

Joyce Bader, MS

This paper explores the application of Bowen family systems theory to the practice of organizational consulting by comparing three different theoretical roots for a consultant's practice: Frederick Taylor's Scientific Management, Kurt Lewin's Action Research and Murray Bowen's family systems theory. The paper compares the impact of these three different orientations along eight dimensions of the consultant's practice. The author suggests that family systems theory, as a theoretical base, can offer the consultant new approaches to refine practice and resolve problematic dichotomies while also potentially changing the nature of consulting.

Consultants to organizations come to their work from a variety of professional and educational backgrounds—from psychology, sociology, education, business, economics, management, and organization development, as well as from careers as managers and leaders inside organizations. Because of these diverse roots, the field of organizational consulting does not have agreed upon criteria for competency or effectiveness. Each consultant applies his or her own thinking or theoretical orientation and abilities garnered from life experience.

For the past twelve years I have worked as an external organization development consultant to leaders and management teams in corporations, government, and nonprofit organizations. During that time, I often reflected on questions of competency and effectiveness in organizational consulting. Initially, my reflections grew from two theoretical perspectives that formed the basis of my academic training and underlie much of organization consulting today—Scientific Management as developed by Frederick Taylor at the turn of the century (Taylor 1915) and Organization Development, an approach to consulting that emerged from Kurt Lewin's work in field theory and action research in the middle years of this century (Lewin 1951).

Gradually, I began to observe my actual behavior in client organizations and to analyze the results of my work. I could see that my consulting practice changed as a result of three obvious influences and one less obvious influence. The three obvious influences were increased knowledge of organizations, increased experience in knowing what worked with client organizations, and specific client feedback regarding effectiveness.

The fourth and less explicable source of development in my consulting practice was my own changed understanding and posture toward my family of origin and the concomitant decreased anxiety I experienced in my relationship with clients as I worked with them. For example, as I began to develop greater ability to observe myself and my family interactions, I also seemed to bring greater observational skills to client systems. As I increased my ability to respond to my family in thoughtful, less reactive ways, I also saw my responses to clients become more calm and thoughtful. Further, as a I began to act in ways that were more consistent with my beliefs toward my family, I also found myself increasingly able to take reasonable stands with clients in stressful situations. Overall I became less anxious and more flexible in my relationships with both my family of origin and my clients.

Intuitively, I understood that these personal changes were producing changes in my approach to consulting but I had no theoretical basis for this understanding. As a result, I began exploring family systems concepts and contemplating their applications to organizations and to my consulting practice.

I found that Bowen family systems theory (Kerr and Bowen 1988) provided new ways to understand myself, my family, organizations, and my consulting practice. The theory did offer insights into why my personal changes influenced my abilities as a consultant. I have come to believe that family systems theory offers both new ways to understand organizations as human social systems and potential new models for the practice of organization consulting. In addition, the theory has particular relevance now in an era of constant social experimentation in organizations, an era of high anxiety among employees, leaders and consultants alike. A theory that explores the role of anxiety in human social systems can provide an excellent frame of reference for consultants and the organizations they serve.

The following chart suggests some of the contributions that family systems theory can make to the practice of organization consulting. The chart compares three types of consulting across eight dimensions. The types of consulting compared are: traditional management consulting, organization development consulting, and "systems" consulting. The label "systems" consulting is being used by this author to specifically refer to consulting methods drawn from a family systems theory base—as opposed to a general systems theory base which derives from different academic roots (Papero 1990). The chart suggests some significant shifts in consulting competency and effectiveness as a result of using family systems theory as a basis for a consultant's practice. In some dimensions the indicated shifts in consulting practice are extensions or refinements of conventional consulting practice. In other dimensions, the changes in practice are distinct and unique to a family systems approach to organizational consulting.

The first dimension on the chart is *theory.* Traditional management consulting practice is herein identified with Taylor's theory of scientific management. The current practice of organization development is primarily an outcome of Lewin's theory of action research. Systems consulting is defined as a potential application of Bowen theory to the practice of consulting.

The second dimension on the chart is *knowledge,* which pertains to the broad fields of knowledge or understanding upon which a given theory is based and upon which a

COMPARATIVE DIMENSIONS OF CONSULTING PRACTICE

	TRADITIONAL MANAGEMENT CONSULTING	ORGANIZATIONAL DEVELOPMENT CONSULTING	SYSTEMS CONSULTING
THEORY	Scientific Management: Frederick Taylor	Action Research: Kurt Lewin	Family Systems Theory: Murray Bowen
KNOWLEDGE	Technical/Specialized	Organization Process/ Generalized	Natural/Family systems
MODEL	Closed/Mechanistic systems	Open/Organic systems	Natural systems
POSTURE OF CONSULTANCY	Expert: Consultant manages consultancy	Collaborative: Consultant & client manage consultancy together	Differentiated: Consultant coaches client toward managing self in the system
PROBLEM ORIENTATION	Content	Process	Emotional process: content and process
IDENTIFIED CLIENT/FOCUS OF WORK	Leader	Leader and groups	Consultant/Client relationship
CONSULTANT ACTIVITIES	Problem-solving, advising	Action Research; Facilitating group learning	Defining self and coaching client
OUTCOME ORIENTATION	Content problem solved	Increased capacity to improve organizational process	Increased overall functioning in content and process

consultant working from this theory might derive his or her understanding of organizations. Each of these three types of consulting is based on a rich and diverse knowledge base. This discussion does not mean to be reductionist but rather to point to the general and conventionally accepted understanding upon which each theory tends to focus and to build upon this to understand how a particular knowledge base might influence a consultant's practice.

The knowledge base of traditional management consulting is typically seen as quantitative and technical, focused on the factual basis of a particular aspect of work such as financial management, manufacturing, inventory control or any of the many areas of organizational work. The knowledge base of organization development consulting, in contrast, is usually seen as a more qualitative approach, based on how people behave particularly in regard to learning and changing in group situations. Systems consulting is based on the understanding of family and natural systems and is thus potentially both qualitative and quantitative.

Over the years, as each of these theories and knowledge frameworks has been discussed in the literature, *models* (Morgan 1986) have emerged for looking at organizations. These models are evocative and can substantially inform a consultant's practice. Scientific management tends to view organizations as closed/mechanistic systems. This informs traditional management consulting in a wide variety of ways. For example, a powerful belief of a traditional consultant would be that it is possible to work on part of an organization without influencing other parts and, as an extension, that the environment will not have further impact on the system. Traditional management consulting operates within a model that the work can be controlled and implemented in a linear, defined, and cognitive fashion.

The organization development model, on the other hand, views organizations as open and organic systems that have constant and interacting inputs and outputs both internal to the system and in relation to the environment. This view encourages attempts to understand organizational life and implement change in nonlinear, connected, and experiential ways.

Systems consulting, based on Bowen theory would take a similar approach in that the view of organizations is certainly organic. But Bowen theory takes this understanding much further. Organizations are seen *as actual natural systems.* From a family systems framework, the organization is not abstracted through a model but rather seen occurring naturally. As an extension of this factual view, organizations are likely to share characteristics attributable to other natural systems. This view would encourage attempts to understand organizational life in both linear and nonlinear, defined and connected, cognitive and experiential ways.

The *posture of the consultancy* is often a logical extension of these ways of understanding organizations. The posture of the consultant in traditional management consulting is expected to be that of the expert in control and taking responsibility for fixing the client's problem. Consultants are brought in to the organization, the client describes the problem, and then assumes a dependent "whatever you say" posture toward the expert consultant.

Organization development consultants, on the other hand, have collaborative relationships with clients to solve problems. Organization development consultants do, however, take a very active role in the process of problem-solving with the client. Usually they collect and summarize information about the organization, contribute to the in-depth diagnosis of the problem, and recommend approaches to resolution.

The posture of the consultant in a systems consulting practice would be that control and responsibility for the situation would clearly lie with the client. The client's management of self in the system would be a key variable in the consultancy. In addition, the consultant's self-management in the client-consultant relationship would also be a key variable. The consultant's work would be to interact with the client in a calm and neutral manner, thereby enhancing the client's ability to learn and function more effectively in the organization. Few consultants practice in this manner. The challenge is in *not acting* for the client on his or her problem. Rather, the consultant would serve as a sounding board and coach for the client in understanding and taking action in the situation.

The fifth dimension on the chart is that of the *problem orientation* of the consultancy. In traditional management consulting, the problem orientation is toward the content of the particular technical problem. A classic example would be how effectively time and resource are being used in a particular work process such as a manufacturing process. Another example might be what the organization's human resource policies are. In contrast, the organization development consultant has typically focused on the ways people work together through examining key organizational processes such as communication, decision making and conflict resolution.

With systems consulting, the orientation is toward the emotional process of the system, defined as the automatic interactions of organisms toward each other in a system (Comella 1994). With this orientation, which is not a "problem" orientation, the consultant would support the client in gaining an understanding of the emotional process of human beings in organizations generally and in the client's organization specifically. For example, client and consultant might work toward understanding how anxiety affects human functioning in the organization and on ways that anxiety could be reduced and functioning potentially increased. With emotional process as the focus, systems consulting is an approach that would integrate both content and process in an effort to understand and improve organizational functioning.

Traditional management consulting and organization development consulting both attend to both content and process. In both cases, however, there is a distinction made between content and process with one predominating. If applied with real understanding, however, emotional process could integrate content and process orientations into one holistic perspective on organizational life, thus eliminating a dichotomy that has troubled organizational consultants of every persuasion.

A problematic dichotomy for consultants is the *identified client or focus of the work.* Traditional management consultants have typically had a great deal of clarity about who is the leader. In the expert consulting mode, the leader, who manages resources and implements solutions, is the obvious pivotal person for the consultant's work. This clear focus has become blurred over time as social science research has shown that involvement produces commitment. Solutions were not implemented unless key people and groups were involved in the problem-solving process.

Organization development consultants, on the other hand, fully recognize the importance of involvement and influence on commitment and implementation. As a result these consultants tend to view both the leader *and* key groups as the client. A first effort of most organizational development consultants is to define key people close to the problem, seek information from them, and work with them, as a group, to understand the problem and seek solutions. While this approach often produces energy and productive commitment, it can also raise anxiety as lines of authority and ability to implement solutions may become increasingly confused.

In a systems consulting approach the identified client and focus of the work is the consultant-client relationship. In this frame the "client" is not so much a particular person or group of persons but rather the new social system created by the entry of the consultant into the organization. The consultant's management of self in this new social system or set of relationships, is critical to the work. This ongoing management of self, as a defined entity in a new system, can have a profound influence on how the organization understands and acts. In this model, the client dichotomy—leader or group—is less of a problem. While Bowen theory might indicate that work with a key functioning individual will more likely produce change in the system, the theory would also contend that differentiation on the part of any member of the system can alter system functioning.

In the case of *consultant activities* within an organization, Bowen theory does not so much offer a refinement of Taylor and Lewin's perspectives, or a resolution of difficult dichotomies, but rather a distinct and new perspective on how a consultant might work with a client organization. In traditional management consulting, the consultant's activities are direct advice and problem-solving. For this model to be effective, the client must be willing and able to take advice and implement it.

In organizational development the consultant's activities have typically followed a version of Lewin's action research model which includes collecting and analyzing information with the client, arriving at a shared understanding of the situation, and agreeing on joint actions to be taken to change the situation. The consultant's primary activity is as a collaborator in group learning and change (Weisbord 1987).

In systems consulting the consultant's activities would focus on defining a self to the client and on coaching the client to understand him or herself and then define self in the social system of the organization. Helping the client to understand himself in the social system of the organization is not particularly new to the field of organization development consulting, although it may be underemphasized and underdeveloped as an approach to change.

In contrast, the consultant's definition of self to the client is notably a new activity for the field of organization consulting. It could easily be argued that defining a self is frequently referenced in organization development literature— for example, the "authenticity" of the consultant is often discussed (Block 1981). But, this usually means building trusting client relationships that facilitate the work. Authenticity is thus seen more as a precursor to successful work rather than as the work itself.

Defining a self to the client implies a highly self-aware and conscious approach on the part of the consultant. The consultant must pay as much attention to his or her own functioning with the client as to the client organization itself. The differentiation of the consultant in the process of the consulting work is a new kind of awareness and work in the field of organization consulting. The field has not focused on the consultant's awareness and action as a central concern. While this focus is yet to be well developed, this author envisions the consultant as more of a distinct entity, a learning resource or catalyst to the client as opposed to an expert or collaborative problem-solver.

As to the *outcome orientation* the traditional management consultant is interested in solving the content problem presented by the client. The organizational development consultant is typically interested in the client's increased capacity to improve organizational processes. The systems consultant is interested in increased overall functioning of the social system in a way that simultaneously influences content and process since these are inseparable in this framework.

This broad overview of three potential methods of organizational consulting could be elaborated in great depth and detail. Generalization naturally produces some distortion and oversimplification. The intent of this discussion is to stimulate both the author's and the reader's thinking.

The author's view is that Bowen family systems theory which is just emerging has the potential to lead to powerful changes in the field of organizational consulting. Some of these changes represent refinements of tried and true practices based in traditional management consulting practice. Other changes represent opportunities to resolve old and troublesome dichotomies that have hindered successful work with organizations. However, some of the changes in consultant practice suggested by Bowen theory are entirely new frames of reference for the field. This new orientation to the consultant's practice requires open-minded and thoughtful consideration and development to serve organizations in an age of unprecedented anxiety and change in the workplace.

REFERENCES

Block, Peter. 1981. *Flawless Consulting.* Austin, Texas: Learning Concepts.

Comella, Patricia A. 1994. "A Brief Summary of Bowen Family Systems Theory." *Family Center Report* 15: 2-4.

Kerr, Michael and Murray Bowen. 1988. *Family Evaluation.* New York: W. W. Norton & Company.

Lewin, Kurt. 1951. *Field Theory in Social Science: Selected Theoretical Papers.* New York: Harper & Row.

Morgan, Gareth. 1986. *Images of Organization.* Beverly Hills: Sage Publications.

Papero, Daniel V. 1990. Bowen Family Systems Theory. Boston, Massachusetts: Allyn and Bacon.

Taylor, Frederick W. 1915. *The Principles of Scientific Management.* New York: Harper & Row.

Weisbord, Marvin. 1987. *Productive Workplaces.* San Francisco: Jossey-Bass.

2

THE ORGANIZATION AS AN EMOTIONAL SYSTEM

THE ORGANIZATION AS AN EMOTIONAL SYSTEM

Introduction

Three papers comprise this section of the proceedings. The three authors have tried to present a broad picture of the emotional process which operates in human work systems or, as Kathleen Wiseman might put it, their view from the bleachers.

A core concept of Bowen family systems theory is that emotional process operates in all human relationship systems and that the human species shares this aspect of functioning with other life forms. Indeed, Darwin's theory of evolution by natural selection is a theory about relationships in an ongoing process which has resulted in the diversity of life on Earth. Each of the authors in this section has drawn inspiration from examining and thinking about emotional process in the human and other species and from viewing human social systems as natural social systems.

Dr. Bowen, too, drew upon his knowledge of other life forms in developing his theory about human functioning. In his interview with Kathleen Wiseman, Dr. Bowen provided a glimpse into the process which he used in developing Bowen family systems theory. In responding to questions about the potential value of models of the behavior of animals belonging to other species, Dr. Bowen replied:

> Well, I didn't have anything to observe except the [human] families. So I used a model from evolution . . . and I tried to make it point by point consistent: the humans with animals.
>
> I would say every time there [was] a discrepancy between the animal model and the human, I would go back to look for another animal model. And this had to do with forms of life that were absolutely necessary for each other. I found a book in biology that has thirty-six different stages between parasites and symbiosis. . . . Symbiosis on the biological level means one form of life which "facilitates" another form of life. . . .

In "Life at Work: the View from the Bleachers," Kathleen Wiseman describes her quest for neutrality of perspective about the functioning of humans in the workplace. She draws upon her experience as a consultant to family-owned businesses and her insights into parallels between members of nonhuman and human social species in their perceptions and responses to threats in order to present her ideas about the role of leadership and the role of the consultant in organizational functioning.

The second paper, "The Emotional Side of Re-Engineered and Re-Invented Work Places," is by Patricia A. Comella. Ms. Comella discusses why chronic anxiety is endemic to the work place and why restructuring has the potential to limit flexibility in functioning at the very time the organization is most desirous of finding new and creative ways to survive in the global marketplace. She also touches briefly on the contributions Bowen theory can make to managing functioning in the emotional system of the work place.

In "Anxiety and Organizations," Dr. Daniel Papero, Director of Training at the Georgetown Family Center and author of *Bowen Family Systems Theory* (1990: Allyn and Bacon), draws upon the research of Robert Sapolsky into the functioning of leaders in baboon troops. Dr. Papero explains how anxiety may be viewed as a relationship phenomenon, and how anxiety appears to affect the functioning of leaders, thereby pointing in the direction of explaining leadership as a relationship phenomenon.

LIFE AT WORK: THE VIEW FROM THE BLEACHERS

Kathleen K. Wiseman, MBA

This paper describes my observations about relationships and interactions in work systems during times of change and about the tendency toward bias while working in or consulting to those systems. I view the patterns, forces and functioning of the system through the lens of Bowen family systems theory.

Murray Bowen, MD, a researcher and psychiatrist affiliated with the Menninger Clinic (1946-54), National Institutes of Mental Health (1954-59), and Georgetown University Medical Center (1959-90), developed a theory of human functioning and behavior which views the human family as a multigenerational, natural living system in which each member's emotional functioning affects the other members' functioning in predictable ways. While the theory was originally developed from research on the family system, its description of human functioning and relationship processes is equally applicable to the workplace.

During the twenty-five years I have consulted to organizations—small partnerships, large corporations, family firms, and government agencies—I have discerned relationship forces and counter forces that operate in the organization and in the individual. In my practice as a consultant, I have observed that although individuals may be able to articulate elaborate explanations for their actions (Kerr 1981), they actually tend to act automatically. These automatic behaviors fall into patterns that we can observe in the natural world.

I have had two challenges. My first has been to redefine what "help" means, because the traditional modes of helping organizations, such as providing survey-feedback, organizational diagnosis, and direct intervention with specific solutions offer at best only short-term remedies that do little to help the organization develop new capacities for the future. My second challenge has been to resist the influence of personal relationships on my perception— to find a neutral space from which to observe human interactions objectively as they are subjectively reported. By being more factual, and less actively diagnostic, I have found that others could begin to do the same for themselves. I believe that if individuals can discipline their thought processes to be based more on the objective observation of facts, they can develop a greater flexibility that enables them to make calmer, more thoughtful decisions. I am not seeking to separate emotional and intellectual processes artificially. I am attempting to describe the facts of emotional process and its contribution to an individual's functioning, thinking and decision making. Emotional process is driven by that part of our brain that is more instinctual and automatic. Becoming increasingly aware of emotional process allows one to explore calmer responses to change.

With increased understanding of the following three axioms, based on Bowen theory, people can better manage the challenges they face at work:

- Humans and their work systems are similar in function to other life forms and are natural social systems (Comella 1994);
- Employee [individual] and organizational [system] functioning tend to be more automatic than thoughtful; and
- The ability to manage self at work, in family, or in social interactions by observing automatic behavior separates humans from other forms of life and enables the development of more thoughtful adaptations to change.

Without observing our own reactivity when faced with a changing situation, our reactions continue to be more automatic than thoughtful — on the part of consultants as well as that of our clients. Deeply entrenched patterns of processing information create a filter through which we perceive data and personal interactions. These perceptions control how we "see" events and interactions and influence how we respond. These patterns are the result of thousands of years of encoding adaptive responses on the brain (Kerr and Bowen 1988).

Bowen posited that people can choose how they conceptualize life events and human functioning with the following metaphor: Picture yourself standing on the sideline at the 50-yard line of a football game, having a close-up appreciation of individual actions and reactions. From that vantage point, you can describe individual characteristics and attributes and make judgments about individual skills and abilities. Alternatively, you can climb to the top of the bleachers and see patterns and forces as groups of individuals act and react to each other over time. Individual characteristics, so important from the 50-yard line, diminish in relation to the broader perspective provided by distance. Broad discernment of patterns provides the viewer with multiple levels of inquiry. Bowen family systems theory uses a bleacher view of man's functioning.

One way we can learn to stand in the bleachers to observe ourselves and our work systems is by thinking about the patterns and forces of systems in the natural world. Consider, for example, the following questions connecting seemingly unrelated nonhuman behavior to human conduct in the work environment: Can variations in the grunting of a vervet (Morris 1990) as it leads its troops onto the open plain provide insight to a CEO leading a woman's apparel firm that is experiencing a 50% loss in sales? Can the structure and function of the Australian paper wasp's hive provide a model for increasing productivity in the news room of a daily newspaper? Can the cooperative hunting behavior of a pride of lions in Kenya increase the effectiveness of a self-managed team at an automobile assembly plant in Tennessee? These analogies do not imply that we can describe or predict human behavior from animal behavior. Rather, this is a way to observe and question human interactions at work within the larger framework of evolution and automatic biological processes.

From the bleachers we can observe the biological and evolutionary life force for togetherness and the counterbalancing force for individuality. In a pride of lions, a troop of vervets or a hive of wasps, the collective allows for survival strategies of greater complexity and success. The coordinated hunting pattern of individual lions acting together decreases the risk of predation and improves their ability to forage, while providing for the self and the young (MacLean 1978).[1] These are natural survival mechanisms in the animal world. The force for togetherness in humans supports dependence, connection and affiliation. This force is biological and has evolutionary value for the individual and the organization. Business organizations provide the connectedness needed to increase the chance for survival of both the individual and the collective.

The forces of individuality and togetherness create an often unrecognized, underlying tension in all of life, including the workplace. These forces operate on all of us who have chosen to work together with others in an organization. Just as individual nonhumans join with others of their species to pool resources toward a common outcome, employees in an organization have made a choice to join together to maximize their chance for survival. This collective of individuals initiates, promotes, and sustains efforts that move the collective into the future. Individuals contribute intellectual capital and functioning toward a goal larger than they believe they can achieve on their own. They are committed by their membership in the group to the future of the group. Embedded in the individual goal is the goal of maintaining the collective. Also embedded in each individual is the counterbalancing need to succeed on his own and to survive and be recognized as a self. To varying degrees, each of us seeks autonomy and self-achievement as a distinct and separate entity from others (Kerr and Bowen 1988).

Every individual in an organizational system attempts to balance the interplay be-

---

[1]Based on extensive comparisons of the brains of reptiles, lower mammals, and higher mammals, MacLean concluded that, although the human brain has expanded to a great size, it has retained the basic features of its ancestral relationship to reptiles, early mammals, and recent mammals. These basic features make it possible to distinguish three formations in the human forebrain that are radically different in structure and chemistry. These three formations constitute a hierarchy of three brains in one, or what MacLean has called a 'triune' brain.

The three formations of the brain described by MacLean are the reptilian brain (R-complex), paleomammalian brain (limbic system), and neomammalian brain (cerebral cortex). . . . There exists a complex interrelationship between the R-complex, limbic system, and cerebral cortex, an interrelationship that has been beautifully described in the following hypothetical example presented by science writer Anne Rosenfeld:

> "Let us take a simple example—and allow ourselves a little room for conjecture—since we do not actually know exactly what role any of the three brains serves in ongoing complex human behavior. Each major component of our triune brain seems to react somewhat differently to the same sensory stimulation. For example, if we accidentally bump into an old "flame," our neocortex may rumble into its well calculated verbal pleasantries, spinning out the person's name, asking about what's happened, keeping up its chitchat, all the while taking in countless bits of information about the person before us and perhaps trying to tell our limbic system to be still. The limbic system, however, swamped with messages from above and below, inside and outside, swirling with memory and old desires and fears, is by no means quiescent. Its messages, through other, lower parts of the brain, may send the heart racing, hands freezing, stomach churning, face flushing, and sexual responses activated despite our attempts at neocortical cool. Or perhaps we are torn with feelings of anger and a desire to escape this discomforting encounter. But we keep on chatting pleasantly. Meanwhile, our reptillian brain is stirring, too, running our body through a parade of habitual gestures and 'body language' that probably signals our conflict—perhaps we keep shaking hands overlong or somehow feel obliged to scratch a suddenly itchy ear." (Durrell and Durrell 1987)

tween the need for individuality and for togetherness. This balance is affected by events and processes that continuously influence the organizational system and the individual contribution of its employees. We act at times for self, at times for the group and at times for both simultaneously. When we act for togetherness, we are essentially contributing part of our self-functioning and our individual autonomy to others to further the well being and success of the collective. This may coincidentally serve the interests of the individual, but there are times when the group demands too much from an individual. When that point comes, the individual's anxiety is heightened which, in turn, may increase the system's anxiety.

It is difficult for individuals to know how to say "no" to the system and still stay connected to it. The goal is for each individual to understand the amount of self he or she can contribute, while still maintaining a sense of self. This continuous management of self and togetherness is made more difficult by an anxious system's demand for affiliation and group harmony.

The choice between promoting the self and helping to move the organization into the future requires ongoing assessments. The decisions are not conscious ones; they occur in portions of the brain that are more instinctual than thoughtful — initiated in the reptilian and limbic system and rationalized by the neocortex (Hermann, 1994).[2]

When change—and accompanying anxiety—increase in a workplace, balancing the trade-offs between the forces for individuality and togetherness becomes more difficult. Anxious people and anxious systems tend to move toward togetherness (Kerr 1981). Anxious togetherness tends to diminish individual contributions to group productivity. Anxiety changes the nature of individuality and togetherness. With all the changes influencing the workplace, we are finding more anxious, not more thoughtful, togetherness. While it may calm anxiety, it doesn't allow thoughtful perception of and reaction to change. Anxious togetherness is like alcohol: It allows people to relax in the short run, but detracts from the ability to manage the underlying problem in the long term. If people could recognize and better manage their own anxiety, they'd do better in their togetherness. A togetherness that is generated by heightened anxiety has little tolerance for individual variation and actions. During times of rapid or intense change, the group's need for mutual reassurance and comfort tends to suppress new ideas and creativity and diminish the capacity of a work system to reflect, encourage and tolerate each individual's unique contributions. Risk of organizational failure increases as the need for togetherness stifles creative responses to external changes.

Over the last 25 years, individuals have been encouraged to work in teams. Teams have been created to increase production, to solve problems, and to facilitate communications. Based on the assumption that if one head is good, more heads are better, we have overlooked the implications of important characteristics of the force for togetherness. Togetherness has advantages and disadvantages at the workplace.

---

[2]Based on Paul MacLean's research, the two older brains are thought to control genetic and instinctual behavior. The more evolved neo-cortex is more adept at learning new ways of coping and adapting.

Advantages include dampened anxiety, calmer employees in the short term, and improved productivity in the short term. Disadvantages include diminished individual creativity, more time spent thinking about maintaining togetherness than on the goals of the group or its individuals, and decreased profitability and effectiveness in the market place over the long term.

A togetherness created to dampen anxiety diminishes individual and organizational creativity. The move toward togetherness, even if it is recognized as having a negative impact on effectiveness, is a way of managing anxiety. It is an adaptive process that makes it difficult to address change in the environment that created the anxiety. It is possible to see this adaptive response as it is happening in the organization. If a move toward togetherness comes with little regard for the value of an individual's contribution, the organization is focused on calming the anxiety and may lose its ability to respond creatively to the threat in the environment. It is as if the adaptive process keeps the team on the field playing the game but inhibits its capacity to develop new game plans. Understanding the forces for togetherness and individuality can improve the individual's and the organization's ability to cope with anxiety and react thoughtfully to the challenges presented during times of change.

Change as a Natural Biological Process

Organizations of all sizes are encountering change from the external environment and experiencing change internally as change affects their individual employees, groups, divisions and the organization as a whole. At the systems level, traditional, routine production processes—such as order entry, customer service, quality control and product assembly—are continuously being re-engineered and redesigned. Long-term employees are being asked to negotiate short-term contracts. Employees at all levels are threatened with corporate downsizing. The pace of the workplace has also changed dramatically; internal and external correspondence traditionally answered through the exchange of letters after a day or two of reflection are now faxed with responses expected within minutes or hours; e-mail and voice mail now demand more information and opinions from more people sooner than ever before.

These newer and faster communications capabilities seem to be producing less meaningful communication in the workplace for CEOs, managers and line employees alike. The current management literature has not used a natural systems approach to conceptualize this change. The current *ad hoc* adaptation to change has left each of us struggling to learn artificial techniques for short-term relief with little appreciation for change as a continuous, natural process. How can employees barraged with dozens of e-mail messages every day know which are most important, and how to respond? That kind of over-stimulation and arousal strains each employee's capacity to adapt. Yet adapt they must, even if in a more automatic and reactive way.

Seen from the bleachers, change and continuous adaptation are fundamental life processes. Natural systems and organizational systems react to change by losing and gaining balance in a constant effort to achieve homeostasis. All systems, from the simplest cellular life forms to the most complex human organizations, must continually sense their environment, interpret new information, and adjust to new circumstances.

The short-term goal is to regain homeostasis; the long-term goal is survival in the current environment and into the next generation.

As individuals, we adapt to change continually. Over generations our species has been afforded less and less time to adapt to major changes. The most intensely felt changes are a result of sudden, unexpected shifts in the environment and ruptures of significant relationships. The changes can be subtle, such as the increased demands of the fax machine and e-mail, or more obvious, like a decrease in company earnings and threatened job loss. While everyone seems to be aware of changes in the speed of communication or corporate profitability, few pay attention to the effect on the organization of a trusted employee's divorce, the death of the president's mother, an unresolved dispute between the chairman of the board and the CEO, or the reconfiguration of office space. All these changes influence the organization and require adaptation from its individuals and systems.

Eventually, the combination of the changes may exceed any individual's or system's capacity to adapt. Increasing the requirement for adaptation arouses the organism to react more automatically and with less flexibility, triggering limbic responses. All that e-mail may make us more informed, but it robs us of the time to be thoughtful. The adjustments affect an individual's functioning at a physical, emotional, and behavioral level. Some symptoms of this inability to adapt can be seen in more frequent reports of illness, less creative solutions to problems, decreased productivity, increased interpersonal conflicts, and extramarital affairs. These responses are symptoms masking the need for increased flexibility to cope with change.

Overtaxed individuals in an overtaxed system seek to automatically deposit their overarousal on others,[3] when others in the system are struggling just as much to adapt to the same demands, changes and anxiety. Blaming others and the victim mentality that results create less ability to deal with change. This is still adaptation, but narrower adaptation. It results in decreased productivity, robbing the organization and its employees of the satisfaction of accomplishing their goals.

Organizations know intuitively that the rapidly changing world of work demands that everyone working within them must develop an increasing repertoire of adaptability. If the tempo of the music changes, we need to learn new dance steps. Indi-

---

[3] Kerr, Michael E., M.D. and Murray Bowen, MD, *Family Evaluation,* W. W. Norton & Company, p. 134. "The thinking on which the concept of a triangle is based illustrates the thinking on which the entire family systems theory is based. The theory is an attempt to define the *facts of functioning* in human relationships—facts which can be observed to repeat over and over so consistently that they become knowable and predictable. *What* and *how* and *when* and *where* are facts about a relationship that can be observed. Conjecture about *why* something happens is not fact and so the inclusion of such conjecture in the theoretical concepts was avoided as much as possible. While it is a fact that human beings speculate about *why* people do what they do, the content of those speculations is not fact. The triangle describes the what, how, when, and where of relationships, not the why. Triangles are simply a fact of nature. To observe them requires that one stand back and watch the process unfold. Conjecture about why any one person says or does a particular thing immediately takes the observer out of a system frame of reference. The assignment of motive is necessarily subjective and not verifiable; the assignment of function can be objective and potentially verifiable."

viduals who understand that we are all part of the problem will consider developing a greater repertoire of responses.

Viewed from the bleachers, individuals have a better chance to recognize the impact of change no matter how subtle or where it is located in the organization. Humans can learn to what extent their adaptation is automatic or thoughtful. With awareness that change and adaptation are a part of all systems, individuals can recognize that the effort to force others to take responsibility for their own responsiveness to change is as futile as attempting to decrease the rate of change. If an employee is worried about losing his position, it would be futile for him to ask his boss for guaranteed employment; he'd have a better chance to adapt and survive — possibly in a different workplace — if he were to take responsibility for self and improve his skills for his own or another position. For the organization to manage successfully in a changing environment, each individual, whether manager or employee, does best developing his or her own capacity to respond with thoughtful solutions that are of mutual benefit to the individual and the organization.

A Leader's Role in Managing Change

Sociobiologist E. O. Wilson defines leadership as the capacity to initiate and sustain group movement (1975). This definition aids in thinking about work systems as natural social systems because it allows leadership to be seen as a natural system phenomenon in the life of any organization. A primary responsibility of any leader in a nonhuman or human social system is the innate or learned capacity to assess whether or not any given change is a threat to survival.

A broad view of the external environment and its impact on the organization helps to separate real from imagined threats. This is accomplished by observing objectively the facts of the change, and having an awareness of one's own automatic responsiveness. Attempting to evaluate the details of change is less important than having the internal confidence that one can manage oneself through it. This confidence comes from viewing life events as a part of an orchestrated process with the individual's role quite small. It separates the initial, anxious response from the more thoughtful one that allows us to adapt to change regardless of how initially threatening it might appear to be. It is the knowledge that learning, patience, and developing a less aroused brain allow for more effective adaptation to change. This does not mean that we do not rise to meet the occasion; instead, it means that thoughtful responses, coming after those that are automatically generated, are more successful at stimulating novel adaptations. A less anxious brain has more capacity to be creative and resourceful.

At the same time that leaders are scanning the external world, they must constantly assess and manage the internal environment of the organization — the interdependencies, the anxious togetherness, the automatic reactions of individuals, and the responsiveness of these individuals to each other. This goes beyond managing in the traditional sense. It requires an ability to recognize patterns and be in contact with the emotional, reactive process of the organization. It requires an appreciation for the calming and anxiety-producing forces and continuous assessment of what is happening in the togetherness. Leaders need to manage the relationship between the organization and outside forces impacting it and the internal reaction of individuals moving toward togetherness.

During the three years that a ladies' apparel firm experienced dramatic losses in sales, its most important internal resources, the employees, became anxious about the changes they perceived and imagined. Layoffs, job reassignments, and absent leadership strained the employees' ability to function. Facts were overwhelmed by speculation about worst-case scenarios. Productive adaptation became more difficult, as teams formed that spent more time blaming the environment and other people than looking for solutions. Meanwhile, the company's founder and leader, preoccupied with changes in her nuclear family, was less able to think about external or internal threats to the company. She did not have the life energy to put the events into perspective and devise creative strategies. Without a view from the bleachers of the external environment, the employees were increasingly paralyzed by their internal speculation. Unlike the lead vervet who forays into the open to assess the environment before uttering the cry that informs the pack to move into the open, the president functioned less as a leader, allowing the organization to react randomly to the environment. Predictably, the organization grew more anxious about the forces of change and became unable to make factual assessments of the risks of predation. The company survived, but as a much smaller entity, and only after the president installed an interim leader to help design and implement necessary changes.

Leadership is the continuing ability to see change in the big picture of the external world and the smaller pictures of relationships in the organization's internal world. Becoming more objective about the facts presented by these pictures improves decision-making, but it is the leader's personal response and self management in response to these facts that shapes the emotional process of the organization. A leader's ability to initiate and sustain movement depends on how the organization perceives the leader's ability to respond to the internal and external change. If people are confident the leader can manage these forces, their anxiety is lower, allowing them to move successfully into the future.

Consultants who Manage Change

Should organization development consultants take the "bleacher view" as they help organizations manage and adapt to change? I believe this broader vantage point helps consultants understand the functioning of work systems.

Approximately fifty years ago, the field of organizational development came into being as an academic discipline that studied how individuals and groups function in organizations. Over time, organizational development joined management training and general business consulting as a profession to provide solutions to workplace dilemmas. I believe that the functioning of the people in the field changed as the focus changed from research to problem-solving. The researcher's effort focused on observing facts to prove or disprove assumptions; for problem-solvers their emphasis shifted to intervention.

People who are attracted to the role of consulting to others in business are drawn to function in anxious organizational systems, seeking emotionally responsive togetherness. They are "comfortable" functioning in triangles. Based upon my research in my own family and research with other consultants, I believe that organizational consultants occupy a functioning position in their families of origin that provides them with needed feedback during times of anxiety. This attracts them to similar functioning and feedback in work systems. Regardless of the consultant's feeling of comfort when immersed in an anxious work environment, it is familiar and compelling at a cellular level. The consultant is drawn to work that requires him to be on call to intervene automatically and provide help and advice to any system. This is an emotional formatting, an automatic way of being tuned to the world. It is not a value driven choice to do good.

For those consultants who are frustrated when they have intervened in workplace dilemmas only to find resistance to change or the problem surfacing elsewhere in the organization, Bowen family system theory provides a way to think differently about the role of the consultant. A consultant who takes the bleacher view contributes lasting value to the organization as it responds to change. The ability to view change as a natural process, to discern patterns from individual behavior, to tolerate automatic responsiveness without seeking immediate relief, and to challenge the system to greater levels of adaptation provides the kind of assistance that is of long term value.

Consultants who see their role as relating to the system while focusing on the management of their own emotional reactivity to clients will enable others to better manage the anxiety in themselves and in their organizations. Consultants should resist the need to change others or function for them. Instead, they would be more effective focusing on their own responsiveness to others as they respond to challenges in the workplace. Calmer, more thoughtful consultants who think about the functioning of natural systems when confronting challenging situations can stimulate more novel and creative thinking and problem solving in leaders than those who offer empathy and advice, however well-intentioned or cleverly disguised. Less anxious leaders can be more objective about the problems facing their organizations and are far more able to institute solutions to crises as well as endemic problems in their organizations.

The work of consultants is to "think" systems and to provide knowledge about how systems function—not to provide answers. It helps for consultants to look at themselves as the client—impressions, automatic responses and emotions—throughout the process. Consultants who can look at the field from the bleachers remain genuinely curious about the changes they observe while managing their own anxiety and can provide valuable, lasting assistance to systems and individuals challenged by change.

In summary, thoughtfully managing our response to others and encouraging others to learn about systems thinking can stimulate a similar capacity in others. A natural systems approach to thinking can provide business leadership with increased flexibility to assess the phenomena of change and to generate calmer, more creative and productive responses throughout their organizations.

REFERENCES

Comella, Patricia A. 1994. "Review of Primate Social Systems." *Family Systems:* Washington, DC: Georgetown Family Center.

Dunbar, Robin I. M. 1988. *Primate Social Systems.* Ithaca, NY: Comstock Publishing, Cornell University Press.

Durrell, Gerald, and Lee Durrell. 1987. *Ourselves and Other Animals.* New York: Pantheon Books.

Hermann, Ned. 1994. *The Creative Brain.* Kingsport, Tennessee: Brain Books.

Kerr, Michael E. 1981. "Family Systems Theory and Therapy." In *Handbook of Family Therapy.* Alan Gurman and David Kniskern, eds. New York: Brunner/Mazel.

Kerr, Michael E. and Murray Bowen. 1988. *Family Evaluation.* New York: W. W. Norton & Company, Inc.

MacLean, Paul D. 1978. "A Mind of Three Minds: Educating the Triune Brain." In *Seventy-Seventh Yearbook of the National Society for the Study of Education.* Chicago, IL: University of Chicago Press.

MacLean, Paul D. 1990. *The Triune Brain in Evolution: Role in Paleocerebral Functions.* NY: Plenum Press.

Morris, Desmond. 1990. *Animal Watching*: A Field Guide to Animal Behavior. New York: Crown Publishers, Inc.

Wildon, Edward O. 1975. Sociobiology: The New Synthesis. Cambridge, Massachusetts: The Belknap Press of Harvard University Press.

THE EMOTIONAL SIDE OF RE-ENGINEERED AND RE-INVENTED WORKPLACES

Patricia A. Comella, JD

This paper is about the emotional side of restructured workplaces. The views expressed here arise out of the author's belief that a human organization is a natural social system which responds automatically to forces which threaten its survival or well-being or those of its members, just as do social systems elsewhere in nature, be they human or nonhuman. The views expressed also reflect the author's belief that nonhuman social systems may offer insights into the automatic (emotional) side of human social systems. Such automatic responding is encompassed by the terms *"emotional process"* and *"anxiety"* as used in Bowen family systems theory (see Bowen 1978; Kerr and Bowen 1988; Papero 1990; Gilbert 199). Bowen family systems theory is the product of the research of Murray Bowen, MD (1913-1990) into the behavior and functioning of the human family, one example of a natural social system.

In a *natural social system* (see Dunbar, 1988 for a discussion of nonhuman social systems as an outcome of the forces of natural selection), reciprocal relationships exist between the system itself and its members. These relationships have an emotional component. Through their membership, individuals derive benefits not otherwise realizable either fully or in part and automatically accept constraints on choice and functioning as a condition of membership. The system itself extracts contributions from its members but, since it cannot survive without members, automatically limits what it demands of its members. When the survival or well-being of the system is threatened or the conditions for survival are harsh, members of the system tend to accept greater constraints on functioning to enhance survival or ensure the continuation of benefits. (The naked mole rats of Africa offer an example of a highly constrained nonhuman social system in an exceptionally challenging environment; see Sherman, Jarvis and Alexander 1991). At some point, the constraints on functioning may exceed the limits of the system or its members to adapt and instabilities or symptoms may develop, including movement of members from one social group to another or the formation of new groups. (Regarding nonhuman species, see Fossey 1983, concerning emigration of female gorillas to new social groups; Moss 1988, concerning fragmentation of elephant families on the deaths of matriarchs).

General systems theory has been able to capture some elements of the functioning of human social systems (Senge 1990), as have individually-based theories of organizations (Bader 1995). However, neither theoretical approach captures the emotional component of organizational functioning sufficiently, particularly during times of heightened stress. Application of Bowen family systems theory, particularly when coupled with an understanding of natural systems as a response to the forces of natural selection (Darwin 1859), has the potential to contribute to understanding organizations as natural systems.

One response of organizations to threats to their existence and well-being has been the "re-engineering" and "re-invention" phenomenon of recent years, which is operating globally at many different levels and in many different sectors of society and the economy. Restructuring government and industry has become commonplace in the last years of the twentieth century as part of the effort to adapt to an increasingly populous world, diminished resources, a global marketplace, institutional instabilities, rapidly changing technologies, shortened response times, and an infrastructure regarded as obsolete or inadequate for successful functioning in a rapid response environment.

The focus of re-engineering and re-invention is change; specifically, achieving enhanced responsiveness to the needs of the marketplace in a cost-effective, efficient manner so that the organization may survive or enjoy continued well-being. Through the restructuring process, the relationship systems which defined the organization historically are redefined, often dramatically and disruptively.

Restructuring produces an inevitable emotional impact on the functioning of an organization and its members. These impacts have been conceptualized more if not exclusively as impacts on individuals and their functioning, rather than as impacts on a system's functioning. There is a rich literature on the management of organizational change which conceptualizes the individual as largely autonomous in determining or changing his or her own functioning within the social system of the organization. (See Covey, 1989; Senge 1990; Cohen and Brand, 1993; Bader, 1995). Recognition of the organization as an emotional system which has a regulatory effect on the behavior and functioning of its members appears to be in its infancy. In this paper about the emotional side of restructured organizations, the author explores the ramifications of re-engineering and re-invention from the natural systems perspective of Bowen family systems theory. The author examines how understanding of emotional process, as defined and described in the theory, may contribute to understanding how organizations and their members function during times of high stress and anxiety occasioned by change, in particular, by re-engineering and restructuring.

Characteristics of Re-Engineered and Re-Invented Workplaces

From a natural systems perspective, re-engineered and re-invented workplaces are seen to embody continuing change, chronic anxiety of an endemic nature, and potentially impaired flexibility to adapt. The chronic anxiety is a product, in part, of the continuing change; the diminished flexibility to adapt, a product, in part, of the endemic anxiety.

Re-engineering and re-invention by their very nature stress the organization on a continuing basis and potentially threaten functioning at both the individual and organizational level. The stressors and threats are related, at least in part, to continuing disruptions in the relationship systems defining the organization and the continuing change. The disruptions are also related to continuing pressures from the external environment to which the organization perceives it must respond successfully if it is to survive or enjoy continued well-being. The disruptions appear to be inherent to the re-engineering and re-invention processes. Under circumstances of continuing change, disruption, and threats to survival and well-being, chronic, endemic anxiety will be present.

Anxiety limits flexibility to adapt and to make choices not related to responding to the threat. (For a discussion of the effects of chronic anxiety on functioning, see Kerr, 1988; for a discussion of anxiety and organizations, see Papero, 1995, elsewhere in this section.) The social system and its members automatically focus on the threat and organize themselves to respond to it. In doing so, they automatically limit their potential to make choices not related to avoiding or mitigating the threat. Managing the anxiety presents challenges to each person in the organization, particularly to those in the key functioning positions traditionally called leadership positions.

Among the significant changes which disrupt the relationship systems defining an organization are "downsizing" (or "rightsizing") and "flattening" the organization, changing the organization's leadership, moving toward "self-managed teams," and introduction of "continuous improvement" or "total quality management" processes. "Downsizing" or "rightsizing" the organization involves "doing more with less." Within a relatively brief time span, significant numbers of employees (sometimes hundreds to thousands of employees in a large organization), many of them long-term, may be separated from the organization and their functions redistributed among the remainder. "Flattening" the organization involves reducing the number of mid-level managers in an effort to reduce the number of strata between the lowest and highest levels in the organization's hierarchy. As with downsizing, managerial functions are redistributed, thereby broadening the span of control of surviving managers and increasing the number of employees under each manager's oversight. The broadened span of control may involve oversight of new subject matter and the acquisition of new substantive knowledge about operations. Loss of institutional memory is a likely consequence of downsizing and flattening. Changes in key leadership positions may accompany the restructuring efforts. Often, the new leaders have been selected for the aggressive methods which they have employed in restructuring other organizations. The newcomers may have limited knowledge of the organizations of which they are assuming leadership.

There may also be shifts toward new modes of operating within the relationship systems. Expectations of long-term membership in relationship systems may diminish. For example, there may be a move toward "self-managed teams," whereby groups of employees come together to accomplish particular purposes over limited periods of time, functioning somewhat independently of the organizational hierarchy. Team members are expected to define their *modus operandi* and structure their relationships according to what is necessary to accomplish the team's purpose. Each team member is a key person with respect to the team's functioning. Team members may find themselves variously and perhaps simultaneously functioning as leaders and followers, as process facilitators and subject matter experts, as spokespersons and listeners, as thinkers and doers, as managers and workers. Upon accomplishing a purpose, members are likely to disperse and join new teams in new roles to accomplish new purposes. Some team members may leave the organization entirely and join another, or remain unemployed.

"Continuous improvement" or "total quality management" processes may also be adopted. These processes start with the premise that improving the ability to meet customer needs and expectations is always possible. The organization and its members continuously challenge themselves to discern customer needs, exceed customer expectations in meeting those needs, measure progress in doing so, and adjust as necessary to ensure improved quality.

Concepts of self-managed teams and continuous improvement involve tacit assumptions about the autonomy and ability of individuals and organizations, despite the levels of chronic anxiety within the systems, to effect the desired goals and objectives of the restructuring once the individuals have received the power and authority to act from management ("become empowered"). Occasionally, there is some recognition of limitations in functioning arising out of the changes. For example, there may be recognition that morale has decreased in the restructuring and that improved morale is necessary for success. However, there does not appear to be recognition that emotional process, as defined in Bowen family systems theory, may be setting limits on what changes are realizable under the circumstances. A natural systems view of the organization as an emotional system offers insights into constraints on individual autonomy and functioning, as well as the overall functioning of the system.

Restructuring of Mobil Corporation—A Case in Point

The restructuring of Mobil Corporation, as described in a June 19, 1995 article in *The Washington Post* (Southerland 1995), illustrates the effects of the restructuring process and the limited awareness of the organization as an emotional system. The article cites general approval in the financial community over the cost-cutting implications of Mobil's downsizing. From the article, it appears little significance is attached to the emotional costs of the downsizing, except at the individual level. There appears to be no concept of the organization as an emotional system. According to the article:

> [Mobil] stock surged to a record high on June 6 after Dean Witter analyst Eugene L. Nowak's glowing report on Mobil's cost-cutting and prospects.
>
> Lucio A. Noto, 57, who took over as Mobil's chairman and chief executive in March 1994, is downsizing the company more quickly and aggressively — and some say more ruthlessly — than many analysts had expected. Because of that, and his overall commanding direction of the company, analysts expect Mobil to continue to shine.
>
> Big oil companies such as Mobil can no longer dictate terms in many developing countries and they must compete with well-financed, state-owned oil firms that have entered the refining and marketing field around the world.
>
> Many of Mobil's European competitors . . . now possess oil field technology that equals Mobil's. And the history of the oil industry indicates that

sooner or later a Middle East oil crisis will erupt, disrupting the best-laid plans and projections.

Nearly every investor-owned oil company has been sharply cutting its work force and trying to increase efficiency. . . .

Consequently, the timing of Mobil's decisions, the energy it throws into projects and the quality and dedication of its remaining employees become extremely important.

Meanwhile, Noto may face his toughest challenge in maintaining staff cohesion, morale and productivity as he pursues both downsizing and ambitious financial goals.

At its Fairfax [Va.] headquarters, the company is entering a painful and difficult period. Mobil said last month it would eliminate 1,250 jobs in Fairfax by the end of March 1996. The reduction, among the largest by a single area company in recent years, will slash the company's work force here by nearly a third. Altogether, the company will cut 4,700 jobs worldwide, or about 9 percent of its initial work force of 51,000.

But middle and lower-level employees at Fairfax headquarters say the latest downsizing announcement has damaged morale there. The job cuts have been good news, however, for Mobil's bottom line. . . .

But as Noto himself acknowledged at the company's annual shareholders meeting, the downside of downsizing is "the loss of many loyal and trusted employees."

Emotional Process and Restructuring

In the preceding paragraphs, the author discussed re-engineering and re-invention from a natural systems perspective, based on the concepts of Bowen family systems theory. The focus of the description was on the sources of stress and anxiety inherent in the restructuring process. Discussion of emotional process and restructuring continues in this section.

A fundamental assumption of the theory is that emotional process automatically operates in all human relationship systems. An organization is no exception. An organization as a whole and its members automatically respond to what is happening in the relationship systems of which they are a part, particularly where survival or enhancement of well-being is involved. This is the nature of emotional process. The intensity of emotional process exhibits variation according to the individuals comprising the relationship systems and the circumstances to which they are responding.

When an organization's survival is at stake or perceived to be at stake, anxiety is the most likely response. The same goes for individual members of the organization when their existing relationships with the organization are threatened. The anxious responding automatically focuses the energy of the system and its members around the threat, channeling and narrowing the choices for responding. The intensity of focusing and channeling is related to the intensity of the threats as perceived. In the extreme, when anxiety is sufficiently high, energy is directed almost exclusively to alleviation of the threat through alleviation of the anxiety.

Variation exists in the intensity of the threat and its likelihood of occurring, as well as in individual responses to the threat. When the threat persists over an extended period of time, the anxious responding becomes chronic. Re-engineering and re-invention by their very nature are sources of chronic anxiety as they subject the organization and its members to continuing change and adjustment in efforts to survive and remain competitive.

Anxiety, whether in response to an imminent threat or to a chronic situation, limits the flexibility to perceive the full range of choices potentially available and limits the ability to make decisions based upon consideration of the potential choices. The automatic tendency is to consider only changes which avoid or mitigate the perceived threat. When anxiety is sufficiently high, the organization and its members can be expected to experience difficulties in carrying out such critical activities as long-range planning. The planning horizon tends to become truncated and the planning more risk-averse.

This has ramifications for efforts to re-engineer and re-invent. Almost always, they are undertaken when change is perceived to be necessary for the organization to survive or improve its position in a highly competitive marketplace. In other words, re-engineering and re-invention are responses to threats. This means that anxiety goes hand-in-hand with re-engineering and re-invention. Paradoxically, one objective of re-engineering and re-invention is to move to more competitive organizational arrangements and processes, where there is enhanced capability to adapt to market conditions. However, the anxiety inherent in the re-engineering and re-invention processes imposes limits on flexibility to adapt and to make choices. Additionally, re-engineering and re-invention result in the severing of ties to existing relationship systems which define the organization and require the development of new defining relationships. Reestablishing new relationships and maintaining them are a source of stress to the individuals involved and can be expected to produce anxious responding of varying intensity in at least some of the individuals. Again, paradoxically, the activities characteristic of re-engineering and re-invention are also sources of the diminished flexibility which attends anxious responding to threatening situations.

In situations of heightened stress and threat to an organization's survival, the customer focus of re-engineering and re-invention may also heighten anxiety within the organization, particularly if the customer itself is experiencing threats to survival. This is because anxiety is "contagious," moving through relationship systems as *triangles* and *interlocking triangles* (Bowen 1978).

Re-engineering and re-invention efforts may also make key leadership positions in the organization vulnerable. As the Mobil example illustrates, the actions taken by change agents brought into an organization as leaders to restructure and bring the organization through critical periods following downsizings are likely to increase anxiety within the organization and diminish flexibility. The change agents themselves may magnify the anxiety if they are not able to establish and maintain a calm presence. Bowen family systems theory predicts that a leader who is able to function more calmly, more thoughtfully, and less anxiously has the potential to diminish anxiety and increase flexibility in a social system.

Bringing Natural Systems Theory to Re-Engineering and Re-Invention

The effects of re-engineering and re-invention on an organization and its members is heightened anxiety and diminished flexibility at the very time heightened flexibility and enhanced functioning are most needed to survive and remain competitive. The "doom and gloom" picture is a natural consequence of an organization's being an emotional system which responds anxiously to re-engineering and re-invention.

It is only a partial picture, however, of how natural systems function. A natural systems theory not only offers insights into the nature of emotional process and anxiety, it also offers insights into the management of anxiety and change.

A natural systems theory of human functioning in social systems such as organizations provides a way of looking at leadership and leadership's contribution to what is happening within the system. If dysfunction is occurring in an organization, a natural systems theory holds that the leader has played a part. From this it follows that the leader may contribute to "fixing" the dysfunction in the system by taking responsibility for his or her contribution to it and by taking steps to eliminate or diminish that contribution.

Conversely, a natural systems theory provides a way of looking at symptoms of dysfunction in an organization. It holds that the most vulnerable parts of the organization are most likely to display such symptoms of dysfunction in the organization. From this it follows that treating the symptoms will not "fix" the organization unless perhaps the symptom is an indicator of lack of basic skills or knowledge to do the job. (In this latter case, an appropriate fix might be education or training of the incumbents or replacement of the incumbents with persons having the necessary skills or knowledge.) "Fixing" the organization, instead, requires attending to one's own functioning in the relationship system, starting with the leader.

A natural systems theory also provides a way of looking at "super stars" and "under achievers." In the well functioning organization, each person has a job to do. The jobs are well-defined; each person is doing his or her job responsibly *and* is allowing others to do the same; there is respect for individual variation; and each person understands and respects the rules of the system (Bowen 1982). A natural systems theory tells us that in a well functioning organization no one should under achieve or over achieve. Either posture suggests dysfunction in the system. If there is a super star, it is reasonable to expect that elsewhere in the system someone else is underfunctioning. A natural systems theory also tells us that the leadership of the organization has a role in bringing the functioning back into alignment.

A natural systems theory may also offer insights into the design and functioning of self-managed teams. For example, the movement to self-managed teams appears in part to be a reaction to rigid, dysfunctional hierarchies. If this perception is accurate, then the move away from hierarchy and toward self-managed teams has an emotional component which may obscure functional ways of organizing a team to accomplish its mission. In this regard, hierarchies in nature provide ways of managing complexity, as well as ways of managing access to scarce resources and the stresses of living in a social system (Bonner 1988; Dunbar 1988). In other words, to reject a hierarchically organized team in reaction to experience with dysfunctional hierarchies may result in rejecting a time-tested, functional way to organize a particular team and get a particular job done.

The foregoing are not meant to be exhaustive of the contributions a natural systems perspective may bring to understanding and functioning in re-engineered and re-invented work places. They are provided to illustrate how a natural systems theory, in particular Bowen family systems theory, may inform the workplace about how the organization may be conceptualized as an emotional system and about what is to be expected when an organization embarks on a process of continuing change to survive and compete in the marketplace.

REFERENCES

Bader, Joyce. 1996. "Rethinking the Consultant's Role." *The Emotional Side of Organizations.* Washington, DC: Georgetown Family Center.

Bonner, John Tyler. 1988. *The Evolution of Complexity by Means of Natural Selection.* Princeton, New Jersey: Princeton University Press.

Bowen, Murray. 1978. *Family Therapy in Clinical Practice.* New York: Jason Aronson, Inc.

———. 1982. Introduction to *Understanding Organizations, Applications of Bowen Family Systems Theory.* R. Sagar and K. Wiseman, eds. Washington, DC: Georgetown University Family Center.

Cohen, Steven and Ronald Brand. 1993. *Total Quality Management, a Practical Guide for the Real World.* San Francisco, California: Jossey-Bass Publishers.

Covey, Stephen R. 1989. *The Seven Habits of Highly Effective People: Restoring the Character Ethic.* New York: Fireside.

Darwin, Charles. [1859]. *The Origin of Species by Means of Natural Selection or the Preservation of Favoured Races in the Struggle for Life.* London, England: Penguin Books Ltd.

Dunbar, Robin I. M. 1988. *Primate Social Systems.* Ithaca, New York: Comstock Publishing Associates of Cornell University Press.

Fossey, Dian. 1983. *Gorillas in the Mist.* Boston: Houghton Mifflin Company.

Gilbert, Roberta M. 1992. *Extraordinary Relationships: A New Way of Thinking about Human Interactions.* Minneapolis: Chronimed Publishing.

Kerr, Michael. September 1988. "Chronic Anxiety." *The Atlantic Monthly.*

Kerr, Michael E. and Murray Bowen. 1988. *Family Evaluation: An Approach Based on Bowen Theory.* New York: W. W. Norton & Company.

Moss, Cynthia. 1988. *Elephant Memories, Thirteen Years in the Life of an Elephant Family.* New York: Fawcett Columbine.

Papero, Daniel V. 1990. *Bowen Family Systems Theory.* Boston, Massachusetts: Allyn and Bacon.

———. 1996. "Anxiety and Organizations." *The Emotional Side of Organizations.* Washington, DC: Georgetown Family Center.

Senge, Peter M. 1990. *The Fifth Discipline, the Art and Practice of the Learning Organization.* New York: Doubleday Currency.

Sherman, Paul W., Jennifer U. M. Jarvis and Richard D. Alexander. 1991. *The Biology of the Naked Mole Rat.* Princeton, New Jersey: Princeton University Press.

Southerland, Daniel. June 19, 1995. Flying High at Mobil: Oil Giant is on the Fast Track after Downsizing Program. *The Washington Post.*

ANXIETY AND ORGANIZATIONS

Daniel V. Papero, PhD

A business founded in a market system has as its principal function its own propagation. It seeks to do this by earning a return on capital invested in it, and its success endeavor is measured by its profitability. A measure of its functioning, therefore, is its ability to return a consistent profit on its operations. When a business grows beyond a sole proprietorship, that growth rests in large measure on the ability of its employees to bring their talents and skills to the task at hand. The functioning of employees, therefore, represents an important component of the company's effort to propagate itself and distinguish itself in terms of profitability.*

A stroll through the business and management section of a good bookstore leads one to conclude that organizations currently find the topic of individual functioning in the organizational context a pertinent subject. Managers are advised to create highly effective people through a regimen for the development of proper habits, exhortation and even, occasionally, threat. Thinkers and activists also look at the functioning of organizations themselves, focusing on communication, strategic planning, the definition of mission, efficiency and a host of other variables believed to be important to enhancing individual effectiveness and organizational productivity. While many of these areas are undoubtedly important, family systems theory suggests that a more basic variable may form the distant drumbeat of personal and organizational functioning, a protean rhythm that sets the pace and challenges the ability of individuals and of organizations to function at their best.

This basic variable, anxiety, affects both individuals and the organization as a whole. People often think of anxiety as a psychological phenomenon or state and, indeed, it falls within the current system of diagnostic categories of psychiatric evaluation. The classification recognizes that anxiety is broader than mental, that the term describes a condition or state of the entire organism or individual. Within the diagnostic categories one finds several classifications of anxiety, such as panic disorder and various types of phobias. All of these apply to the individual alone, and do not touch on a linkage between the state of the individual and his or her position in a relationship network.

---

* As a person relatively unfamiliar with contemporary theories of business and business operations, I am indebted to Mr. Nordahl Brue of the Bruegger Corporation, Burlington, Vermont, for taking his time to read a draft of this paper and to offer suggestions as to how it might be better presented to a business audience. I found his thinking insightful and helpful, and he bears no responsibility whatsoever for my interpretation of his ideas.

Family systems theory views any of the various classifications of anxiety as an expression of the condition of the individual organism. Family systems theory also posits that the condition of the individual cannot be separated from the condition or state of the relationship network in which the individual lives and functions. The markers of the condition of the individual, therefore, mark the condition of the relationship network.

The use of the term relationship network, while accurate, inadequately describes the nature of the group, unit, or perhaps even superorganism (a whole comprised of multiple individuals). Family systems theory, extrapolating from the human family, proposes that units or groups of individuals are connected, each to the others in their various constellations, in a manner that links the functioning of each (physiologically, mentally, and behaviorally) to the functioning of all the others. Some are more vitally linked than others, who are more peripheral. Each person both contributes to and reflects the condition or state of the unit physiologically, mentally, and behaviorally. The interdependence constitutes species-typical behavior of the human and of a large portion of animate life.

Clearly individuals bring to the unit differing capacities for functioning. Some constitutionally display traits that move them into positions of leadership, while others slip into the positions of subordinates. Yet family systems theory maintains that how well each functions either as chief or subordinate is influenced by how the group as a whole functions. Said somewhat differently, the condition of each person (physiologically, mentally, behaviorally) depends to some degree how the group or unit is managing the pressures to adapt to changing conditions. For example, how well the leader leads may relate directly to how well the followers follow. How the leader leads and the followers follow both shapes and reflects the condition of the unit.

The neuroscientist Robert Sapolsky describes clearly the interplay of individual and group in his studies of a baboon troop in Kenya. He notes that physiological functioning changes with social position and an animal one year to the next may be quite different physiologically as its social position changes within the group (Sapolsky 1992). He goes on to propose that the physiological correlates of rank, particularly of dominance, depend upon the type of society in which the rank occurs. With the term *type of society* he refers to whether the society is stable or unstable.

He describes in particular a period of social instability in the group of baboons. He notes that typically in a baboon troop, when an alpha (most dominant) male nears the end of his prime, a beta male, occupying the number two position, is ready to move into the alpha slot when the incumbent falters. During the period he describes, however, no beta was clearly waiting to inherit the alpha position. Instead, positions two through seven had formed a coalition to harass the old leader, who was quickly deposed. Subsequently the coalition rapidly dissolved, and the group entered a period of social instability. No clear hierarchy emerged among the victors. Coalitions formed and dissolved quickly, even several times within a given day. Behaviors reflected a dramatic increase in dominance interactions and aggression and a decrease in feeding and mating behaviors. During this period, according to Sapolsky, the psychological advantages of dominance disappeared. For the half dozen animals at the top of the hierarchy, lack of predictability and lack of control characterized life. Furthermore, the physiological advantages of dominance, present during previous stable periods, vanished. The highest ranking animals no longer enjoyed the lowest basal cortisol concentrations (a measurement of physiological stress) nor the fastest elevations during stress (a measure of flexibility of response). Viewed through the lens of family systems theory, the animals had lost flexibility of response.

From this study and others showing similar findings, Sapolsky concludes that a single physiological profile of dominance does not exist among social primates (Sapolsky 1992). The physiological profile depends, instead, upon the type of society in which it occurs, the critical variable being whether the society is stable or unstable. He further states: "It is my feeling that the psychological advantages and disadvantages of dominance, varying according to social setting, are the critical variables in this stable/unstable dichotomy." (1992, 276-77) Those advantages can be generally described for the individual as a sense of control, of predictably accessible outlets for frustration, and a broad, predictable relationship network around the particular animal. These characteristics vanish during a period of instability.

The instability of the group is actually one of perception, based presumably in each animal's perceived lack of predictability and lack of control in the absence of a clear group structure. That perceptual instability leads to each individual's focus on the relationship system, on the position of each with regard to the other(s). The focus on the other(s) coupled with the increased interactional intensity results in the various behavioral indicators of increased instability in the group.

Sapolsky's description of the baboon troop as stable or unstable approximates family system theory's use of the term anxiety applied to the unit. The unstable unit is reflected in the changes in physiology, mental process, and behavior of the unit's members. Instead of the dichotomous concepts of stable and unstable, family systems theory views the condition of the unit ranging along a broad continuum from very stable to very unstable with many variations between the extremes. In the mid ranges of the stability/instability continuum (in family systems terms the continuum of the intensity of anxiety) the condition of the unit might be reflected in the functioning of a portion of the group, perhaps in a few peripheral relationships or in the functioning of a few individuals.

Again extrapolating from knowledge of the human family, various markers reflect the changing condition of the unit. Intensifying anxiety for the individual is marked by heightened sensitivity to others in the group, shifts in perception and interpretation of events and behavior, and an increasing automaticity of behavior. A characteristic feeling is that of helplessness and fear. Aside from the markers of individual distress characteristic of changes in the condition of the individual organism, relationships predominantly express the shifting condition of the group from more to less stable. As with Sapolsky's baboons, interpersonal encounters—aggression, conflict, postural bluffing (often in what appears to be the human variant of dominance interactions)—emerge and recede. Alliances also appear and dissolve, a process family systems theory incorporates in the concept of triangling. The various emerging markers of increasing instability (i.e. anxiety) reflect shifting physiology, mental process and behavior of the participants. If the anxiety is sufficiently intense and the instability severe, the various markers of "mob process" emerge—intense efforts to extrude one individual or one group leading even to violence, stalemated polarization between subgroups, panic reactions based on a shared perception and consequent fear, and so forth. Family systems theory defines these processes as emotional and automatic, predictably repeating to reflect the intensity of anxiety and the degree of instability in the group.

A most remarkable quality of anxiety, so well-known to humans that it often is overlooked, is its infectiousness. The physiological, mental, and behavioral markers of anxiety tend to spread upon exposure from one person to the next to the next. Sometimes the spreading of anxiety leads to a dampening of intensity; at other times the spreading is accompanied by rapid intensification of anxiety. Whether anxiety spreads and whether it intensifies as it spreads depends upon the interplay of at least the following variables: the severity and magnitude of the actual stressor(s), the state or condition of the relationship network at the time of the stressor (where it would fall on the continuum from unstable to stable), and the ability of key individuals to maintain functioning (both mental and behavioral) in the face of the changes and pressures in the network marking the intensification of anxiety or increasing instability.

If anxiety spreads and becomes more intense, the characteristic markers of instability appear. If sufficiently intense, large numbers of people become involved, and one can speak accurately of a storm of anxiety sweeping through the unit, displaying in intense version and on a large scale the characteristic markers of anxiety in the unit. Among the more prominent examples of large storms of anxiety one can include the witchcraft persecutions of Europe and North America in the late sixteenth and early seventeenth centuries, any number of investment frenzies and their corresponding financial panics, and even, perhaps, the polarizations of large nation-states, for example that of the United States and the Soviet Union during the so-called cold war.

If Bowen theory's description of the relationship between anxiety and functioning in the unit is accurate, what then can be drawn from this perspective that may be of use to organizations and businesses as they attempt to position themselves in the shifting climate of modern society? The first may be simply the basic idea that when the intensity of anxiety decreases, the ability of the individual and the unit to function at a more efficient level increases. The people who form any work group represent a portion of the anxiety equation. To the degree that such people recognize, understand the impact of, and possess skill in the management of anxiety, the organization should be able to maintain a high level of efficiency in functioning in highly uncertain, difficult environments. If the concept of differentiation drawn from the Bowen theory is accurate, some will automatically possess such knowledge. Others may be able to acquire a satisfactory degree of mastery through effort and experience. If the critical personnel in an organization have developed a degree of competency, and can operate with the skills of anxiety management, their functioning in the relationship network can help stabilize others whose skills are not so well developed and practiced.

How leaders emerge and conduct themselves, therefore, takes on heightened importance. An important task of a leader concerns maintaining stability in the group. Sapolsky discusses the characteristics of animals that rise to dominant positions in a troop. He writes about the style of the animal, how it achieves and manages its rank within the group Sapolsky 1992). Analyzing ten years of data on the behavior of the animals, Sapolsky and his researchers found subsets of animals that show certain extremes of behavior (styles) and that low basal cortisol levels characterized a certain stylistic subset of dominant animal.

These animals displayed the following behavioral characteristics: 1. They were excellent at discriminating between threatening and neutral interactions with social rivals, and 2. If a rival was determined to be threatening, these animals tended to initiate the fight. Even though in general Sapolsky's researchers determined that initiating a fight is not usually a successful strategy (initiators typically lose 80% of such fights) these animals mostly initiated winning fights, implying that they were picking their fights carefully, suggesting social knowledge, control, and general savvy. 3. Once the fight had occurred, these animals were best at determining whether they had won or lost. 4. If the animal lost the fight, low basal cortisol levels were associated with those animals who most often displaced aggression onto third parties. Sapolsky refers to this behavior as an outlet for frustration. 5. Finally, lower basal cortisol levels were found among those animals who spent the most time grooming and being groomed by nonestrus females and interacting with females and infants. In short, Sapolsky's research demonstrates that a fully flexible stress response, indicative in terms of this paper of efficiency of functioning, and a set of behaviors described previously characterize the group of animals that consistently maintain high ranking positions within the baboon troop.

In writing about the functioning of the human family unit, Dr. Bowen wrote the following:

> Operationally, ideal family treatment begins when one can find a family leader with the courage to define self, who is as invested in the welfare of the family as in self, who is neither angry nor dogmatic, whose energy goes to changing self rather than telling others what they should do, who can know and respect the multiple opinions of others, who can modify self in response to the strengths of the group, and who is not influenced by the irresponsible opinions of others. . . . A family leader is beyond the popular notion of power. A responsible family leader automatically generates mature leadership qualities in other family members who are to follow. (Kerr and Bowen 1988, 342-43)

Generalizing from Sapolsky's research and from Bowen theory, one can speculate about the characteristics of people who may become effective leaders, particularly during periods of accelerating anxiety in the organization. First of all, effective leaders will likely have good control of their own emotional reactivity. They will have the ability to establish relationships and remain in contact with the various factions in the organization that push for rapid, fix-it change and the victory of narrow self-interest. The ability to remain in contact with intense, conflictual others is necessary if the potential leader is to employ knowledge of triangles to help position him- or herself in a manner to reduce the intensity of anxiety in the system and produce greater stability.

The ability to discriminate among threats and challenges to the organization will certainly be an important characteristic. Leaders who are functioning efficiently will recognize situations that must be responded to and those that do not represent a significant challenge to the organization. They will also tend to initiate the response to the challenging situation and will quickly and accurately assess how effective their response has been. These three characteristics, the efficient assessment of threat, the initiation of the response, and the assessment of effectiveness check and reinforce one another.

People who may become effective leaders will have developed what Sapolsky calls outlets for frustration and what Bowen theory refers to as the management of emotional reactivity. Whether such mechanisms involve displacement of aggression remains to be seen. Clearly the human displays this characteristic, but it is less clear whether it is a component of effective leadership. This linking of Bowen and Sapolsky is not exactly accurate, since the concept of outlets for frustration incorporates the mechanisms that Bowen theory refers to as anxiety binding, but the notion of mechanisms for the management of the stress response/anxiety is common to both. In a sense all of the characteristics listed above are psychological, a matter of perception, of attitude, of mindset. No one has said it better than Sapolsky. ". . . the psychological filters with which those external events are perceived alter the resultant physiology with at least as much potency as the stressor itself . . . .For us clever primates, life is filled with ambiguous events, and we differ as to whether we quench life's thirsts from glasses that are perceived as half full or half empty." (Sapolsky 1992, 280)

The subject of psychological filters leads again to Bowen theory, and the subject is more complex than simply half empty or half full. The view of the glass as half empty comes out of a position of high anxiety and personal sense of loss of control and lack of predictability. When individuals and units can shake the pervasive filter of helplessness, anxiety decreases and functioning improves. Knowledge of how the emotional system of the unit operates can assist in reducing helplessness. Leaders may well need the skill of recognizing the difference between the content and the process of organizational situations. While the content of anxiety or instability shifts with the wind, the process of how people and the group act remains relatively predictable. For example, the emergence of the alliance process in the group, triangling in terms of Bowen theory, can occur around all sorts of issues when the anxiety is sufficiently intense. Knowledge of how triangles function and how particular triangles operate as well as developing the skills of detriangling can all be important aids to reduce helplessness in the anxious climate of the organization.

Many of the skills developed to manage one's own emotional reactivity derived from family systems theory can assist the individual and the leader's efforts to remain functional in the face of intense group instability. Such skills include the ability to listen to and comprehend the other's perception of the situation, an ability to grasp what the other believes he or she is facing. The leader will have to have a deep interest in the welfare of the entire organization and be able to retain that interest in the face of forceful pressures to follow the quick-fix proposition of one or another group or the appeasing gestures that lead to long term confrontation and disruption. He or she will have to have some capacity to maintain the position that family systems theory refers to as emotional neutrality, characterized by not taking sides in response to emotional pressures to do so, the capacity to observe while participating, and the paradoxical stance of full involvement without becoming too concerned about the outcome of the endeavor. The leader will have to be able to distill facts from the cauldron of intense feeling and communicate about those facts to feelingful others. He or she will have to present thinking about those facts that is not heavily laced with personal subjectivity.

Beyond addressing the challenges of leadership, what does family systems theory have to offer the contemporary corporation or organization? First and foremost may be the lesson, hard-learned in families, that change-oriented, fix-it approaches that focus on changing the behavior of someone else to quell one's own anxiety are not only ineffective but can make the problem worse. They are expressive of the unstable condition of the unit. Family systems theory would posit that the identified problem, whether in an individual or in a relationship or a network of relationships, reflects the condition of the group, its position on the stability/instability continuum. Approaches that focus on the problem without including the overall condition of the unit appear much more likely to be ineffective or even counterproductive. Slower, long-term approaches to problems, approaches that focus on the system that has produced the problem, may be more effective than an approach that promises a quick fix. A corollary would suggest that what seems to be the easy way may not be the best way to improve functioning within an organization.

Whether such a measured approach is feasible in an anxious organization remains to be seen. The discomfort generated by the intensity of anxiety or degree of instability in the group will emerge typically as a strong pressure to relieve discomfort quickly. All things being equal, the pressures for quick relief will be self-centered on the individual or the subgroup, leading to conflict and potential polarizations as the self interest of the various groups clash, heightened by the discomfort of anxiety. The outcome can be increased discomfort, anxiety, and instability, leading to even more intense pressures for rapid solutions which relieve discomfort. The leadership qualities noted above will have to emerge in this climate.

REFERENCES

Kerr, Michael E. and Murray Bowen. 1988. *Family Evaluation: An Approach Based on Bowen Theory*. New York: W. W. Norton & Company.

Sapolsky, Robert M. 1992. *Stress, the Aging Brain, and the Mechanisms of Neuron Death*. Cambridge, Massachusetts: The MIT Press.

3

HUMAN SOCIAL SYSTEMS

HUMAN SOCIAL SYSTEMS

Introduction

The human family is a social system. Dr. Bowen developed the majority of the concepts of Bowen family systems theory through observations of members of human families. He recognized that there are other human social systems and that emotional process appears to operate in these systems as well. When he finally believed that he had a sufficient factual basis to support the concept of societal emotional process, he added that concept to the theory.

Human social systems vary extensively in size, composition, and purpose but exhibit fundamental patterns of functioning at the emotional level. These patterns are described by the eight concepts of Bowen family systems theory. Family-owned businesses, prisons, government bureaucracies, multinational ventures and the society as a whole are but a few examples of human social systems.

This section on societal emotional process leads off with a paper by Dr. Ann Bunting, a clinical psychologist in Shelbourne, Vermont and an editorial consultant to the Georgetown Family Center's journal, *Family Systems*. Her paper, "Bowen Theory: Potential Applications for the Field of Corrections," describes her efforts to apply Bowen family systems theory to the design of prison systems. Her paper focuses on her work as a member of a committee composed of public and private sector professionals whose purpose has been to design a private prison with the goal of returning productive citizens to society.

In the second paper, "Consulting to Russian-American Joint Ventures," Dr. Katherine Baker, president of Intercultural Training Associates in Washington, DC, discusses how she has applied Bowen family systems theory to assist her in achieving neutrality in observing and thinking about the emotional process operating in joint ventures. Emotional process often exhibits itself among the principals in joint ventures as a focus on the cultural differences to explain why there were problems in the relationship system.

The third paper, "Violence in the Workplace: A Family Systems Perspective," is by Dr. Walter H. Smith of the Western Pennsylvania Family Center, Pittsburgh, Pennsylvania, and an editorial consultant to *Family Systems*. Today in the United States there is much societal anxiety about violence in the family and the workplace, especially where children are involved. Dr. Smith presents his perspective on violence as a symptom of fundamental and basic emotional processes in human life. He presents a case study of murder in the making by an employee of an organization in which aggression was a routine pattern of functioning.

Before proceeding to the three papers, the editors have included a discussion of two social systems with which Dr. Bowen had great familiarity. One was the Georgetown Family Center, which he founded. The other was the 110 year old Bowen family business. In his interview with Kathleen Wiseman, Dr. Bowen described these two social systems.

Georgetown Family Center

I've had a business [for thirty years]. The name of that is the Georgetown Family Center. It was a collection of people who were in training with me back in the early days who I believed were motivated to work on themselves rather than on saying the problem isn't there or blaming someone else. The problem is still there. I would say the personnel of the Family Center is absolutely unique in being the only one that has not changed its functioning position in thirty years. We have lost a handful of people. Every family institute that was started twenty-five to thirty years ago has had a major disruption within the first few years of its life. It's literally been pulled apart, which would be the equivalent to a family business failing. Every single one. And I bet we are the only one that is still running under its original charter.

I started out with a working proposition which said that if any disharmony occurs within this outfit, I played a part in it. And if I don't get critical of things and I try to fix my part in it, the business will give back. And it has. Now that doesn't mean I've been 100 percent successful because I've flip-flopped more than I'd like to admit. But I'm able to see it and get on top of it. And we're still carrying on thirty years later.

Bowen Family Business

The family business was started 110 years ago with my great-grandfather. Then when he died he turned it over to my grandfather for another fifteen years, then he died and turned it over to his son and his son's sister, who was my mother. My mother married Dad, who was sort of a turned-on, hard-working fellow and the business went for about forty to fifty years with Dad and his brother-in-law running it. Mother got involved in it and all of Dad's and Mother's kids got involved in it a little bit, at least till they got away to college and that sort of thing. It went into a hell of an upheaval in 1959, which was about eighty years out. And that's when Uncle was influenced by his wife. He was sort of a passive fellow. But his wife got into a spat with Dad about running the business. And, well, when he got into the thing with Uncle's wife, they got into a big fight. I remember one big fight, when Dad bought a new ambulance, which was fairly expensive, and she didn't like it. And she slapped Dad one day and knocked his glasses off. Then they got into a deal in which my younger brother bought out my uncle's half of the business and Dad gave little brother his half for moving back home. So little brother has now taken it over and is running it. Twenty years, and now my brother's oldest son has become a partner with my brother running it and he married a girl from the local hospital there. They have two daughters, so one of these days my brother will bow out and turn it over to his son, which I would guess would be another ten years, which would be 120 years. And I don't know where it'll go from there. I don't know what will happen, but it can't continue forever.

[As to the principles that made it successful], I don't know. There are so many doggone things you can go into. Generally, it went to the one who was most responsible for self in the total family. And each transfer did that. My great-grandfather started it, he passed it on to his oldest son, who was the most responsible for his parents during their later years. Then he passed it along to his son, then to his daughter, my mother. Dad was the responsible one. He was the one who put the fire into it and kept it going and built it up. So Dad was the responsible one. And that went on for about fifty years and he passed it on to the son who had done the most to move back home and take over. Dad had worked a number of years for essentially no money. They gave him a place to live and he gradually bought out my uncle and is passing it along to his oldest son. The other two sons moved away.

BOWEN THEORY: POTENTIAL IMPLICATIONS FOR THE FIELD OF CORRECTIONS

Ann Bunting, PhD

For the past two years I have been part of a committee comprised of public officials and private professionals whose purpose has been to design a private prison that would return productive citizens to society. My interest in joining the committee was the challenge of applying the concepts of Bowen theory to the field of corrections. I came to the committee with experience as an expert witness in court cases pertaining to child custody disputes and to questions about terminating parental rights. Additionally, I had clinical experience coaching parents of children and spouses of mates with behavior problems.

This paper will describe those aspects of the project which are relevant to Bowen theory. Two significant questions the committee addressed from the beginning were: how much change is possible for prisoners and what kinds of variables influence the process of change for people who violate basic societal and personal norms.

The concepts from Bowen theory most useful to these questions were differentiation, cut-off, multigenerational and nuclear family emotional process, and societal anxiety.[1] The three areas focused on were the prison structure, family relationships, and community contact.

Goals of the Committee

The United States has one of the highest rates of incarceration of any country in the world.[2] The actual result of such high rates is that the goals of punishment and containment are addressed, albeit imperfectly, while the societal goal of rehabilitation is impeded. Since there is very little successful rehabilitation, public safety from the behaviors of those who are imprisoned is limited only to the time they are in prison. Once released, many offenders return to criminal activities. Some are released with more skills and determination to carry out criminal behavior. The costs of crime are high in terms of loss of life and property before and after incarceration and in terms of the costs of imprisonment (roughly $25,000 per prisoner per year in the state in which the committee works).

The goal of graduating productive citizens is a reflection of the desire to think long term about criminal behavior in the hopes of eliminating some of the negative consequences to society of crime and of opening the possibility of more positive consequences to society from rehabilitation.

Defining the mission of the project and the means of funding it remain central preoccupations. All along, there have been temptations to deviate from agreed upon ideas in order to meet the needs of the current corrections system in our state, to get funding, or simply out of impatience to get going. The committee defined goals and assumptions about variables that bring about change.

Change requires an emphasis on individual functioning and consistency in structure and contact over time. The committee decided to develop a two year program for prisoners. Program officials are to develop specific rules for functioning on the part of prisoners within the setting and clear expectations for performance in educational and vocational arenas and within family and community relationship networks.

Change also requires some level of personal initiative and belief in the principles upon which the program is based. One way to test out individual motivation and to reinforce the importance of personal responsibility is to have a program which prisoners must apply to enter and from which they can be expelled if they don't meet the basic requirements. Thus, willingness to take responsibility for entering the program and for making use of their time in prison became two major criteria for acceptance of prisoners. This is in contrast to accepting people solely on the basis of the type of crime they committed or by simply accepting everyone.

The desire for maximum choice in hiring and firing personnel, in training staff, and in defining directions and programs for the prison led to the decision to work towards a privately run prison. Also a private prison might be better able to hold firm in its principles in the face of societal anxiety. Society has an impact on how prisons function primarily through local, state and federal politics which influence funding, and secondarily through the media.

A decision was made to explore the possibilities of using the program to "incubate" new businesses and to develop a self-supporting financial base. This idea is related to four goals: (1) To provide a financial incentive to prisoners in the form of stock ownership or salary and to increase their capacity to contribute directly, while in prison, to family, society, and their own future. Money earned would go towards some form of restitution to society for the crime(s) committed, to family support, and to savings for use at discharge. (2) To prepare prisoners for life after prison through the acquisition of skills and a network of business relationships. (3) To contribute to the state's economy so that prisons become more of a positive force in the state and to decrease the societal projection process which often defines prisons and prisoners in harsh and/or simplistic terms. (4) To gain independence from financial sources which might have conflicting goals and which might be withdrawn.

Community contact is an important facet of life which is often overlooked in prisons. Therefore, the committee emphasized the development of programs such as child care or repair centers and of facilities such as restaurants and meeting rooms, all of which serve a positive function in the community. Such facilities and programs have the potential to decrease the societal projection process and to increase the sense of responsibility of prisoners to the larger community. Long-term change is reinforced by a thoughtful transition from prison to home and community and by appropriate placement in a job or educational program.

Follow-up contact with graduates and their families is an important way to stay in touch and to learn. This was considered necessary to provide ongoing support and to measure the efficacy of the program over time.

Family Relationships

The efficacy of including family members as a significant aspect of a prisoner's experience while incarcerated is slowly gaining acceptance across the nation. Unwittingly, many prison programs have reinforced the process of cut-off which often exists as a component of the prisoner's multigenerational family emotional history. My challenge in thinking through this area has been twofold: how to present the *idea* of multigenerational process as a potentially significant force for change in a way that makes sense to the committee and the wider public, and how to incorporate the *process* of multigenerational contact into the structure of the ongoing program as well as have it available as one of the "therapies" from which inmates and their families could choose.

Multigenerational process is an idea that makes sense. While the importance of family is recognized in many prisons today, most programs focus upon parenting skills and potential inclusion of very young children within the prison structure. This is, of course, primarily true for female prisoners. Spouses are also included. Least likely to be included are parents, grandparents, siblings, aunts, uncles and cousins.

One aspect of societal anxiety that influences this process is the tendency on the part of the public and prison officials to blame families for producing offspring with criminal behavior. The idea that these same families might be useful in producing more functional behavior seems contradictory. This view is reinforced by many of the prisoners who blame family members and society for their misbehavior and/or incarceration.

To understand the potential significance of family attachments in producing long-term better functioning, I believe, one needs to have the idea of the family as an emotional unit as defined by Dr. Murray Bowen.[3] His theory places the family in an evolutionary context and defined some of the processes which might account for a wide variety of functioning among humans.[4] The concept of differentiation and its emphasis on the difference between thinking and feeling within the individual and among family members suggests a process of thinking through, step-by-step, more constructive ways of functioning in relationships. The concepts of anxiety and reactivity and the use of triangles to mediate these processes give clues for understanding what is going on in self and within relationships. They also provide a more objective way of evaluating the functioning of self and others.

The work of Dr. Bowen also implies that constructive functioning of humans is dependent upon significant relationships with multiple members of one's family and of society. The processes of anxiety and reactivity inhibit the development of multiple relationships and tend to foster a few intense relationships which cannot sustain continued and calm contact for any consistent length of time.[4]

One of the ways prisons can be useful to family functioning is the containment of behavior that has made family members anxious. Thus, it provides an opportunity for family members to calm down and to think about the problems in the family more clearly. Similarly, a structured environment in which the prisoner's access to alcohol and drugs is restricted opens the possibility of clearer thinking. The restriction of these kinds of behavior also means the prisoner has to find other, more constructive ways, hopefully, of alleviating anxiety. Given that family members might be calmer and prisoners more restricted, there is the possibility of all attending to family relationships in a more responsible way. This is even more feasible within a prison structure that encourages them to do so.

The development of more thoughtful behavior and of the capacity to allow differences to emerge among family members has the promise of leading to more contact within the nuclear family and between the generations as well. This, in turn, helps defuse the intensity of the relationships formed in prison and gives the prisoner the possibility of staying out of the waves of anxiety which can sweep through a prison. The prison population might, therefore, function at a higher level if more contact within and between generations were fostered.

I would like to propose to the committee that one of the requirements for entry into this program be the willingness of the applicant to think about family relationships and to learn about family emotional processes. This might be indicated initially by a willingness to provide facts about the family across several generations and to think through a series of questions about his or her own ways of functioning around family members. A further set of questions would focus on clarifying underlying assumptions and beliefs many family members share. A related requirement might be the willingness of at least one family member, and hopefully more, to participate in the prison programs and to think about the family relationship system.

Regular weekend and evening programs in which family members could participate give both the inmate and the family time to be together in a calmer environment. In this case, the prison officials as well as other prisoners and their families have the opportunity of functioning as a neutral pole on a triangle when anxiety increases between family members and prisoners. I also think it would be useful to give responsibility to family members as well as inmates for planning and carrying out these events.

I would like to explore the development of incremental increases in privileges based on the capacity of the inmate to take responsibility for him- or herself within the prison and upon the ability of the inmate and family members to function responsibly around each other. This might include time outside of the prison spent in the company of family members. Modern technology might make this feasible through electronic surveillance systems. The significant point is that the prisoner and the family members would have to negotiate with each other and with the prison officials for these incremental increases in privileges. As a third step, the inmate and the family would have to negotiate with relevant community members (such as friends of children and their families, or the local police station) in those instances when time out of prison occurs. Such a structure of negotiations has the potential of providing experiences of resolving anxiety-provoking differences constructively and in mutually satisfactory ways. Finally, I would like to see the possibility of including interested and talented family members in the businesses run by the prison and in the programs offering service to the community.

Community Contact

The various avenues for increasing community contact have been touched upon in the other sections of this paper. The role of the institution itself in society is the first area of consideration. Within this program, several ways in which the institution might contribute to the community pertain to activities like a repair shop, a restaurant or a day care center. A more significant contribution, and a more difficult one, is the development of businesses and/or the training of inmates to fill needed roles within the state. In a state such as ours, which has suffered from a long recession, successful new businesses would be welcomed.

The idea of providing individual prisoners and their families more access to the community has been captured in the ideas described in the prior paragraph. However, an even more significant arena for establishing contact would be in the home community or neighborhood of the inmate. This is an especially difficult task because there is resistance on all sides. Nevertheless, part of the task of rehabilitation means taking responsibility for the crimes committed and being able to handle oneself in the presence of emotions exhibited by threatened parties. Some of those emotions entail feelings of shame and distancing on the part of family members and feelings of fear and disapprobation on the part of the local community. While initially anxiety-provoking, such efforts on the part of prisoners, families and communities could lead in the long run to calmer contact, reduced distortions and better understanding of life's complexities.

It is not clear at this point whether this program will ever become a reality. Two things of interest have happened, however. First, given the quality of leadership demonstrated by the man who organized the committee, the ideas developed by the members have been spread throughout the state and within the corrections system. They are alive and under consideration. If we don't pursue them, it is likely others will. Second, we have found a program which has already actualized many of the ideas (although not those about family) and has a twenty-five year success rate.[5] We may at least be influential in bringing that program to the state. It's been a project well worth our effort.

END NOTES

[1]There are a number of books which explain the eight concepts of Bowen theory. I refer the reader to Murray Bowen. 1978. *Family Therapy in Clinical Practice.* New York: Jason Aronson, Inc. and Michael E. Kerr and Murray Bowen. 1988. *Family Evaluation.* New York: W. W. Norton & Co..

[2]The committee members were given many sources which reported this fact. One example is: Paulette Thomas. 1994. "Making Crime Pay; Triangle of Interest Created Infrastructure to Fight Lawlessness." *Wall Street Journal,* May 12, A6.

[3]See references in note 1. Additional source is Bowen-Kerr Interview Series. 1979. "Family Systems Theory and Therapy: An Overview." *Videotapes and Audiotapes on Family Systems*

Theory and Therapy. Pamphlet produced by the Georgetown Family Center, Washington, DC.

[4]Ibid. The following article is an example of how an evolutionary context can be helpful when thinking about the development of the family as a unit and the shaping of family functioning over time: Robert Noone. 1994. "Intergenerational Attachment and the Family." *Family Systems* 1:2 (114-125).

[5]Many articles have been written on the Delancey Street Foundation. Two examples are: Gross, Jane. 1991. "Ex-convicts Are Serving Blintzes Instead of Time." *The New York Times*. December 18, and Raine, George, 1993. "Drug Czar Taps into Delancey Street." *San Francisco Examiner*. November 28.

References on Criminals and Prisons

Cadwalader, George. 1988. *Castaways: The Penikese Island Experiment*. Vermont. Chelsea Green Publishing Company. An objective and thought-provoking account of one effort to rehabilitate hard-core juvenile delinquents. One of the sub-themes is the story of how societal process, as reflected in the state corrections system and in academic debates, influenced the structure of treatment programs in Massachusetts over the past 25 years.

Gilmore, Mikal. 1994. *Shot in the Heart*. New York: Doubleday. A biography of Garry Gilmore. A complex approach to the question of the development of criminal behavior. A broad historic, religious and multigenerational background is given as well as an account of Gary Gilmore's individual life course and his interaction with various correction systems.

Harris, Jean. 1986. *Stranger in Two Worlds*. New York: MacMillan. She brings an educator's experience and thinking to her observations about the range of human functioning that makes up a prison population and to her description of the inadequate response of the corrections system to the problems.

CONSULTING TO RUSSIAN-AMERICAN JOINT VENTURES

Katharine G. Baker, DSW

Intercultural Training Associates, Inc. (ITA) came into being in 1992 when a number of Russian and American colleagues with experience in both countries formed a partnership offering consultation to Russian-American joint ventures that was based on Bowen family systems theory (Bowen 1978; Kerr and Bowen 1988; Papero 1990). The Soviet Union had recently collapsed, and its successor states were starting to develop free market economies. Many Russian and American entrepreneurs sensed the enormous possibilities of huge new consumer markets and they were rushing into partnerships with each other, creating new companies or joint ventures. The Americans were supposed to supply Western economic know-how, while the Russians would supply the local resources and cheap, well-educated labor. Almost as fast as these joint ventures were formed, many began to fall apart. Frequently these business failures were blamed on "cultural misunderstanding." Russians and Americans didn't "know" each other and had launched into working with each other in a state of cultural ignorance. ITA's partners believed that Bowen family systems theory might prove useful as a mediating approach to understanding Russian-American joint ventures.

Complaints on both sides tended to reflect stereotypical thinking. The Americans complained that Russians did not know what a contract meant. They would sign agreements and then not be committed to them. Americans described Russian managers as rigid and authoritarian, making decisions without consulting with their American partners. They thought Russian workers lacked energy, initiative, and a sense of responsibility or accountability in their work.

The Russians complained that their American partners were "ignorant and arrogant." Americans pushed their way into agreements without developing solid relationships with their new partners. They were superficially friendly and smiled a lot, but did not know how to connect on the "deeply spiritual" level that was necessary to develop trust in a Russian partnership. According to the Russians, Americans were uncultured, driven by time constraints, insensitive, and acted as if they knew all the answers. They were also naive about the harsh realities of doing business in Russia and were easy to fool.

As ITA began to consult with bicultural business enterprises, the partners came to understand that joint ventures involved considerable financial and personal risk on both sides. American investors risked corporate capital, as well as the company's time and resources. The Russians had fewer financial assets to risk, but they risked time, resources, and the uncertainty of participating in Western-style economic and financial structures that were completely new to them. Bowen theory offered useful descriptors for understanding the relationships in joint ventures. The inevitable *anxiety* associated with these risks transformed itself into a focus on the "faults of the other," and on the behavioral and psychological differences between Russians and Americans in the workplace. Complex, *interlocking triangles* developed between Russian and American managers and their subordinates, as well as with their boards of directors, Western corporate headquarters, and other providers of investment capital. For example, a Russian manager would form an alliance with Russian workers in which the American partner-manager was on the outside; or an American manager would form a special relationship with a Western board of directors (and capital source), which would fail to consult the Russian partner when making key financial decisions.

ITA also saw these business relationship failures as imbedded in the wider context of a post-Cold War *societal emotional process* which could be described as repetitive cycles of reactivity. For fifty years there had been rigid international polarization, with the United States and the Soviet Union locked in a superpower nuclear standoff. From the point of view of family systems theory, one might describe the post-Cold War years as a period in which an intensely *reactive togetherness* movement began to develop. The former archenemy superpowers were determined to become partners in a world still grappling with anxiety fueled by a continuing nuclear threat, dramatic political changes, and pervasive macroeconomic instability. The United States tended to define itself in an *overfunctioning* role, as Congress allocated funds to help the *underfunctioning* former Soviet Union overcome seventy years of economic mismanagement and socio-political totalitarianism.

The Russian reaction to this U. S. effort was mixed. They both welcomed and were suspicious of the *togetherness* effort. They were pleased to be the recipients of grants, loans, and training to jump-start their moribund socialist economy, but they resented the implication that Americans (and other Westerners, as well as Japanese) knew what was best for them.

The Russians in some ways accepted the *underfunctioning* label that the Americans had given them. Clearly their standard of living lagged far behind those of the American, Japanese, and Western European market economies. But they responded to offers of help with a combination of embarrassed humility and demands for respect as a former superpower. This *reactive* ambivalence led to heightened *anxiety* on the American side. Americans have always preferred that the recipients of their largesse be grateful, and the Russians were not unreservedly grateful. They were not sure they wanted a completely Western-style market economy if it meant giving up national pride and self-respect in the process.

The reaction of an increasingly conservative American Congress to this Russian ambivalence was a drastic reduction in aid and training programs. Difficulties began to develop in the wider geopolitical arena when the United States and Russia attempted to work together as post-Cold War international partners; at the same time, political problems began to emerge within Russia as so-called economic reformers clashed with regressive nationalists in establishing viable new governmental and economic structures.

As with most *reactive togetherness processes*, the relationship between the United States and Russia was supposed to be "sweetness and light" on all international, organizational, and interpersonal levels in order to contain the *societal anxiety* that had been expressed in the old days by mutual threats and posturing. This paper cannot address the *management of anxiety* at national and international levels. But at the organizational level, when the inevitable frictions developed in Russian-American business joint ventures, the search for scapegoats was on, and "culture" became a convenient catchall term for explaining away some of the broader contextual and process issues.

In offering "cross-cultural consultation," ITA accepted the initial problem definition of Russian-American joint ventures as lying in the realm of "culture," but also worked with clients to move beyond that narrow focus on differences toward the kind of understanding that family systems theory could bring to the underlying relationship processes that fueled the conflict.

What is culture and how can it fit into a systems view of human relationships? From the anthropological point of view, culture is a broadly descriptive framework for understanding a range of individual, family, group, organizational and societal behaviors and values within a social species (Bourguignon 1979, Kluckhohn and Strodtbeck 1961, Spiegel 1982). The concept is usually applied to humans, but is also used to describe the behavior of other social mammals (Bonner 1980, Goodall 1990, Moss 1988, Trivers 1985, Wilson 1975). Culture, in this anthropological and ethological sense, includes behavior, communication, and language patterns, aspects of family structure (such as male and female roles), interactional patterns in organizational systems (such as leadership styles and norms for decision making), and subjective domains such as the arts, religion, and values.

Spiegel cites Kluckhohn's model of culture as being limited to five basic arenas within which humans function: time, activity, the relationship orientation, the man-nature orientation, and the basic nature of man. Within these five arenas, Spiegel states that "although there is variability. . . . [it] is neither limitless nor random but occurs within a range of three possible solutions for each [arena]" (Spiegel 1982). For example,
(1) Time: past, present, future.
(2) Activity: doing, being, being-in-becoming.
(3) Relational: individual, collateral, lineal.
(4) Man-nature: harmony-with-nature, mastery-over-nature, subjugated-to-nature.
(5) Basic nature of man: neutral/mixed, good, evil.

Spiegel concludes that

> "all possible solutions are in varying degrees present in the total cultural structure of every society, and every society will be characterized not only by a dominant profile of first-order value choices but also by substitute second- and third-order choices. Differences among various cultures are based on the pattern of preferences for each of these solutions in a dominant-substitute profile of values." (1982)

Using this model to understand patterns within Russian-American joint ventures led to a focus on differences and polarization. In the Spiegel model, Russians have been described as "past" oriented, centered in "being" rather than "doing," "collateral" in their relationships and with a view of the basic nature of man as "evil." Americans were described as "future" oriented, valuing "doing," "individualism," and with a basic view of man as "good." Russians and Americans overlapped in their shared value of "man's mastery over nature." This emphasis on differences did not lead to smoother, more responsible working relationships within joint ventures.

Another model for analyzing cultural variation is the use of an "emic-etic" axis (Brislin and Pedersen 1976). These terms have been usefully borrowed by cultural anthropologists from linguistics (Brislin, Lonner, and Thorndike 1973). In linguistics a phon*emic* analysis records sounds which are meaningful in a specific language. A phon*etic* analysis records all sounds, whether or not they are used in a given language. The term *emic*, therefore, as used by cultural anthropologists, refers to specific cultures and their differences. The term *etic* is a theoretical attempt to incorporate many different systems in cultural descriptions (Brislin and Pedersen 1976).

When an *emic-etic* axis is used to describe a range of approaches to cultural analysis (see Table 1), the *emic* end of the axis focuses on the many *differences* between cultures, and the *etic* end of the axis describes the *universalities* within the human species. This author believes that both positions can be extreme and driven by *anxiety*.

Often the *emic* position's focus on differences can lead in the direction of conflict and *cut-off*, and away from the ability to put energy into productivity and joint problem solving. For example, an *emic* analysis of Russian-American joint ventures would focus on the many behavioral and attitudinal differences one might encounter in developing a bicultural working team. An *etic* analysis would search for underlying commonalities, which can be useful in keeping the focus on objective tasks to be accomplished in a business setting. However, this approach can push too strongly in the direction of *togetherness*, masking real differences. For example, an *etic* analysis of a Russian-American joint venture would tend to deny differences and to assume that because all the employees are human, they probably approach their work in similar ways.

TABLE 1: CULTURAL AXES

LEVEL OF ANALYSIS	EMIC	BOWEN THEORY	ETIC
Focus	Focus on differences between groups	Focus on facts, objectivity	Focus on similarities
Assumptions	All cultures are different	Neutral about cultural issues	All cultures are the same
Emotional Process	Cut-off	Differentiation	Togetherness

This author believes that most observations of human similarities and differences in cultural behavior are rooted in the subjective experience of the observer. For Russian-American joint ventures, the negative cultural stereotyping described earlier in this paper generally expresses *emic* assumptions, but probably also reflects an *underlying anxiety* generated in the pendulum swing from Cold War enmity to post-Cold War friendship.

For ITA, cross-cultural consultation with joint ventures occurs at a different level of observation. The focus is not on *emic* differences or *etic* similarities, but shifts to the middle ground of a more objective assessment of the facts of the organizational relationship system. Bowen theory has provided a useful frame of reference for understanding these factual observations. The theory has drawn attention to internal organizational *anxiety, triangles, projection processes,* leadership based on responsible self-management, and an assessment of the wider *societal emotional context* within which the organization functions. With a calmer, more neutral work environment in which "cultural differences" are no longer the central issue, joint ventures can then proceed with their work.

An example of a joint venture that failed because of the focus on cultural differences was a project involving a large American production company and a Soviet government ministry. In 1986 when this joint venture was formed, Soviet law required that the Soviet partner retain 51 percent ownership. The objective of the project was to increase productivity in the joint venture's plant. The company's engineering, sales, marketing, and administrative staff were headquartered in Moscow. The production plant, located one thousand kilometers east of Moscow, employed two Western managers and seventy-five Russian workers. Many of the Russian workers were brought to the United States for short-term training. They learned quickly and were competent, diligent, and bright. Sales also went well, and productivity and income increased exponentially from 1986 to 1990.

Serious problems, however, developed in three areas: management, marketing, and financial controls. As described by an American participant in the project, "Soviet society and business management have always been pyramidal, with all power and decision making resting in the managing director at the top. He wields and exercises power, and expects that his commands and orders will be followed." This participant described the managing director of the joint venture as "a little Stalin," whose leadership style discouraged responsibility and creativity and created a "deadening psychological atmosphere." In addition to his professional responsibilities, the managing director decided who got use of a company car, who would get an apartment, a vacation, a dacha, and other privileges.

The deputy director was an American who spoke Russian and initially had a very positive attitude toward Russia and the project. However, he soon began to report that the managing director was "a typical Soviet," who never consulted him on any decisions and accused him of talking to other people in the company behind his back. Blaming others absorbed considerable emotional energy at the top levels of leadership in this company.

The American partners believed that the Russians needed American technological know-how, but reported that they felt ignored in the areas of management, marketing, and finance. There was no marketing plan and no need to cultivate clients because the Russians believed they did not need a plan. Clients would come to them, they thought, through the Soviet government's central planning ministry (Gosplan) since Soviet businesses depended on the company and needed its products. Financial reporting was scant, and did not link sales with costs and profits.

Within a year the American deputy director had to be replaced because he felt depressed and was unable to function effectively. Over the next five years three more American deputy directors were replaced. By 1991, the joint venture no longer had an American deputy, and a complete management impasse had been reached.

The American partners in this joint venture simply gave up trying to work with the Soviets. They concluded that in the future they should negotiate 51 percent control of any company in which they planned to invest, and should insist that the managing director, the marketing director, and the financial manager all be American. The Russian conclusion was more ambiguous; they had won the battle (they had kept their people in charge of the joint venture), but lost the war (the Americans had pulled out).

ITA was not involved as a consultant to this joint venture while these difficulties were developing. However, it provided an assessment and analysis to the American partners after the venture fell apart.

An *emic* assessment of this joint venture would have focused on the cultural differences in management style and communication patterns in the company. It would have asserted that these differences were crucial to the long-term breakdown in productivity and cooperative management for the joint venture.

An *etic* assessment of the joint venture would have focused on the universalities in the two joint venture partners, suggesting that the reasons for the management breakdown were common to business failures in all parts of the world. In other words, the same misunderstandings could have arisen between two American partners or two Russian partners. All humans face the same basic struggles to make organizations work effectively.

Using a family systems approach to assess this joint venture, ITA acknowledged some truth in both the *emic* and *etic* analyses, but made an effort to find a middle ground that would neither whitewash differences nor overemphasize them. This approach to assessment attempts to gather facts and maintain objectivity. It acknowledges differences which are deeply rooted in history and could be described as part of a *multigenerational process* at the organizational level. In addition, it examines long-term patterns of *anxiety* and their manifestations in an organization. A range of *anxiety*, as well as patterns of functioning over time, are realities for organizations as well as for families.

An attempt to understand the historical evolution of the joint venture's functional management style inevitably led to some acceptance of differing processes and less polarization into warring camps. Neither partner in the joint venture had put much energy into developing a direct, respectful relationship with the other before beginning to define the other as culturally "wrong." Both sides had tended to blame the other for all misunderstandings without taking responsibility for their own part. In addition, each side had attempted to form an alliance with the bicultural board of directors in order to isolate and devalue the partner. This kind of *triangling* did not occur with the production plant, probably because it was a thousand kilometers away and difficult to contact by telephone or mail. The production plant, in fact, continued to function relatively smoothly and effectively even as the administrative headquarters in Moscow fell into disarray.

In the end, both the Americans and the Soviets used *cut-off* to handle the anxiety generated by their inability to form a direct, respectful relationship with each other. The American company gradually withdrew its capital investment without really understanding the underlying dynamics of the problem. The Soviets decided to carry on alone, with mixed results. Just as in a polarized divorce, the partners may be doomed to repeat these patterns of conflict and *cut-off* if they decide to participate in future Russian-American joint ventures.

ITA recommends that companies seeking to form joint ventures with partners from different cultures fully grasp the historical, political, social, and economic context of the partner. In joint ventures involving Americans and Russians, this includes some recognition of the *anxiety* generated by the historically adversarial Cold War relationship and an understanding of how the relationship might translate itself into an unrealistic 180-degree pendulum swing—from overly intense friendship to enmity and back again. Through an objective acceptance of the historic context, respectful relationships can develop in which goals, objectives, responsibilities, decision making, and accountability are clearly defined and redefined over time. When observed on this broader, neither purely *emic* nor etic level, "cultural differences" are no longer a central focus, but can become a way station along the road to effective long-term partnership.

REFERENCES

Bonner, John T. 1980. *The Evolution of Culture in Animals.* Princeton, New Jersey: Princeton University Press.

Bourguignon, E. 1979. *Psychological Anthropology: An Introduction to Human Nature and Cultural Differences.* New York: Holt, Rinehart and Winston.

Bowen, Murray. 1978. *Family Therapy in Clinical Practice.* New York: Jason Aronson.

Brislin, R. W., W. Lonner, and R. Thorndike. 1973. *Cross-Cultural Research Methods.* New York: John Wiley.

Brislin, R. W., and P. Pedersen. 1976. *Cross-Cultural Orientation Programs.* New York: Gardner Press.

Goodall, Jane. 1990. *Through a Window: My Thirty Years with the Chimpanzees of Gombe.* Boston: Houghton Mifflin .

Kerr, Michael E., and Murray Bowen. 1988. *Family Evaluation: An Approach Based on Bowen Theory.* New York: W. W. Norton.

Kluckhohn, F. R., and F. L. Strodtbeck. 1961. *Variations in Value Orientations.* Evanston, IL: Row, Peterson.

Moss, C. 1988. *Elephant Memories: Thirteen Years in the Life of an Elephant Family.* New York: Fawcett Columbine.

Papero, Daniel V. 1990. *Bowen Family Systems Theory.* Needham Heights, Massachusetts: Allyn and Bacon.

Spiegel, John. 1982. "An Ecological Model of Ethnic Families." In *Ethnicity and Family Therapy.* Edited by M. McGoldrick, J. K. Pearce, and J. Giordano. New York: Guilford Press.

Trivers, Robert. 1985. *Social Evolution.* Menlo Park, California: Benjamin/Cummings.

Wilson, Edward O. 1975. *Sociobiology: The New Synthesis.* Cambridge, Massachusetts: The Belknap Press of Harvard University Press.

VIOLENCE IN THE WORKPLACE: A FAMILY SYSTEMS PERSPECTIVE

Walter H. Smith, Jr., PhD

This paper focuses on a common behavior in human life: violence. My past efforts on the subject have focused on violence directed towards children by family members. I have always believed violence is a mere symptom of more fundamental and basic emotional processes in human life. Human violence, wherever it occurs, is more similar than different, despite our tendency to categorize it by where and how it occurs. This paper is part of an effort to extend my understanding of human violence in the workplace. It draws upon clinical cases and my work as a consultant to organizations.

I define violence *as aggression which results in harm and injury and significantly controls and limits life*. Violence is not inherently right or wrong and occurs routinely. Aggression is simply a basic human emotional condition of life. Human survival depends on our ability to take action and control our environment and living conditions. Humans are particularly adept at observing the environment and initiating actions which appear to be in their best interests. Building sophisticated shelters, storing and preserving food, and providing medical care are simple examples of these actions. Violence is another example. (The arresting actions of a police officer and military actions of soldiers are violent. Humans, like many living species, act to hurt and injure others to maintain and foster survival and quality of life).

In my clinical experience with sex offenders, violent parents and others, humans are violent when they *perceive* a need to use aggression in response to threats to survival and quality of life. No one wants to injure others. But most humans will do so under certain conditions where they perceive they have little choice to sustain survival and quality of life. When and under what conditions humans perceive the need for violence varies greatly. These variations include acts by some which most humans do not accept as reasonable acts to protect interests.

Background

Murray Bowen, MD, developed a theory which understands individual functioning as an aspect of an emotional system (Bowen 1978, Kerr and Bowen 1988). Human emotional systems include family, workplace, and society. In emotional systems individuals are so strongly attached that it no longer makes sense to view their actions as separate from each other. Understanding the functioning of the emotional system as a whole can better explain and predict individual experience than understanding the individual experience in isolation from the emotional system. Human emotional systems have naturally developed over long periods of time and are guided by basic forces which influence living things on Earth.

Families are natural emotional systems. In my view, work and social emotional systems are a product of both culture and evolution. The division of labor and tasks in social groups appears to be a part of human evolution. Certainly these characteristics can also be observed in other social species. Yet, human creativity has influenced the shape and nature of workplaces and societies. The creation of governments, economies, and social traditions has greatly influenced and shaped our natural tendency to be social.

Emotional systems vary in their levels of functioning. Family systems theory accounts for these variations through the concepts of differentiation and chronic anxiety. Differentiation is the relative ability of members of an emotional system to regulate and direct their own functioning despite stress and anxiety. Both emotional systems and the individual members of emotional systems have varying levels of differentiation. However, the members of emotional systems have levels of differentiation which do not vary greatly and change little over a lifetime.

Anxiety is the automatic response to threats and perceived threats. More than the experience of nervousness, anxiety encompasses the entire range of physical, relationship and behavioral responses to threats. An increase in appetite when stressed, distancing in marriage with conflict, and complimenting a boss when insecure, are all examples of anxious responses in which a person could report not experiencing fear or nervousness. The intensity of anxiety varies across and within emotional systems. These variations are important in understanding the ways family, work and social systems function.

Violence and Regression in Emotional Systems

Violence is another symptom of human functioning and reflects attempts by individuals and emotional systems to cope with stress and anxiety. An employee attacks another when acute anxieties are high, relationships are polarized, threatening and conflictual, and there appear to be few or no alternatives. With enough anxiety, violence can become a routine way of behaving, as individuals constantly perceive threats to their survival. Violent people are doing just what humans and other forms of life have done throughout history: using aggression to respond to threats and perceived threats.

An emotional system in which increased violence occurs is an emotional system in regression. Regression is the automatic response of a family, work or social system to chronic anxiety. When anxiety is high enough, the emotional system can be overwhelmed and revert to more automatic, primitive ways of functioning. Differences, once honored and respected, become a point of conflict and contention. The workplace polarizes into factions, and gossip and aggression increase. Employees become territorial and coalitions are formed. Problems in organizational performance are attributed to certain individuals and specific groups. Employees are hired based on personal characteristics and their potential to contribute to the strengthening of certain coalitions over others. Employers begin firing "poor performers" assuming their absence will improve productivity. Employees begin preparing for lawsuits and grievance actions. Leaders begin to abstain from taking responsible action or become autocratic and dictatorial.

Regression in emotional systems is not caused by a single event or condition. Instead, it is the system's way of managing persistent threats to its survival. The system is like any other living organism. When threatened, it mounts a response and defense. When the threat persists, the organism becomes consumed with defending and remains perpetually reactive to the environment and itself.

Events which are threatening routinely occur in work systems. In work systems with a lower level of functioning, real threatening events can trigger an atmosphere in which actions which ordinarily would not be perceived to be threatening are perceived to be so. For example, a mental health center perceives the need to respond to the threats to its income and future because of managed care. This change is an appropriate response to anticipated threats. Instead of viewing staff members who resist the change as part of an expected result, they are viewed as threats to the organization's future. Managers then push these staff members to comply and conform to the changes, thereby increasing their resistance to change. Staff members form coalitions, some for change and some against it. The staff members against change argue that clients will be harmed. Some staff members respond to these arguments by changing their point of view. Managers interpret these actions as a threat and begin to identify the leaders of the opposition and to examine their work behavior as a basis for disciplinary actions.

This process of escalated, polarized, and reciprocal functioning of managers and staff are illustrative of emotional regression. Once the process begins with a real event, it is perpetuated by perceived threats and the process of regression takes on a life of its own. The more threatened each side becomes, the greater the risk for violence.

Dr. Murray Bowen described this process in his theory. The concepts of societal regression and nuclear family emotional process describe the movement of anxiety in family and social relationships. In highly regressed work environments, aggression is common and useful. Aggression becomes a means of protecting one's survival and quality of life. It's every person for himself or herself — and for good reason. It is as if members of a regressed system are functioning in a survival mode, scanning the environment for threats. Staff members are working defensively to avoid becoming the focus of negative attention. When one employee acts to injure or kill another, it is common to view this act as unusual, rather than as an aspect of routine aggression in the environment. Certainly, physical threats and death are serious matters. However, this behavior often occurs in the organization where aggression is necessary to cope and manage one's survival in the work environment.

The polarization and side-taking behavior during a regression foster the overall functioning of an emotional system during the regression. Initially, polarizing relationships decrease the conflict and emotional tension due to individual differences. Typically, polarized factions distance and this calms the work environment. Polarization also simplifies the complexity of organizational problems and tensions. "If only the other side would cooperate, the organization would function more effectively." The organization may function as if the threats to its existence are to be found in particular employees or others outside the organization.

However, polarized relationships reduce an organization's flexibility and individual members become locked into stances and positions they have to defend. This lack of flexibility makes the organization less responsive and adaptive to the environment. Relationships and factions are less cooperative. Decisions for the future can be based more on the polarizations than on the best interests of the organization. In a polarized workplace, challenging a decision or position can be interpreted as a threat. In a highly polarized workplace, mere differences can be interpreted as a threat.

Clinical Case

Routine acts of violence which I have observed in the workplace include sexual harassment, staff firings, physical altercations, and discrimination. I will present below one of the more dramatic cases of violence in the workplace.

John was referred by his stepsister to psychotherapy upon his arrival from an another city. The previous day he had aborted his plan to kill his boss and his boss' superior by driving to Pittsburgh instead of to work. His plans were elaborate and detailed. He had devised elaborate ways of entering the work site and shooting his employers. The five hour driving time to Pittsburgh provided a buffer and greatly helped to limit his ability to act on his urges.

John worked for seven years as a skilled professional in a ten-person unit of a large government agency. The workplace was described as a generally hostile environment with a highly authoritarian group leader. The supervisor was positioned to sit and observe his staff at work each day. Routine threats of personnel actions were made to influence staff behavior and work performance. John survived for many years by being compliant and masking his strong emotional reactions. He did not form or join coalitions and was perceived as somewhat distant. He routinely observed other staff members come under scrutiny and face disciplinary action.

His work performance became a target of scrutiny during his last two years of employment. His response was to fight back against personnel actions, greatly polarizing his relationships with his boss and his boss' immediate superior. The more John resisted personnel actions the more he became a focus of concern. He anticipated being fired, which would ruin him financially. He believed his employers were racially motivated and this heightened his sense that "somebody had to do something to stop those people." He filed numerous grievances through his union and finally hired an attorney and filed suit on the basis of discrimination. He said he simply wanted to be left alone to do his job. In response to these actions, his supervisors initiated several personnel actions and eventually John was placed on probation. John's anticipation of a poor probation evaluation and subsequent firing prompted his plans to kill his bosses.

John is the middle son of three male children. His father is a quiet man who has had three wives. He murdered his first wife with a knife and spent a few years in jail. He never actually married John's mother. He married his third wife in 1981. John described his relationship with his quiet father as distant but warm. His stepmother was the dominant figure in the household and she and John had a history of verbal clashes. A major event and loss for John

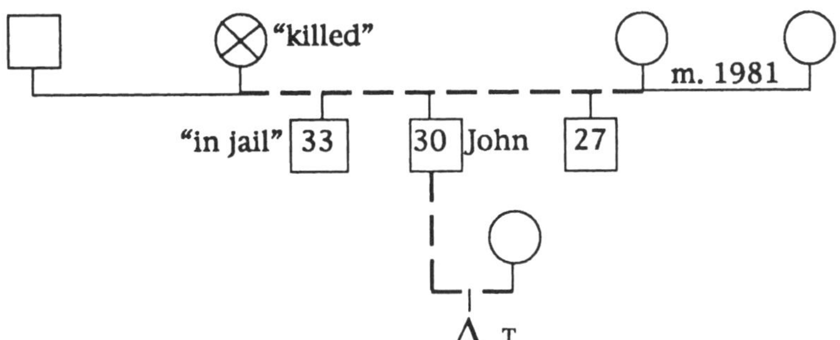

was his girlfriend's abortion in 1985. John left Pittsburgh shortly after this event and wanted to "begin again" in another city.

John's primary presenting symptoms included severe depression, agitation, and extreme suspicion. His responses to the workplace were clearly related to his family of origin. He viewed himself and his father as victims of an overbearing stepmother and mother, each the authority figures in the family. Yet each of these women was more defined by the father's helplessness than he was by their dominance. Nevertheless, John engaged in verbal battles with his stepmother to reduce her range of control in the household.

His girlfriend's abortion triggered strong feelings of loss and anger toward her. He strongly identified with the child and left Pittsburgh to distance from the pain of the experience.

John viewed his job prior to the workplace conflicts as tense but meaningful. He enjoyed his work and used his income to develop real estate investments. When John became the focus of management concern, relationships quickly polarized and both John and the managers used aggressive acts to manage their perceived threats. The intensity of John's response is based in his family of origin. Yet, conditions in the organization were an important part of John's plans to seriously injure his employers.

Summary

Violence is aggression which results in injury and harm. In work systems where there are perceived threats, violence can be routine. The perceived threats are related to the functioning of the organization and the levels of its stress and anxiety. Any workplace can become a threatening environment with enough anxiety. Some work environments require little stress to become violent. In lower functioning organizational environments, responses to real threats can trigger a regression and the organization can begin responding to perceived threats. Polarization of relationships during regression is an aspect of perceived threats and resulting violence. Violence is a natural outcome under certain circumstances in human existence.

REFERENCES

Bowen, Murray. 1978. *Family Therapy in Clinical Practice.* New York: Jason Aronson, Inc.

Kerr, Michael E. and Murray Bowen. 1988. *Family Evaluation: An Approach Based on Bowen Theory.* New York: W. W. Norton & Company.

4

DEFINING A SELF WITHIN SOCIAL SYSTEMS

DEFINING A SELF WITHIN SOCIAL SYSTEMS

Introduction

Bowen family systems theory postulates that the basic emotional functioning of each human individual is defined in the crucible of the relationship of an individual and his primary caretakers and is an outcome of a multigenerational family emotional process. Out of these crucibles come individuals imbued with the precepts and patterned responses to life's challenges they have absorbed from those persons most important to them, in particular, the primary caretakers, who are usually the parents. These precepts and responses define the range of flexibility to make choices in response to life's challenges, particularly when the individual or social systems of which he is a part are under stress.

Families and individuals within families vary in the degree of flexibility they have to make choices in response to life's challenges. Through the process of "defining a self," individuals over time and with continuing effort may increase their range of flexibility to make choices. In the process of defining a self, individuals make systematic efforts in the context of significant relationships to come to know what they stand for and to act accordingly, while remaining in contact with those most significant to them around the issues presented. They take responsibility for their thoughts and actions; in sum, they take responsibility for themselves.

The process of defining a self can become a life's work. Each challenge in life often is an opportunity to clarify what one stands for and to chart a course consistent with that stance. And each opportunity taken has the potential to bring the individual to heightened capacity for responsible functioning in the social systems to which he or she belongs.

Without such an effort, many individuals automatically adopt the precepts and imperatives of the family emotional process as their own, amalgamating these with others borrowed from the other social systems of which they are a part, such as church, school or fraternal organization. While capable of guiding an individual under fortuitous life circumstances, unquestioning acceptance of this amalgam of precepts may prove insufficient during times of crisis which "try the human's soul."

In his interview with Kathleen Wiseman about emotional process in family-owned businesses, Dr. Bowen discussed some thoughts around the concept of becoming a responsible self as part of defining a self and its relation to the family emotional process. On the subject of family emotional process, Dr. Bowen described how patterns of functioning are transmitted automatically from generation to generation and accepted unquestioningly by the new generation:

> I would say that the average person believes what he has been taught in the early months of infancy, by pretenders And I would say that most parents are pretenders. And they have been taught as if they know the facts of life, this is eternal truth and they continue to believe that for several generations. In other words, your kids in the present generation will act like they're being taught by the Messiah and they accept it as truth. They in turn transmit it to their kids, and they in turn transmit it to their kids and it sometimes improves a little bit. It can improve, it can get worse. But there's a part of it that can't improve and that's where family theory comes in.
>
> A child/parent is going to have child/children. And most people are out there pretending to be parents when they are really children. And the degree to which one is a child and only pretending to be grown up, is going to soon give that to his spectrum of kids, automatic, that's everybody. A family business is made up of all these people. . . .

Dr. Bowen discussed how a focus on managing self in significnt relationships is an essential component in being a responsible self in all social systems:

> [People who make efforts to function responsibly in a social system become important to the members of that social system. They do it primarily by] working on self instead of being critical of the others. The human being is dependent on important others so that the responsible person has to be responsible for others on whom he is dependent. You can't ignore them. *Being responsible means being responsible for self without being critical or mean to the others. And it means respecting the person on whom one is dependent.* That has to do with the concept of altruism which has been worked out pretty much in animal families. *In other words you cannot be just for self.* You have to be aware of your dependence on others and work with them too. Be aware of them, but always keep the focus on self. And I would say the lesson for a person is in being less critical of others. . . . Every time somebody gets critical, they are going to make it worse instead of better. You can't become critical of other people, important people, or it will become worse.
>
> And it goes that when one person can focus on self and not focus on what's wrong with the others, he can serve as a working model for others, then another, then another, and then others will pull up a little bit. And over time they will pull up a fair amount.

The authors of each of the four papers in this section describe their efforts to be and become responsible selves as they attempt to function responsibly in important relationship systems. In "Leadership from the Viewpoint of Bowen Theory," Paulina McCullough describes the stages of her thirty-year journey to function responsibly in charting a course which included establishment of the Western Pennsylvania Family Center, serving as its first director, and passing the baton to the second director.

The second paper, "Consultant as Sponge: An Evolutionary Journey," is by Judith S. Ball. Ms. Ball, an organizational consultant, uses the sponge as a metaphor for exploring how the consultant may be brought into an organization in a time of crisis in order to "solve" the presenting problem and end up instead occupying a key position in the organization as an absorber of the organization's anxiety. Ms. Ball discusses her efforts to explore her own propensities to become an anxiety sponge as an outcome of the multigenerational emotional process operating in her family of origin.

In the third paper, Selden Dunbar Illick, Director of the Princeton Family Center, describes her efforts and the efforts of other faculty members to design and teach a course about Bowen family systems theory in the academic setting of a degree-granting institution. The goal of the effort was to design and teach the course so that the course itself and its presentations were themselves applications of Bowen family systems theory. Realizing the goal was an exercise in the process of defining self in the relationship systems of the Princeton Family Center, the administration of the Trenton State College School of Nursing, and the classroom of graduate students enrolled in the Family Health Nursing Master's Program at the college.

"A Graduate Nursing Course Using Bowen Theory" is by Dr. Gail Hilbert, Graduate Program Coordinator at the Trenton State College School of Nursing. Dr. Hilbert describes her efforts to define herself to the administrators who had to give approval to what would be a nontraditional course presented in a nontraditional manner; namely, the course in Bowen family systems theory taught by members of the Princeton Family Center faculty. Dr. Hilbert also describes her efforts to manage her anxiety as she prepared for an accreditation visit for the program.

LEADERSHIP FROM THE VIEWPOINT OF BOWEN THEORY

Paulina G. McCullough, MSW

In this paper a thirty-year quest to introduce family systems theory ideas to professionals in the Pittsburgh area is recounted. The original idea which involved others grew to become a permanent educational organization. My thinking on how leadership functions evolved in the course of this venture. The stages that this project covers, the ideas behind the project, and its most salient features are reviewed.

Traditionally it is assumed that a leader is one who has to act on others. Even in instances when it is recognized that a leader interacts with others, the avowed purpose is to monitor directly and influence their actions in keeping with organizational objectives. The present example examines a method by which leadership is exercised from a blueprint of principles. Actions are based on those principles rather than on arranging, managing, or otherwise influencing relationships with others.

A cursory review of organizational literature defines leadership as an individual theoretical construct. On the one hand, leadership is defined as a set of psychological and behavioral characteristics. Models come from history, politics, and group theory, to name a few. The connections between a leadership role and an organization are established primarily by how much consonance there is between the leader and the goals of the organization. The notion of "power" or the capacity to influence others seems to be quite central to these definitions. Exceptions are the book, *Understanding Organizations* (Sagar and Wiseman, eds. 1982) and some of the literature on family owned businesses. In the latter the role of the entrepreneur and transitions, especially succession, seem to be the main foci. The bulk of both organizational and corporate literature describes goals which mirror the strivings of society at large (and, by extension, what a leader should attempt). At the risk of oversimplifying, emphasis is on success, profitability, and the bottom line.

Leadership, for the purposes of this paper, is defined as the combination of evolving ideas occurring within an environment in interaction with people. Leaders and others establish a reciprocal arrangement; the leader is the person who charts the direction and others recognize the value of the enterprise and become part of it for varying lengths of time.

Ideas, in this case a whole theory of human behavior known as Bowen theory, are central to the exercise of leadership. Bowen theory turned to evolution for its model, frequently studying other species to understand what is natural for groups about leader selection. In the study of whole families Murray Bowen was able to see a natural group in action and described its characteristics in detail. Leadership is one of the functions that give families a direction. Leadership emerges from the unit in interaction and is patterned following a dynamic interactional exchange involving all members. Bowen theory extends the scope of how the family leader emerges to multigenerational patterns and how they are transferred from one generation to another. Thus *that leadership exists* is true in all families. But *how the leader emerges* is determined by the interaction within the family unit. The concept of differentiation assesses individual functioning and accounts for how individuals interact and occupy different places in a group. Differentiation accounts for the fluctuations of families and their members (and may be extended to other human aggregates) and the differences in functioning of the unit and of its members. Individuals are in continuous interchange in a series of interlocking triangles, the building blocks of emotional systems.

Bowen defines the leader as inextricably linked to a set of conditions. A leader emerges, but the timing of that emergence is guided by pervasive patterns of human interaction geared toward keeping the entity whole. Using the theory as a blueprint, predictable patterns in the functioning of human groups and their institutions become visible and provide a way for a leader to establish goals and to operate within these human systems. Responses to change and pitfalls along the way are knowable and may be anticipated. The person in charge may anticipate and thus be more prepared for the reactions, responding more appropriately or cogently to the situation.

What follows in abridged form are some of the salient elements that coalesced to put me in a leadership role. The antecedents of my journey stretch far into the past. The initial thirty-year life span occurred within an extended South American family who, although not as colorful as the one in Garcia Marquez' *One Hundred Years of Solitude*, had some of the same ethos and commands. In 1960 my nuclear family moved to the United States. I was first exposed to Murray Bowen's developing ideas about family functioning at Georgetown University, and they were consonant with my previous experience. I studied the concepts and applied them to my own family and assumed that I would continue to put them into practice upon my return to Chile, I remained in Pittsburgh instead. The physical location is secondary to the intellectual/emotional search.

Stages of the Journey

The first stage, *groundbreaking*, lasted nine years. It represents the efforts of one person, in an environment that previously did not know of Bowen theory, to establish a system to make this body of knowledge known as a distinct and viable method of exploration and research. The second stage, the *takeoff stage*, lasted approximately ten years. During this period a beachhead was developed and a distinctive method of teaching family systems emerged. Receptive ears (attached to humans) were found who first learned and then assisted in the dissemination of ideas. The third stage, or *consolidation*, now in its tenth year, was punctuated by the creation of an organization, the Western Pennsylvania Family Center. The original objectives were continued but from a central and more stable, permanent location conducive to the growth of original goals. A more permanent home would facilitate the search for new vistas.

I held a leadership position until about four years ago. Some of the aspects of the search and the ensuing growth will be represented as *organic.* As in most transitions, it is most appropriate to regard succession as part and parcel of other events. In this instance the move toward succession was an anticipated one, necessary to both institutional goals and to preparing for changes in my family. The view toward a change in leadership had been there since the beginning. It was part of a shift from identifying programs based on individuals to pursuits grounded on overall missions and goals. Subsequent to my resignation as Director three deaths occurred in my family. Concomitantly, offspring pursued their own life courses. As for myself, I think of the present stage, for lack of a better term, as *rehearsing solitude* and, perhaps, being mindful of the philosopher Plato's dictum as "practice dying." I will add that, based on past history, "practice dying" will be a rather active pursuit.

Laying the Groundwork (1966-74)

Ideas. In the 1960s family systems theory, as it was known, had expanded from the studies of families with a schizophrenic offspring and a clinical focus, to an extension of the principles to all families. The scale of differentiation came into being then, quickly followed by "differentiation of self in the family of origin" and the concept of interlocking triangles. From Bowen's initial articulation of the seminal idea of the family as a unit, new concepts came into being.

Environment. Psychiatry and the mental health community in Pittsburgh in the middle sixties did not know about family therapy. My beginning expertise stood out even before I became a formal part of a family therapy clinic. In fact, it was the early acknowledgement by others of this viewpoint that led to my being hired by the largest psychiatric establishment, Western Psychiatric Institute and Clinic. Thus, the environment was initially curious and receptive to the ideas. Originally family systems theory was presented as a body of knowledge, first as an elective course to psychiatric residents and then to community mental health workers. As it became clearer what making these principles basic to one's work (and moreover, to one's life) signified, the instructors combined systems ideas with traditional psychoanalytic and group ideas. In effect, systems theory became diluted at best and "washed away" at worst.

Individual. For myself my initial intent was to maintain a systems perspective in an otherwise traditional milieu, namely, the human sciences and the human services which functioned overwhelmingly out of individual paradigms. In professional meetings Bowen had advanced the belief that where he was concerned he knew of no individual who had been able to stay current with family systems ideas as a whole in a different environment (not based on systems premises). An extension of the dictum was that it would take more than one person to establish firm grounding. Premonitions notwithstanding, this first stage was one of flying solo. Clinical practice with families lent some aid, in that studying many families validated the theoretical construct for me and also became a vehicle by which to practice increasing emotional detachment. Family systems literature, periodic attendance at conferences and individual systems consultation on family and other systems were also crucial at this stage. The environment, although recognizing some value to systems ideas, homogenized them to fit with traditional individual views. Parenthetically, despite an effort to keep me in their midst, my point of view was amalgamated with the rest and lost its distinctness and its potential contribution. Clinical practice was the exception. A sense of aloneness and even futility would surface at times. The image of "rowing upstream" came to mind.

Interaction. There are the predictable issues involved in introducing a different variable into an environment. My overall response to the quest was how difficult and protracted the whole grounding process had become. Intellectual knowledge of systems theory did not make navigating much easier. Another variable was anxiety. Most of the time I underestimated both the power of group togetherness and my own reactivity to occupying an outside position. In short, I overestimated my own capabilities. If I go back to the metaphor, "At high tide I swallowed a lot of water." All in all, groundbreaking represented an enlightening, humbling, and sobering process.

Review. The unfolding process could be regarded as one of "organic growth." It consisted of a vision or a rough intellectual sketch, the details of which could take place in a variety of ways. It was predicated on the assumption that the vistas which emerged would point toward further steps. Teaching as part of a traditional cadre subverted the ideas, for the most part, and neutralized my usefulness. I knew then that finding a forum where systems theory would stand on its own was crucial if the efforts were to be continued. Changes in the environment provided that opportunity.

Takeoff Stage (1974-85)

One factor which led to this new stage, the takeoff stage, was that family systems ideas had grown and become part of the family therapy movement. At the same time, Bowen reaffirmed the connections of the theory with the natural sciences.

In Pittsburgh, a long standing ideological and organizational history was discontinued when the largest psychiatric hospital—ensconced in psychoanalytic theory and also involved in primate research—replaced those frameworks by one whose objectives promulgated eclectic psychiatric teaching and practice and mostly pharmacologically based research. A family therapy clinic was created in 1974 of which I became a part. This new shift offered the opportunity for a distinct (although mostly mobile) basis of operation in the form of a course for professionals to study their families.

The new situation offered many more alternatives. In effect it became a laboratory to study ideas, leaders and individuals in interaction. From a theoretical standpoint, the goals were to conceptualize family systems theory further as well as to evaluate the teaching/learning interaction; in other words, to extend and refine how the ideas were understood and presented. In terms of the participants, objectives were to determine who were the people who applied to the course, who embarked in the course of study, what were observable applications of their learning, and who broadened their field of vision to add their efforts to the common undertaking—in sum, how one learned about learning.

One outcome was that those with unusual motivation made their thoughts known.

Those who offered to become part of the course became instructors. Three years after the first course was offered trainees planned and executed the first Pittsburgh Family Systems Symposium. The courses and symposia, although operating on a shoestring continued to exist into the next stage. Paradoxically, the lack of outside support reinforced motivation of those who were interested.

Although I became a leader from the onset, I had not coached on extended family before and I regarded the exploration as a reciprocal undertaking. Furthermore, I saw coaching on extended family as an extension of how I had practiced family therapy—another method by which to test family theory and my understanding of it. About four years into the course I realized that, frequently, learning about extended family was seen as a way to "fix" the family; it was used as technique. A corollary was that learning for most participants was regarded as an application rather than an opportunity to enlarge one's understanding of systems. This realization resulted in the addition of lectures and other exercises that would aid in a better mastery of the field of study.

In the interactions with the institution and the broader environment, progress was slow and often precarious. Despite the fact that courses were well received and well attended, there was no assurance from one year to the next if they would continue. Subtle thwarting of the efforts were visible in that endorsement of any project (with some notable exceptions) meant that the whole enterprise had to be planned, financed, and carried out as a distinct and viable endeavor. As tensions in the institution grew, there was negative projection toward questionable ventures; the course and accompanying accoutrements were no exception. Continued existence and support became less reliable over time. My observation of the larger entity, plus direct feedback from readings and knowledgeable others, made it obvious that the degree of autonomy and opportunity to grow would not continue.

I resigned my position as staff member in the early eighties after approximately ten years in the organization. Shortly after my resignation the family therapy clinic was discontinued, a further demonstration that the institution as a whole based the decision, at least on the surface, on financial considerations; in other words, family therapy was not thought to hold great promise. My association with the entity continued mostly through the annual conference and symposium which parenthetically were held at Western Psychiatric Institute and Clinic until this year. Soon after I separated from the institution interested individuals who were potentially more instrumental in planning for the future convened as a think tank. Goals were discussed: (a) The need to build a more stable operating system, where things were not dependent on the vagaries of an administration which was not committed to family systems ideas or willing to support those who were. (b) The need to be directed toward identifying any future program on the basis of ideas rather than people. (c) The need to lengthen the program to more than one or two years, and rather, offer an educational environment which would allow people to pursue ideas as far as they wished. (d) A chance to gain broader exposure as a way for motivated trainees to surpass what had been set as yardsticks heretofore.

Consolidation (1985 to the Present)

Then and now it is easier to witness readiness than to put words to it. If the present description is accurate, the creation of the Western Pennsylvania Family Center was a logical corollary to what came before. Roughly twenty years have elapsed since the first course was designed.

Prior to its actual creation at least a handful of people had asked to be part of an organization if one were ever created. A couple of efforts in the past had started but not prospered. Six professionals became the original founders. Initially there were no outside sources of support, although after a couple of years there were sizable grants made. Institution building was probably similar to most such undertakings. Central preoccupation included establishing internal coherence as reflected by faculty, syllabus, programs, and members and subsequently engaging in board formation. After five years I stepped down from being director of the Center. A succession process was announced and, after alternatives were considered, a new director, Cynthia Larkby, emerged as the leader.

What was learned from the quest? The Western Pennsylvania Family Center will have been in existence for ten years this coming September. As far as ideas, individuals—both in scope and reach—have gone further than at any previous time. The three presenters at this conference provide a sample for how each one is grappling with the possibilities. In April of 1994 individuals who took the first course on extended family in 1974 came together for a reprise. The subject of that meeting was explored in a paper presented at an international meeting of family therapists. The composite was illustrative of how the long view of human behavior changes with a systems perspective. For the next symposium this coming June former trainees have been invited to present their ideas and results have been promising. The long quest provides a different gauge by which to measure movement. Thus, whether looking at oneself, fellow faculty, or students, fluctuations over the course of many years can be viewed more accurately in terms of establishing overall functioning.

Those people who form part of the organization know that responsibility for oneself and toward others is fundamental; moreover, they become cognizant of the fact that individual initiative is highly valued. They are not subject to the hiring and firing that seem so prevalent in society at large. All things considered, participation in the Center, whether by faculty, participants in courses and programs, or as part of the membership has slowly increased.

As all human aggregates, this new entity is not outside the laws of human functioning. Anxiety, a common denominator in all human associations, is part and parcel of the proceedings. Although ameliorated by the knowledge of systems, its presence is visible on many occasions. Ebbs and flows, as evidenced by responses to external and internal pressures, are present but amenable to change. There have been critical junctures but they have been successfully resolved. Individual fluctuations are also present. A given individual may excel while another one flounders or seems frustrated. A few times the organization has seemed to flourish while one person appears burdened. Yet, the original founders are still viable and no person has been extruded.

In an organization whose theoretical model is differentiation may one talk of emotional process or even of group process? While I held the position of director I assumed that my views were different from those of the group and I operated out of that assumption. The existence of a "rumor mill," often an intrinsic part of any entity, is mostly quiescent, at least internally. Needless to say, at times there seems to be a faint rumor and—dare I say it?—distinct noise.

On the subject of leadership, however, the creation of the Center has allowed individuals to realize leadership on a variety of fronts. On this score it may be useful to note that despite the change in my titular and organizational role in the Center I have had the opportunity to perform many different functions and my participation has been unambiguously accepted.

There is still much to be done. Research, an avowed goal for many, is only now becoming more probable than possible. In closing I reflect that if a paramount objective of this organization—devoted to learning—is to foster the advent of a new generation of scholars, interested professionals, and lay persons, the first few steps have already been taken.

REFERENCES

Bowen, Murray. 1966. "The Use of Family Theory in Clinical Practice." *Comprehensive Psychiatry*, 7: 345-374.

———. 1972. "On the Differentiation of Self." *Family Interaction: A Dialogue Between Family Researchers and Family Therapists*, James Framo, ed. New York: Springer Publishing Company.

Garcia Marquez, Gabriel. 1992. *One Hundred Years of Solitude*. Cambridge University Press.

McCullough, Paulina. 1993. "The Third Decade: Differentiation and Death." Paper presented at the Georgetown Family Systems Symposium, Washington, D.C.

———1994. "Training in an Extended Family Model: Long-Term Implications." Presented at the Sixth Family Therapy World Conference, Budapest, Hungary.

Sagar, Ruth R. and Kathleen K. Wiseman, eds. 1982. *Understanding Organizations*. Washington, DC: Georgetown Family Center.

CONSULTANT AS SPONGE: AN EVOLUTIONARY JOURNEY

Judith S. Ball, MS Ed.

I am an anxiety sponge. The sponge is a metaphor for exploring triangles and how I function in them—in my family and in my consulting work. I'm curious about what goes into making a human sponge that is so absorbent of other people's anxiety.

First some facts. I was raised in Indiana during the 1940s and 1950s My family was one of fifty Jewish families in a town of about 50,000 people. Indiana was a hotbed of the Ku Klux Klan during the 1920s and 1930s and anti-Semitism was rampant. I am the oldest of four girls and am seventeen years older than my youngest sister. I was born within two years of my parents' marriage and within three years of the deaths of both of my grandfathers. Both my father's parents (Anna and Leo) and my mother's parents (Bessie and Murray) were immigrants to the United States and each couple created a business in which both spouses worked. My mother's family lived in New York City and her parents ran two successful businesses, the second of which was sold after her father's death in 1940.

My father left for World War II in 1943 and returned in 1945. My mother and I lived together in Washington, D.C. while my father was overseas. My mother's family lived in New York City and my father's family lived in Indiana during that time.

AUTHOR'S FAMILY DIAGRAM

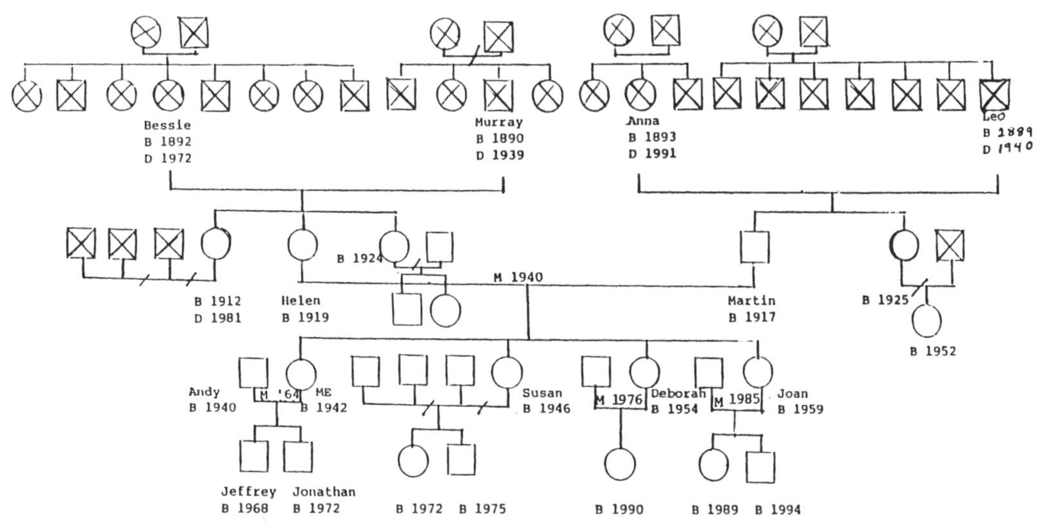

My parents moved to Indiana in 1945 where my father joined his mother in running the family business. His mother Anna worked alongside him until she was well into her eighties. She retired from the business sometime during the late 1970s and my father sold the business in 1985.

My sister Susan was born in 1946 with serious congenital heart defects. She was operated on for the first time when she was three years old. The surgeons were unable to correct the problems and fifteen years later, at the age of eighteen, she had corrective surgery. My mother had a few miscarriages before the birth of my sister Deborah in 1954 and again before the birth of my youngest sister Joan in 1959.

The anxiety in my parents' household was fairly constant and intense. The family triangles, the family business, the geographical distances, the deaths of my grandfathers, my sister's serious medical condition, the anti-Semitism in a small Midwestern town and the usual vicissitudes of life contributed to a highly charged household.

I went to college in Massachusetts and was married to my husband one week after I graduated from college in 1964. We have been married for thirty-one years. After obtaining graduate degrees, my husband and I moved first to Washington, DC, then New York, where our son was born in 1968. We moved back to Washington in 1971 and, after the birth of our second son, I directed programs for a large national women's association for ten years. For the past fifteen years I have consulted to organizations in the general area of organization change, first as a member of a small consulting firm founded and led by a husband and wife. This small firm went out of business in 1991 and I am now working as a designer of corporate training programs.

During the past fifteen years, the following important events took place: My husband's mother moved to Washington, DC from New York City in the mid 1980s and lived here until her death in 1990. My father's mother died early in 1991 at the age of 98. My husband's sister was diagnosed with a very early stage of breast cancer in December 1993. My relationship with the founder of the consulting firm in which I worked became conflictual sometime in 1989. My older son went away to college in 1986; my younger son in 1989. My older son is now a reporter for a daily newspaper in the Southeast and my younger son is on a leave of absence from a graduate program in architecture in California, working now in New York City and figuring out what his next step will be. Both of my parents had been physically well until about eighteen months ago when my mother was diagnosed with bleeding ulcers. The ulcers responded to treatment but occurred again a few months ago. They seem to have responded to treatment a second time and there are no major symptoms at this time.

During the late 1970s and early 1980s I became interested in Bowen theory as much to instruct my professional work as my personal life. I began asking myself: Am I an effective consultant? Do these major efforts to help which my consulting firm engages in really make any difference to corporations in the long run? How do I keep from getting caught up in the problems of my clients and, to what extent am I the problem? Bowen theory introduced me to a new way of thinking about the world and how I function in it. This interest has translated into a continuous journey of learning. I am just beginning to see and understand the important triangles in my life and how I function in them. I am surprised by how long it has taken me to begin to see the way things are in my family and how my functioning in the triangle with my parents is the way I function in most triangles of which I am a part.

The triangle with me and my parents continues to operate this way: There was tension between my parents and my father's mother. And there was tension between my parents themselves. Tension increased in my mother. (She reports that her tension, at least from time to time, had something to do with Dad's anxiety.) She became angry, apparently with me. As a child, mother's anger, even rage, seemed unpredictable and out of control. I would sidle up to my father who had an amazing ability to calm mother down, at least to a simmer from a boil, and he and I would shake our heads in bewilderment and frustration about mother's "crazy temper." I remember being scared, waiting for my father to come home to calm things down, and whenever I could, trying to stay out of the line of fire. There is some rigidity to the way this triangle functioned since I don't recall any occasions when I sided with my mother. When the relationship between my parents was tense, which was frequently, I absorbed anxiety "in the air."

These triangles are garden variety ones, from what I can gather. Dr. Bowen points out in his book on *Family Therapy in Clinical Practice* that a triangle in a state of calm consists of a comfortable twosome and an outsider, with the favored position being a member of the twosome. When, however, the triangle is in a state of tension, the outside position is the preferred one. Gaining closeness or escaping tension describes the shifting forces.

What does this have to do with consulting and professional competence? I believe I respond to anxiety in clients in much the same way I respond to anxiety in the triangles in my family of origin. I gravitate to the position with clients that I am familiar with in the triangle with my parents. My functioning is automatic and predictable: to get out of the line of fire, take sides, often unwittingly, and try to give people solutions to their problems.

I believe that I was triangled in the relationship between the founder of the consulting firm in which I worked and his wife in much the same way I am triangled in the relationship with my parents. I think that as anxiety increased in the relationship between the founder and his wife, some of his focus turned to me. He became dissatisfied with my performance and as our relationship became increasingly tense, I stayed away from the office more—out of the line of fire. This couple was important to me and while it would be more comfortable to just stay away, I knew that doing so would not contribute to my work of defining myself. So I continued to return to the office and stay in touch with these two even as the anxiety and focus on me continued. None of this was easy. I tried to put my energy into defining myself, but the efforts were awkward and anxious. Nonetheless, staying with it, however awkwardly was important to my own learning. By 1991 the firm's founder decided to leave the organization, move further south with his wife and consult by himself. Each member of the firm went his or her separate way. I continue to stay in touch with this couple.

I have been working recently with an organization that creates corporate training programs. I create the training materials but have no responsibility for influencing processes in client organizations. I hypothesized that since I had no responsibility for solving anyone's problems, I would be able to observe the human processes less anxiously and more factually. When I found myself right in the middle of some very anxious situations within the client and consulting organizations I worked hard to focus on defining myself (to me and others) and being responsible for self.

As the anxiety in me and others intensified, I began asking myself questions to help me to stay in touch with the anxiety surrounding me by neither running from it nor giving people solutions to their problems. My presence was probably less anxious which permitted me to ask the following questions. When do "administrative solutions," such as training programs, really improve organizational effectiveness? Are major corporate training programs giant anxiety diffusers? Is the decision to hire a training company an act of triangling in an outsider as a way for corporate management to deal with its anxiety about competition, union organizing attempts, threats of lawsuits, current costs, and the like? Will the problems that led to such "giant administrative solutions" emerge in another form in the organization at other times and places? (I refer to these as "giant administrative solutions" because these training programs cost corporations millions of dollars and they may ultimately touch a large part of the organization.) What are the key triangles in the consulting and client organizations? Is there any relationship between anxiety cascading through an organization and how its leaders function? What is the relationship between the anxiety in clients and the anxiety in their consultants?

I thought I was functioning reasonably well on this project, maintaining a fairly non-anxious presence through two solid weeks of sixteen hour days, until I came home ill at the end of the second week, having caught the same bug which a colleague had. The automatic processes work in wondrous ways! I may have appeared less anxious to others, and even to myself, but my immune system wasn't fooled.

I have learned through this process, however, that the more I can *just be* in the presence of my parents' anxiety and not either run from it, take sides or try to solve their problem, the more I gain flexibility in how I function in other anxious situations such as consulting. I continue to be surprised by the force and subtlety of the automatic processes that operate all the time in me and how difficult they are to identify and override.

I have some new questions about the parental triangle I grew up in. What are the factors that go into the automatic absorption of anxiety that comes so naturally to me? What variability exists in the ways humans are present in the presence of the anxiety of others? What goes into that variability? Can fetuses absorb multigenerational anxiety *in utero*, as manifest in physical defects at birth? To what extent is my position in the triangle with my parents similar to my children's position in their parental triangle?

This sponge will probably always soak up other people's anxiety. The journey in my thinking is just beginning to affect how I function. As my thinking becomes clearer, I hope I become more flexible in my capacity to choose how I function. It is a humbling but hopeful journey.

TEACHING BOWEN FAMILY SYSTEMS THEORY

Selden Dunbar Illick, LCSW

Walking down the halls of Trenton State College Graduate School of Nursing, I was stopped by a former student. " I want to thank you for that course last year in Bowen theory," she said. "I took it because I had to—it was required for my nursing degree—but it has helped me in all aspects of my life. Not just at work, but in my personal and family relationships too."

Designed to teach nurses about organizational functioning, the course offered nursing students an understanding not only of the families they work with, but also of the health care institutions they are working in. But, as this student said, what also happens is that Bowen theory makes a difference in personal lives as well.

Fundamental to learning Bowen family systems theory is learning about the self. Knowledge of the self is also crucial to teaching Bowen theory. For this reason, it is not only the student who benefits in personal, family, and other relationships but the teacher as well. Teaching Bowen theory is not just having a process. Bowen theory is derived from observation of living organisms. And teaching Bowen theory has to do with *living* Bowen theory as well as having knowledge of the theory. Creating that balance requires an understanding of the emotional process which operates continually in all human relationships. Without knowing about how the emotional process operates within the self, one cannot effectively communicate the essence of Bowen theory.

A tenet of Bowen theory is that "the emotionally driven relationship process is present in all families." (Kerr and Bowen 1988, 55). Emotional process is present in all human life. It appears in the form of anxiety, triangles, the individuality/togetherness forces and reciprocal functioning. It is no wonder, then, that emotional process was present among the participants in the course at Trenton State College: a team of seven teachers, a student body of thirteen, the liaison person who brought the Princeton Family Center faculty and the Graduate School of Nursing together, two administration persons at Trenton State College and the Accreditation Committee. For the intensity of the emotional process not to escalate, each person needed to be responsible for managing his or her emotional reactivity. The particular challenge for the Princeton Family Center faculty was not just to explain what it meant to manage a self, but to *exemplify* it as well. Figuring out how to present the material was difficult enough—the tallest order was to *be responsible about managing self.*

The parallels are interesting between what the faculty taught and what they learned. Using the variables of emotional process, a few examples of the emotional process issues the faculty faced in developing and executing this course follow.

Anxiety. Anxiety is constantly present in emotional process. Anxiety moves not only within the individual as a response to a real or imagined threat, but within the system as a whole. Anxiety may be the most fundamental of the four variables of emotional process. An increase in anxiety can lead to an increase in triangling (Kerr and Bowen 1988). And when anxiety is high in a system, the individuality/togetherness forces become unbalanced: movement is away from individuality and more toward togetherness. Anxiety can contribute to the process of reciprocal functioning. If anxiety or stress increases in the system, the over/under functioning positions can be driven to extremes (Kerr and Bowen, 1988). It was crucial that the faculty manage themselves in relation to anxiety in the classroom. Many students arrive in the classroom automatically anxious, concerned about grades, course requirements, and whether they will be able to master the material—not to mention their concerns about how to fit the course into their already full lives. For the faculty to take responsibility for their part in allaying these anxieties, they as teachers had to be as clear as possible about course requirements, grading policy, and, of course, the material. Faculty members also had to manage their own anxiety about being teachers. Some had never done this before and it was important to keep anxiety as contained within self as possible when in the classroom.

Individuality/Togetherness. When anxiety is present, the tendency is for the process to move more toward togetherness and away from individuality. A challenge in the classroom as a teacher is to keep track of one's own thinking and knowledge of theory, and not give in to togetherness pressures to agree with the student who initially may blend and blur some of the differences between Bowen theory and other theories. Often when students first hear the ideas of Bowen theory, there is a tendency to say, "Oh that sounds just like Buddhism," or "That sounds just like structural family therapy." While there are similarities, there are important differences. Remaining respectful of the student's viewpoint and at the same time working to clarify theory as a teacher is critical. When the anxiety rose and the togetherness pressure moved in the classroom, it was a challenge to remember to define a self.

Triangles. Bowen said, "A two person emotional system is unstable in that it forms itself into a three person system or triangle under stress." (Bowen 1978, 478) Triangles form when anxiety is high. When groups or individuals join together to enhance their functioning, it often can be at the expense of others. As teachers, the faculty members had leadership roles and were responsible for running this course as smoothly as possible. There were certain factors that were important to keep in mind. Because this course was team taught and because there was a level of anxiety not only in the students but also in the team of teachers and in the administrators, vulnerability to triangles and interlocking triangles was all-too-likely. Unfortunately, faculty members were unable to avoid triangles. A problem arose when on the last night of class a student burst into tears upon receiving her grade and involved another student. Two teachers were there that night, one of whom was responsible for grading. The two students came to the teacher who was responsible for the grading. The student who had not received the low grade spoke for the one who had, saying that her friend was on trial for the program and would never be admitted with this grade. This was the first triangle. The teacher in the first triangle, unable to manage her own level of anxiety, contacted the second teacher. Furthur interlocking triangles developed when the first teacher, still anxious in spite of talking to the second teacher, contacted the program director. All these triangles and interlocking triangles could have been managed if the first teacher could have managed her own anxiety. She could have observed her own emotional process and dealt directly with the student who received the low grade, recognizing that she had given the low grade based on a well-thought-out set of standards; the fact was, the paper had been below the standard. Bowen said that it is essential always to stay focused on process and to defocus on the content of what is being said (Bowen 1978). In this example, the teachers got caught up in content (student's upset over being on trial) instead of focusing on process (adhering to preestablished standards).

Reciprocal Functioning. As emotional process results in people's occupying different *functioning positions* in the family system (Kerr and Bowen 1988), it also results in people's occupying different *functioning positions* in whatever system one finds self in. If a teacher overfunctions in the classroom, there is a danger that the student could become too dependent on the teacher, thereby not relying enough on his- or herself. The work the student (like all of us) needs to do is observe and listen to one's own internal guidance system in order to learn about emotional process. A subtle but nonetheless important example arose when writing the course objectives. Instead of stating that the student "*will learn* . . ." the syllabus stated that "*Students will be given the opportunity to* . . .". "*Will learn*" can imply that the teacher will overfunction by having to take more responsibility for the students' learning. Whereas "*Students will be given the opportunity to*" alleviates some of the danger of the teacher overfunctioning and places more responsibility on the student.

The course on Bowen family systems theory and organizations is now part of the core curriculum at Trenton State College Graduate School of Nursing and has started its third year. This continuation would not have been possible without the leadership itself in the Trenton State College administration having knowledge of Bowen family systems theory.

It is such a pleasure to work with those who have knowledge about Bowen theory and whose primary efforts are therefore in the direction of keeping the focus on the process and managing a self. A version of this course could be usefully taught to employees in organizations, giving special attention to the people in key functioning positions. These experiences illustrate and suggest that fundamental to learning and teaching Bowen family systems theory is learning about emotional process, the relationship system, and the self.

REFERENCES

Bowen, Murray. 1978. *Family Therapy in Clinical Practice.* New York: Jason Aronson Inc.

Kerr, Michael E. and Murray Bowen. 1988. *Family Evaluation.* New York: W. W. Norton & Company.

A GRADUATE NURSING COURSE USING BOWEN THEORY

Gail Hilbert, DNSC, RN

This paper addresses how Bowen family systems theory was used as the basis for a graduate nursing course in organizational dynamics and how the course was implemented as an innovative move within a traditional profession and a traditional organization. It includes a description of how the graduate program coordinator began to define herself in relation to the traditional accreditation procedure.

Modern nursing, as opposed to care for the sick by family members or religious orders, originated with Florence Nightingale and her efforts to improve the care of the wounded in the Crimean War (Nightingale 1859). Upon returning to England, she established the Nightingale School of Nursing which was financially independent of the hospital and in control of its own activities. This model was implemented at several institutions in the United States and Canada in the 1870s, but all of them eventually came under the control of hospitals, a move which resulted in the staffing needs of the hospital taking precedence over the educational needs of students. These schools, which granted a diploma in nursing, were not associated with institutions of higher education (Dolan, et al. 1983).

During the First and Second World Wars, the Korean War and the Vietnam War, American nurses assumed a role of importance in the military. Many of the nurses who served in the military came to teach in nursing schools. Their influence was reflected in such things as the need for nurses to "be in full uniform at all times," stripes on the sleeves of nursing students to indicate which year of school they were in, and standing at attention when the physician entered the room. Another significant influence on nursing education was that of religious orders which operated many schools of nursing (Kelly 1991). In the 1950s, entering a school of nursing was akin to entering a convent, complete with vows of poverty, chastity and obedience. For example, students who married were expelled from the school.

These religious and military influences on nursing led to a tradition-bound and service-oriented education. The accreditation of nursing schools, which was begun in 1949 and is now conducted by the National League for Nursing (NLN), was based on the Tylerian style of objectives-based curriculum. Ralph Tyler, an American educator, wrote *Basic Principles of Curriculum and Instruction* (1949), which became the "Bible" for nursing educators. Implementing the Tylerian model meant that the curriculum content had to be carefully and tediously documented, with behavioral objectives for each class and course related to course content, unit plans, and end-of-program objectives (Bevis and Watson 1989). Despite the so-called "Caring Revolution" in nursing and a shift to outcome evaluation, the NLN accreditation process still has the potential to be tradition bound and reductionistic.

Even though most nursing education now takes place in two and four year colleges, there are still remnants of the traditional diploma in nursing training. In 1989 this author accepted the position of Graduate Program Coordinator in the School of Nursing at Trenton State College (TSC), an institution which originated as a normal school. Thus the parent institution also had a history of tradition. However, despite this background of conservatism, the faculty of the School of Nursing designed a forward thinking graduate nursing program based on the family as the unit of care. This program embodies the philosophy of Wright and Leahey who state "nursing had come of age with its recognition of the significance of the family to the health and well-being of individual family members. Equally important, nursing has recognized the influence of the family on illness." (1994, 1)

The profession of nursing identifies individuals, families, and communities as clients, but it is rare to have a graduate program which focuses entirely on families. The graduate program at TSC also focused on health, a departure from the medical model which emphasizes dysfunction (Bomar 1989). Family Health Nursing has been defined at TSC as a specialty within nursing that is distinguished by a focus on the family unit as the recipient of care and by the goal of promoting wellness and maintaining the health of families. The faculty designed the curriculum based on an organizing framework for the school which emphasized systems theory, caring, and a definition of health as the synthesis of wellness and illness.

The Master of Science in Nursing (MSN) program at TSC is a 36-credit part-time evening program which prepares clinical specialists and nursing managers. The foundation courses which all students take include nursing theories, perspectives in family nursing, two research courses, and an organizational dynamics course. There are also clinical courses which provide family nursing theory and opportunities to intervene with families in their home environment. The last courses in the program focus on the functional role (clinical specialist or nurse manager) and include a practicum in a setting of the student's choice: acute care, long-term care, or community care.

The course entitled "Organizational Dynamics in Nursing" was initially taught by two adjunct faculty members, a nurse administrator, and a hospital administrator, all of whom based it on traditional organizational and leadership theory. The courses focused on historical and theoretical bases of organizational dynamics, leadership and management, examining the concepts of mission, purpose, strategy, competency, leadership, management, contention and organizational culture, learning and change. However, the two faculty were unable to teach the course the third year it was offered. The course was taught by another nurse administrator who had trained at the Princeton Family Center. Ms. Kance and the faculty of the Princeton Family Center taught this course as a team.

The curriculum emphasized Bowen theory heavily due to the coordinator's exposure to the theory in her graduate education and her experience applying the theory in clinical settings. However, a course taught by a team of adjunct faculty and an organizational dynamics course based on Bowen theory were innovative ideas for the school of nursing. The author took the idea to the School of Nursing Curriculum Committee and the committee rewrote the course description and objectives so that they did not specify any one theory of organizations. Thus, we were free to use the course on Bowen family systems theory.

The course was well received by students and they were able to apply the content of the course to both their understanding of organizations and their work with families. All seemed to be going well until the time came to write the report for initial accreditation of the MSN program by the NLN. The author began to experience anxiety in relation to the need to explain the course content and the fact that most of the faculty teaching it were non-nurses. NLN accreditation is viewed by faculty as a major nodal event which sends shock waves throughout the institution. An initial accreditation visit is even more anxiety-provoking, especially when the curriculum is nontraditional.

The author was not yet tenured and knew the importance of achieving accreditation both for the program and for herself. Her anxiety was also influenced by her functional position in her family of origin. As an only child she often felt responsible for much of what took place in the family and would take action to make things work out. She found herself responding the same way as she prepared for the accreditation visit. As Papero (1990) states, the level of reactivity of an individual and of a group is believed to be the product of several factors: the internal guidance system of any organism which is the result of millions of years of evolutionary development, experiences in the extended family, and the history of the group of organisms interacting with one another in the immediate past. A conversation about this anxiety with one of the faculty from the Princeton Family Center led to a suggestion that the author define herself in relation to the accreditation process by identifying her values about the importance of a nontraditional curriculum and prepare to present that perspective to the accreditation visitors. This helped her to be less anxious about the organizational dynamics course and the entire accreditation process.

The accreditation visit went well, in that the visitors acknowledged the program's unique focus and carefully articulated curriculum. The nursing administrator was present for the faculty interview and articulated the value of family systems theory for understanding organizations. Students were also able to describe how valuable family systems theory was in their practices. The program received full accreditation.

An additional benefit of the process which occurred around the accreditation visit was that the author learned something about defining herself in relation to organizations. She was better able to articulate what she thought was important in a graduate program in family health nursing and conveyed this during the accreditation visit. She was willing to take responsibility for her behavior in relation to curriculum decisions. As Gilbert (1992) explains, becoming comfortable with one's own well-thought-out beliefs, standards, values, and priorities is a step toward freedom from trying to be what one thinks others want one to be, yet it allows one to remain in open contact with significant others in the emotional system.

REFERENCES

Bevis, Em Olivia, and Jean Watson. 1989. *Toward a Caring Curriculum: A New Pedagogy for Nursing*. New York: New York National League for Nursing.

Bomar, Perri. 1989. *Nurses and Family Health Promotion: Concepts, Assessment, and Interventions*. Baltimore: Williams and Wilkins.

Dolan, Josephine, Louise M. Fitzpatrick, and Eleanor Krohn Herrmann. 1983. *Nursing in Society: A Historical Perspective*. Philadelphia: W. B. Saunders Co.

Gilbert, Roberta. 1992. *Extraordinary Relationships: A New Way of Thinking About Human Interactions*. Minneapolis: Chronimed Publishing.

Kelly, Lucie Younk. 1991. *Dimensions of Professional Nursing*. New York: Pergamon.

Nightingale, Florence. [1859] 1992. *Notes on Nursing*. Philadelphia: J. B. Lippincott, Co.

Papero, Daniel V. 1990. *Bowen Family Systems Theory*. Boston: Allyn and Bacon.

Tyler, Ralph W. 1949. *Basic Principles of Curriculum and Instruction*. Chicago: University of Chicago Press.

Wright, Lorraine, and Maureen Leahey. 1994. *Nurses and Families: A Guide to Family Assessment and Intervention*. Philadelphia.

5

CASE STUDIES

CASE STUDIES

Introduction

This section presents four case studies. In many respects, the section is a continuation of the previous section concerning defining and becoming a responsible self. However, since each case study deals with the phenomenon of anxiety, the editors decided to group the papers together.

In the first paper, "Cooperation, Leaders, and Anxiety," Andrea Maloney-Schara, a member of the faculty of the Georgetown Family Center, presents three distinct but related ideas: first, a background on emotional processes essential to understanding the transmission of anxiety in social systems; second, a discussion of an emotionally based strategy for managing the stresses of living in groups; and third, how anxiety in the relationship system disrupted cooperative behavior among the founder and leader of a family-owned business and the members of the family and business.

In the next paper, "The Influence of Anxiety Within a Business," Kent E. Webb explores the relationship between the states of acute and chronic anxiety within the CEO of a business and within the business itself. The business, a mental health care organization that provides outpatient mental health and chemical dependency services within the State of Colorado, is trying to survive during a period of fundamental restructuring of the health care delivery system as part of containing escalating health care costs.

In the third paper, Leslie Ann Fox, president of a health information management consulting firm, presents a theoretical framework which utilizes Bowen family systems theory and guides her efforts to define herself in her relationships with her clients. She describes how she functions within this framework in working with clients in the field of health information management.

In the fourth paper, "The School as an Emotional System," Roger Dillow, an educator and a member of the faculty of the Princeton Family Center, presents his ideas about how Bowen family systems theory may be applied to characterize contemporary American schools as emotional systems. Mr. Dillow offers various models of functioning to illustrate different concepts of the theory. The common thread of the paper is the management of anxiety.

COOPERATION, LEADERS, AND ANXIETY

Andrea Maloney-Schara, LCSWA

"A little bit of knowledge is a dangerous thing" is a useful adage, considering the emotional forces at play in both family and work relationships. Please keep this in mind as three different ideas are loosely woven to give a background on emotional processes, an emotionally-based, cooperative relationship strategy, "tit for tat," and, last, how anxiety in relationships disrupted cooperative behavior between a leader and his family.

The ability to lead is more complex than finding a rational solution to a set of problems. In fact, rational thought often appears to be a lofty goal beset by the frustrations and problems of a world in turmoil, a world that does not respond well to rationality. Rationality can be an attempt to escape from emotional unknowns.

Emotions are part of our ancient evolutionary heritage. How leaders emerge is less well-known. Historically, the focus has been on the psychology of the individual. The emotional process in the relationships has not been considered. Since emotional responses occur mostly outside conscious awareness, patterns of behavior and symptoms are replicated from one generation to the next. There appears to be a nearly genetic sensitivity to past patterns of behavior which then influence the future generations.

All too often, the emotional system maintains behaviors, roles, or strategies that are assumed to have a survival value for the individual. Eventually the group or family benefits. Evolutionary theory spells out these ideas. Murray Bowen, MD, developed a theory based in biology to expand the understanding of human behavior beyond the individual's mental process. The human family was seen as an interactive natural system (Bowen 1978). Others have tried to understand societies as a natural interactive system. Herbert Spencer observed that societies, just as species, have an evolutionary course. Of course for every viewpoint there will always be an opposite. Sidney Hook concluded that "all factors in history, save great men, are inconsequent." (1955)

Other theorists have acknowledged instinctive forces, yet they did not see the interactive, multigenerational adapting nature of emotional systems. Sigmund Freud, assumed that humans had primitive feelings that were projected upon leaders. Leaders were those who could activate these unconscious forces. This was called "the father complex." Social feelings were believed to be acquired phylogenetically. This model, built on observing pathology, noted the range of mental symptoms expressed through aggression. Health rested on the ego's ability to pass through developmental stages without repression. Realistic identification with other people or ideas was possible when the individual's identity was not lost in a need to be a part of the larger group (Hook 1955).

Carl Jung also investigated the role of emotional process in the human. He noted that each human has a preformed instinctive system, "with its own characteristics and universally understandable thought-forms, reflexes, attitudes and gestures." (Jung 1957, 116) Just as animals are born with a general ability to know, so are humans. Inborn tendencies require the stimulation and reinforcement of behavior by the culture and the family. The primacy of the sexual and aggressive drives began to be seen by Anna Freud, John Bowlby and others as secondary to those instincts which enable the formation of social affiliations.

Bowen theory leaves aside speculation on the internal mental process of the individual and focuses on the primacy of the forces regulating social affiliations with the resulting development of patterns of behavior. Theoretically the balance between the two primary relationship forces, not sex and aggression, but rather the force to be an individual and the force to be a part of the group, formed the emotional system (Bowen 1978).

Togetherness predicts the necessity of giving up some amount of individual expression to form cooperative relationships. Individuality predicts a force within the individual to invest in one's own individual life. There is some awareness of this interactive pressure, to be or do for the others. Reactions to adapting to others are often not anticipated. The process can spiral until an individual's identity is compromised and symptoms appear. From a systems perspective the balancing of togetherness and individuality results in a few individuals becoming more vulnerable than others.

This balancing of the two forces can be observed in the formation of reciprocal relationships and interlocking triangles which occur in any system. The way each individual responds to demands is a function of his or her individual strengths, the current stressors and his or her place in the triangles. Traditional families and organizations pressure people to perform and to conform. Those who fail to meet the generally accepted expectations occupy the most uncomfortable positions which are generally the outside of triangles. Those on the outside form their own triangles which reinforce their positions. The greater the pressure, the more polarized and less cooperative the individuals become.

Stressful events are converted to anxiety within the individual. Anxiety and sensitivity to important others regulate the flow of reactivity entering the triangle systems. The ability to be more of an individual, yet less reactive to old sensitivities, may be partly genetic, partly good luck, plus less anxiety and, perhaps, social learning. An awareness of the stressful events, the dynamics in the relationship system and the ability to take a different stance is necessary for an individual to experience social learning.

Social learning is one of the variables that goes into the theoretical concept of differentiation of self. This concept addresses the variability in functioning of both leaders and followers. It is clear that leaders and followers vary in the ability to act on principles rather than react automatically through projection, isolation, conflict, or illness. A differentiated individual is making an effort to understand his or her part in both the forward progress and the difficulties in emotional systems.

The functioning of leaders changes. Most begin to lead by demonstrating the ability to manage relationships during stressful times. Being a leader during stressful times though does not guarantee a fixed state of emotional maturity. Leaders can have difficulty finding adequate responses to the changing external environment. Leaders do have a vision and accomplish goals in a family, in an organization, or in a nation. John Gardner notes that leaders are those that shape and accomplish a purpose in collaboration with or in spite of large organized systems (1990). Leaders can also have ill-defined or destructive visions. Immature leaders may be ultimately destructive.

One indicator of maturity is that leaders are less emotionally reactive to changes in the relationship system of the organization or the family. Often such leaders are interested in furthering more altruistic goals for the larger group. There is evidence that the tendency to formulate principles leading to cooperation in the relationship system has arisen from the inheritance of an emotional guidance system.

One example of the tendency to cooperate is a reciprocal emotional process known as "tit for tat." The process can occur between leaders and followers or between organizations. Robert Axelrod and others have demonstrated that of more than fifty proposed strategies for solving the problem known as the prisoner's dilemma, "tit for tat" had the greatest advantages (Poundstone 1992).

The strategy begins by two individuals cooperating to achieve a common goal. The first stage cooperation: never be the first to defect. However, since it is possible that someone will defect, the others must be prepared for this and have an adequate response. The first individual to defect is the more selfish. He or she will have a momentary gain. When the second individual discovers the defection, or the lack of cooperation, he or she has a choice: do something or do nothing. Doing nothing often reinforces selfish behavior. Doing something tends to disrupt or make the other pay a price for the selfish behavior.

The second stage is retaliation. Retaliation sounds reactive but may not be. The goal is to signal that cooperation between the parties has broken down. Retaliation can range from the subtle—no eye contact, a change in the length of conversations or even the tone of voice—to the more severe: competition or even major conflict. The refusal to cooperate is maintained until the selfish individual signals a willingness to be cooperative again. The price for selfish behavior has become too high.

The third stage is forgiveness. Often selfish individuals are not willing to risk continued retaliation. A form of social learning produces cooperative behavior as a more agreeable stance for both parties. This is not a rational strategy. It is an emotional process that spreads throughout a population because it is successful—more successful than being selfish and being retaliated upon. The predictability and simplicity of these stages makes it possible to notice this behavior in many species.

John Maynard Smith, a biologist, suggested that species evolve behavioral strategies just as they evolve physical characteristics (Pool 1995). If a strategy does not benefit reproduction in some way, it will die out. "Tit for tat" enables the formation of networks of cooperative individuals. Over time cooperative individuals reap a greater benefit from the environment than the more selfish individuals can.

Robert Trivers (1985) notes that reciprocal relationships in which both parties benefit forms the basis for altruism. This behavior is noted to occur in and even between species. Vampire bats feed others based on the degree of association and kinship, birds discriminate against those that invade territory, baboons and monkeys both groom and support those who reciprocate. Dolphins and whales exhibit altruistic behavior towards each other and even towards humans. In addition, restraints in aggression and cooperation can also be documented in the human. Trivers notes the evidence on both sides during trench warfare in World War I (Trivers 1985).

Cooperation in the human and other species promotes better levels of functioning in social relationships. Following simple rules like "tit for tat" appears automatic. Automatic responses allow individuals not to have to devote undue energy to managing emotional disturbances in the group.

When there has been a track record for an organization or an individual to promote cooperative behavior it is unusual to see this behavior erode. However there are times when the automatic response to the lack of cooperation is more reactive and when there may be little possibility for forgiveness. It is as though both the leader and the group are functioning in a lower emotional gear. The hill of life is just too hard to climb. Behavior can deteriorate.

When cooperative behavior in the group deteriorates the leader can overreact. In better times perhaps this leader would not overreact or make unrealistic demands on the group for cooperation. The most difficult challenge for any leader is to let go of expectations for cooperation from the family or even the work group. It is difficult to hold individuals accountable for their lack of cooperation and only retaliate mildly to make a point. Overreactions often occur when the leader, the organization itself, or both, have been stressed and have become more dependent on one another over time. Perhaps the following case will illustrate some of the above points.

Case Example

The originator of any successful family business is a leader. As a middle son of five this leader came from generations where the oldest son had run the family business. The maternal uncle had a clothing store, the maternal grandfather owned a butcher shop, and the paternal grandfather ran a brick factory. His mother was an overresponsible oldest of nine siblings. The father had problems, on and off, with drinking. During the depression the family was able to rely on relatives. The mother hoped the oldest son would rescue the family from difficult circumstances. Not much was expected from the middle son.

After high school, the middle son learned his trade by working in a small business. Eventually, he found an investor who helped him start his own business in another geographical area. He quickly married a local woman who worked beside him. After a few years they earned enough money to buy business property in the area where he was raised. The small business involved his extended family, brothers, and parents. Eventually two of her sisters were involved in the business. However the wife and her family took a back seat to her husband's love of his business. Living through the Depression motivated him to accumulate cash and not borrow money from banks. The money he made grew the business.

This middle son had lots of ideas and became known as an unusual and very successful originator. His energy went into his growing business. It was as important as another child, only this child could take care of everyone in the family. When family problems arose he focused on expanding the business. This was the area where he could succeed.

Over the years other family members were hired. As the originator's children reached adulthood he offered them a place in the business. Eventually stock was issued to reward individuals for doing well in their section of the business. Cooperation and personal responsibility were rewarded. Stock encouraged the children to remain in the business.

Although the originator owned the major share of stock, forty-nine percent, he did not have majority control for tax reasons. This was to become important in the later years as it gave rise to the possibility for selfish action by disgruntled family members.

The business grew exponentially during the sixties and the new growth resulted in the members of the family being required to take more demanding positions. The pressure rose. Family members had to learn new tasks: relating to the community at large, responding to increasing competition, expanding financially and acquiring adjacent property. These requirements for growth put new strains on the talents of these individuals. People found themselves doing jobs that they did not like, and the levels of complaints increased. The individual resolve to cooperate for the benefit of the family and the business was breaking down.

The originator resolved problems by taking strong leadership positions and requiring the others to go along with him. Eventually the business demands, plus the emotional undercurrent in the family, created factions. Coalitions formed. By the time the children of the originator were in their forties and fifties, the mother, who had a lifetime of moderate problems, became seriously ill. Distrust increased and individuals formed clicks. One or two were against the others. The rumors circulated and family fights were reported in the newspaper. Everyone was blamed. Anxiety was up. Anger and hurt overshadowed thinking about principles.

The conflict increased during business meetings. Individual identities were being threatened by the degree of negative comments. Eventually two of the adult children left the family business. One daughter believed that the relationship with the father would be preserved if the two could relate outside of the business. The second left due to the conflict with the father. Both sold their stock back to the company and were given money not to participate in any business in the geographical area. Although money was given, the emotional effect was that the father was disappointed and the adult children saw him as too demanding.

After the first two siblings left, it took a few years before the tensions again rose. The other adult children, cousins or spouses who held stock, formed a majority coalition to bring in an outside manager. This was a rebellion. This coalition briefly resulted in the ouster of the originator. The new manager had no idea of the family dynamics and found his efforts stymied by the wife and others loyal to the originator. Dissatisfaction grew within the new coalition.

Eventually the originator was able to purchase stock from one of the disgruntled shareholders. He returned with the firm intention of establishing and maintaining control. In the following three years all of the original stockholders were bought out, except the son and the originator's wife. Her health was poor and she was very divided on the issues between her son and her husband.

It was during this last year and a half that an outside family member was hired as a consultant. The consultant had two goals: to understand the problems without solving them for others, and to relate neutrally to each individual who was central to the conflict. This was an emotional stance that required a disciplined effort. It appeared to result in better contact between members of the larger family. The mother was able to make some contact with the son. The father was able to think differently about the issues.

The consultant had made the observation that restricting the previous stockholders had made it impossible to cooperate with the family members as future resources for the business. These stockholders had a great deal of money which was no longer able to be used by the corporation. Eventually a cooperative agreement between the father and the son was drawn up. There were constraints, but it was possible for the originator to see the advantages of allowing the son to have a business in the area.

A very few months after this transition the originator's wife died. The originator knew it was in his best interest to marry again. Within a month of his wife's death he married a long-time business acquaintance. The family reacted negatively. However one mitigating factor was that there were several grandchildren in the family business. The originator's obvious interest in the grandchildren made for a more cooperative atmosphere. Not all of the grandchildren could fit into the culture of the organization. Three of the five eventually left. After two of the grandchildren were fired for cause the tension predictably decreased in the organization and increased in the family relationships. The new wife supported the favorite grandchildren. She believed it was best to relate to the factions in the family. It requires strength to overcome the disappointments and hurts of the past and to act cooperatively on principle, but who knows how long this spirit can continue.

The new wife is loyal and has a great deal of business experience. The originator has taken actions to prepare for his wife to take over the corporation should something happen to him. He even borrowed a small amount of money to finish paying off the debts to the remaining stockholders. This family leader has turned to his new wife for the loyalty that at one time he sought from his children. This puts a great deal of pressure on the marriage. As long as the adult children continue to play out the distant negative side the automatic cooperation between the leader and his wife will continue. Perhaps the family members will have less reason for future retaliation; however, the family has not yet found a reason to cooperate.

Summary

Leaders are challenged to participate in any system so as to enable other individuals to accomplish purpose. "Tit for tat" is an emotional process that promotes the tendency for cooperation between all individuals in an ongoing relationship system. When there is a lack of cooperation in a relationship system, the leaders response can range from mild retaliation to revenge. The theoretical assumptions would be that the greater the leader's tolerance for anxiety, the less vulnerable he or she is to reactively being threatened by the actions of others. When individuals are sensitive and need others, problems will arise. Individuals put pressure on one another. At that point cooperation has to be reestablished. Leaders can decrease the reaction to negative coalitions and increase actions that have a positive payoff for the larger group. When there has been disappointment and blame throughout a family or an organization it takes time to understand how the problems and anxiety were generated. Family businesses have greater problems with anxiety than nonfamily businesses, as the patterns, sensitivities, and coalitions at home repeat themselves at work.

There appear to be simple principles that can be relied upon during times of high anxiety to guide behavior. When the relationships between people are seen as part of the intrinsic value of an organization, there will undoubtedly be new ways of observing and testing the guiding principles within the relationships systems to maximize value. Perhaps there will be a method known as cost/benefit analysis of the relationship system. There is always a cost and a benefit to being a member of a family system or an organization. Leaders can and do focus on a specific vision to guide the future direction of the organization, thereby thoughtfully increasing market share, profits, and share holder value. In the future, new knowledge of the relationship system may be included by leaders as contributing to the bottom line for both the family and organization.

REFERENCES

Bowen, Murray. 1978. *Family Therapy in Clinical Practice.* New York: Jason Aronson.

Gardner, John W. 1990. *On Leadership.* New York: Free Press.

Hook, Sidney. 1955. *The Hero in History.* Boston: Beacon Press.

Jung, Carl C. [1957] 1990. *The Undiscovered Self with Symbols and The Interpretations of Dreams.* 1990. Princeton. Princeton University Press.

Pool, Robert. 1995. *Science.* 267:1591-1593

Poundstone, William 1992. *The Prisoner's Dilemma.* New York: Doubleday.

Trivers, Robert. 1985. *Social Evolution.* Menlo Park, California: Benjamin/Cummings.

THE INFLUENCE OF ANXIETY WITHIN A BUSINESS

Kent E. Webb, LCSW

The phenomenon of anxiety affects the functioning of all humans, human families, and human organizations. This paper, a business case study, explores the interrelationship between chronic and acute anxiety within a business and within one of the leaders in the business, the CEO.

Two basic ideas from Bowen theory are applied in this paper. When the functioning of an organization is being assessed it is important to know how chronic and acute anxiety have influenced the functioning of the leadership and the functioning of the business. Specifically, the history of the business and the family history of the company's leaders are key areas to examine. Secondly, if a leader puts in an objective, consistent effort at managing his anxiety as it relates to the family and to the business, the functioning of the leader and the business will most likely improve in time.

This paper describes how anxiety was manifested in a specific business and within its CEO. It identifies the efforts the business and the CEO made to manage and decrease the impact of the anxiety.

Case Study

An attempt is made here to track anxiety within a mental health care organization during its first eight years of operation, from conception of the business, to the loss of a major contract after the initial four years, and to examine the impact of that loss on the business in the subsequent four years. As well, an effort is made to also track the CEO's level of anxiety within the same eight years of operation and the efforts he made to address and manage the anxiety at a personal level.

PPN, the subject of the case study, is a mental health care organization incorporated in 1987 that provides outpatient mental health and chemical dependency services within the state of Colorado. PPN serves health maintenance organizations, national managed behavioral health care companies, and self-insured or self-funded health plans of corporations. PPN is an integrated service network that consists of one hundred thirty independent contractors (mental health professionals which includes physicians, psychologists, clinical social workers, professional counselors, and nurses) and staff clinicians.

PPN is a system of care that monitors quality of care and service as well as the utilization of services. The organization promotes and tracks provider accountability through a client feedback system and review of clinical and administrative data captured in a comprehensive data management and information system.

PPN, P.C.
ORGANIZATION CHART
BOARD OF DIRECTORS
Executive Advisory Committee
CEO
Medical Director
CFO/COO
DIRECTOR CLINICAL SERVICES
DIRECTOR BUSINESS DEVELOPMENT
ACCOUNT MANAGEMENT
NETWORK SERVICES
CLINICAL SERVICES
EDUCATION WORKSHOPS
DEVELOPMENT COORDINATION
PROVIDER RELATIONS
RESEARCH DEVELOPMENT
REFERRAL COORDINATION
CREDENTIALING
ORIENTATION TRAINING
QUALITY MANAGEMENT
CASE MANAGEMENT
CLINICAL MIS
CLAIMS COORDINATOR
OFFICE COORDINATOR
MARKETING
CONSULTING
RECORDS MANAGEMENT
CLERICAL STAFF
PRODUCT DEVELOPMENT
FINANCE ACCOUNTING
MIS DEVELOPMENT

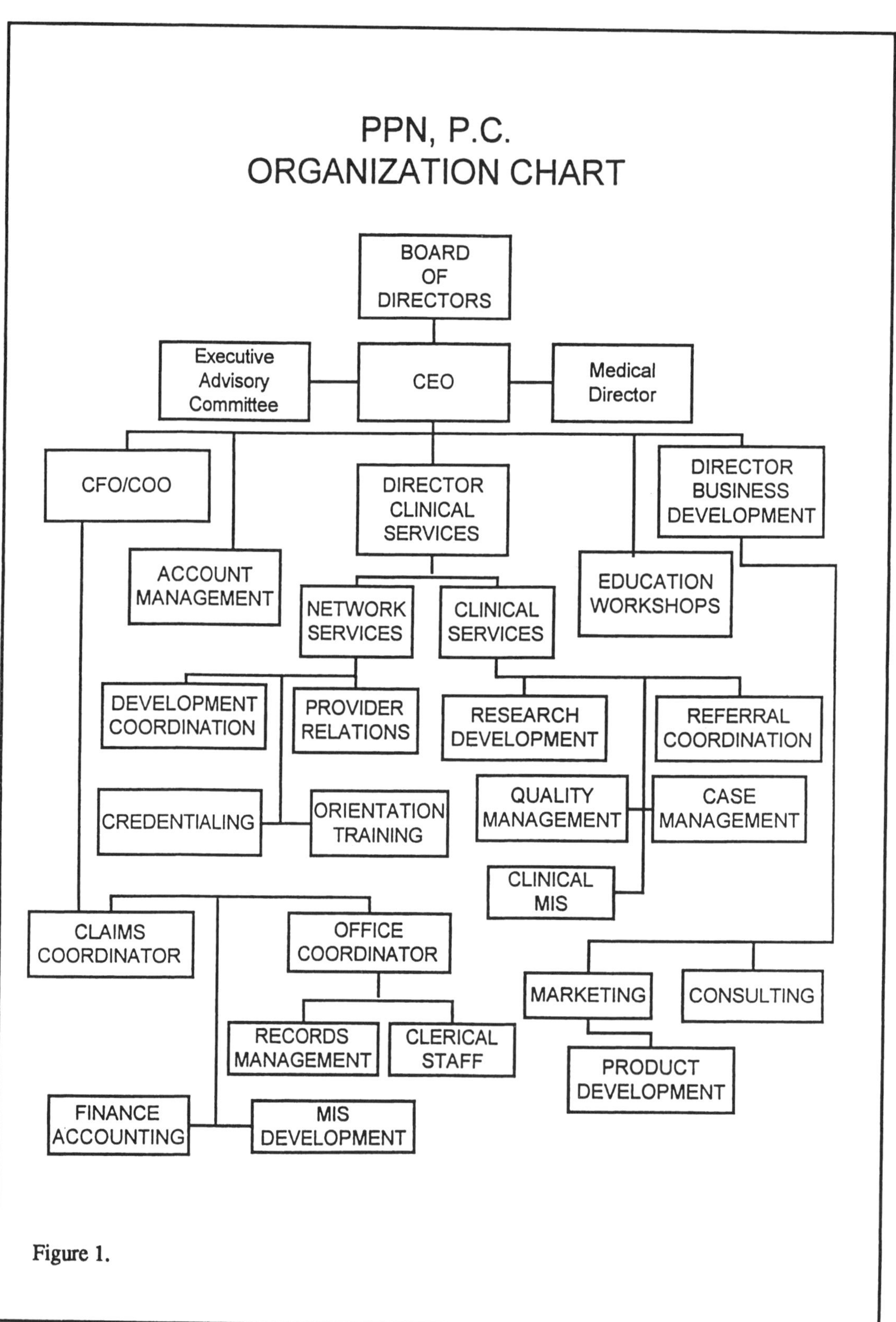

Figure 1.

Structure and Purpose of the Organization

PPN is a small organization with eight employees who have multiple functions and responsibilities both clinically and administratively. PPN has three principles, two of whom are equal majority stockholders and are the managing partners. The other principle presently serves as a member on the board of directors but is not active in the management or delivery systems. The President of the PPN board is also the Chief Executive Officer (CEO) and Director of Clinical Services. The Vice-President of the board is the Chief Financial Officer (CFO) and Chief of Operations (COO). (Figure 1.)

The Origins of PPN

The facts involved in creating PPN were both objectively and subjectively influenced. Objectively, PPN was created to insure a flow of clients for the clinical practices of the principles. The delivery systems for mental health care were just beginning to change in 1987 from traditional private practices with traditional referral systems that included well established fee for service reimbursement models to managed care systems that consisted of panels, networks, and the monitoring of the quality of care and the utilization of services with contractual arrangements as the preferred financial model. The contracts contained a mix of capitation and fee for service arrangements that included discounts from the usual and customary rates established in previous private practice environments.

It was fact that a shift in the delivery systems and financial models was occurring and appeared to be driven by the effort of employers to control escalating health care costs. As a result, a shift was observed in the locus of care which meant care being delivered in the least restrictive setting rather than the most restrictive setting which resulted in substantial financial savings. The shift in the locus of care was a major paradigm shift in the delivery system. It had previously been believed that the most effective care was provided in the most restrictive setting and the least effective care was provided in lesser restrictive environments.

Another fact driving the development of PPN was a shift in thinking in the delivery system that care needed to include and involve the relationship and social systems of the client, specifically the family and the client's community. Previously, the care was most often directed at the individual with little attention paid to the family or the community.

The increased acceptance and use of non-medical doctors in the delivery system was encouraging to the principles of PPN, all of whom were not physicians and therefore benefited from this shift. The shift in the type of providers used to provide the service was another factor driven by the effort to reduce the cost of the service without sacrificing quality. The final factor included the CEO wanting to create an opportunity for himself to develop his leadership, to advance his administrative skills, to address his tendency to move toward emotional dependence and emotional fusion (Bowen 1978).

The CEO was anxious about his inability to establish a full time private practice in four years. He then thought that developing a business with other business partners that sought contracts to provide mental health services for corporations or insurance programs might be a way to secure his practice and financial stability. The CEO was aware that his self-confidence and his self-esteem had declined in response to not having developed a full time private practice. This also contributed to the anxiety he was experiencing about appearing not to be a successful therapist and how this would affect his status in the professional community.

The CEO was doubtful that he could establish a business without depending on others. He was aware of depending on other business partners and on a consultant hired to assist with starting up the business. The CEO observed himself struggling to not take a one down position to the consultant. The consultant also assumed a marketing role within the business and was primarily responsible for obtaining the first major contracts for PPN.

The consultant's success in securing these initial contracts for PPN appeared to be based primarily on the relationship system he had previously established with an insurance company. As the CEO watched and experienced the consultant getting PPN its first large contracts and launching it as a legitimate business, his anxiety intensified regarding dependence on others for his own success. The CEO was also aware of an emotional drive and desire within himself to be in a position of dominance in the organization, to be the leader, to be the "star."

Influence of the CEO's Family of Origin on His Leadership

The CEO's family of origin consisted of many generations of pioneers, farmers, and small business owners. The families migrated from Europe to the East Coast of the United States and westward from Pennsylvania to Kentucky, Missouri, Kansas, and Colorado. The educational backgrounds of the family members gradually increased over the generations from grade school to high school to college, and several to graduate school.

Several basic principles guided the behavior and emotions of many, such as, "Do it yourself," "Stand on your own," "Support yourself," and "Don't give up." Although these sound like statements that might indicate or reflect higher levels of differentiation, as defined by Bowen theory, it appears as though the phrases were primarily principles to aspire to.

The CEO believed his level of differentiation, on the scale of differentiation as developed by Murray Bowen to be between 25-30 on the scale of 1-100. He arrived at this rating since feelings and emotions appear to have been more influential on his and his families' functioning over time than the intellectual system. Other supporting facts for this rating of 25-30 on the scale are: the CEO's drive to be successful was mostly to obtain approval; a major life focus was directed toward finding an ideal close relationship, which appeared to be accurate for most of the family members over generations; fear of being alone; and fear of failing. These characteristics lead to high degrees of relationship dependence and chronic anxiety. Although the families' level of differentiation is low on the scale, the family for the most part has taken care of itself, adding to, rather than taking from society. (Figure 2.)

Significant symptoms developed in the CEO's family of origin, which were as significant, if not more so, than in the families of the CEO's parents siblings and their offspring. The most striking and observable characteristics of the lower level of differentiation began with the CEO's father's death at the age of fifty. His death and the emotional shock wave that followed appear to be a reflection of the high degree of fusion and dependence in the family. Specifically, the CEO's mother remarried nine months after her husband's death an individual who was alcohol dependent and a perpetrator of domestic violence. The CEO's brother was married four times and had a total of six significant relationships. The CEO's first wife committed suicide in 1982 just two weeks prior to the date of the divorce.

As the CEO examined his own personal history and that of his family of origin and his extended family, he became aware of the fact that emotional dependence and the need for emotional dependence increases anxiety even though the initial driving force for dependence is to achieve comfort. This notion is a central idea to Bowen theory and the concept of differentiation of self.

Anxiety and Business

Anxiety was woven into the fabric of the business from inception, with the CEO's personal, chronic anxiety and with anxiety from the subjective emotional factors previously identified that were, in part, driving the creation of the business. The three major emotional forces identified have been dependence, fear, and approval. There were three other principles at the time the business was conceived and in its formative years, therefore; one could assume they were also bringing their own levels of chronic anxiety and inserting it into the business, as well.

Bowen theory defines anxiety as a response of an organism to a threat, real or imagined. The question posed for PPN was, "What might occur for the business if its major

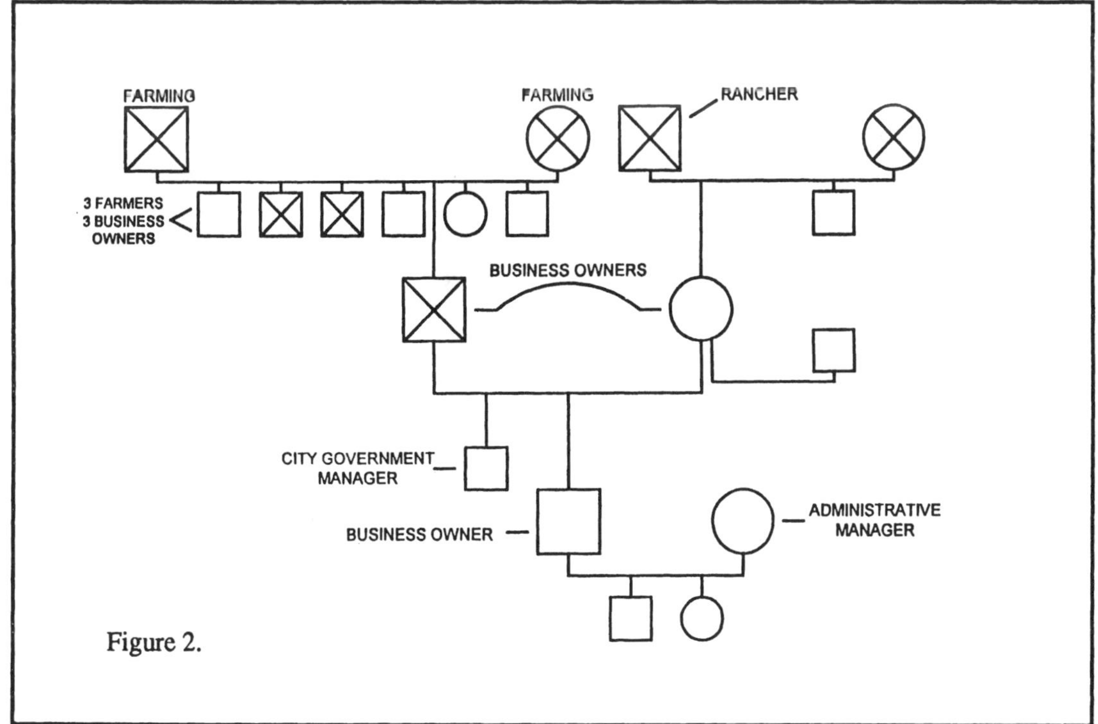

Figure 2.

contract were terminated early in its business life?" Primarily due to forces in the relationship system and a potent triangle between PPN, the consultant, and the insurance company, the contract was terminated in June 1991. The impact and effect of this major event is examined from factual and subjective data from the time the contract was terminated in 1991 to 1994.

PPN's Business Time Line

PPN's growth in numbers of covered lives started with 18,000 in 1988 to 40,000 in 1991. (Figure 3.) The gross revenues of the company increased from $40,000 in 1988 to $250,000 through 1990. As well, the valuation of PPN increased from approximately $80,000 in 1989 to $500,000 in 1990. (Figure 4.) The CEO was aware of increasing anxiety within himself regarding the necessity of maintaining the business at its current levels. This anxiety seemed directly tied to his dependence on the contracts for professional and financial survival.

Midyear, 1991, the major HMO contract was terminated due to several factors outside the control of the business. It appeared the relationship system and emotional forces were the most potent variables. As a result of the loss of business, PPN's revenues and valuation were significantly effected. The number of covered lives were reduced from 40,000 to 20,000. Gross revenues fell from $250,000 to $180,00 and the valuation of PPN shifted from $500,000 to $325,000. On the emotional process side of the equation, the loss generated acute anxiety for both the business and the CEO. Of particular note, was the awareness of the degree of chronic anxiety within the CEO that this life event activated.

Figure 3. Covered Lives

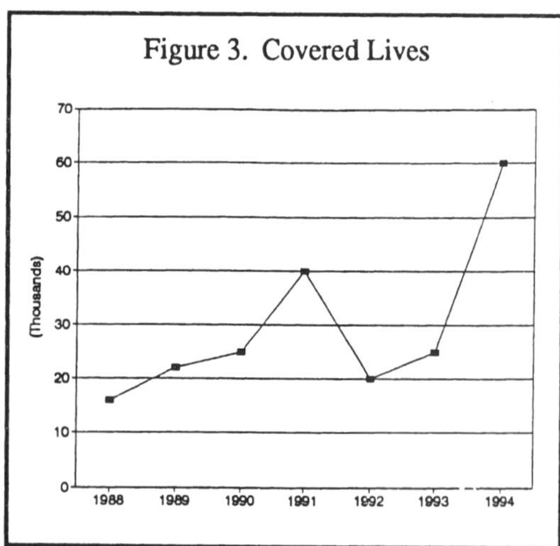

Acute and Chronic Anxiety

Acute anxiety, in Bowen theory, is defined as a response to real threats or to the fear of what is. The real threats with the HMO contract being terminated were (1) the loss of revenue, the loss of clinical business for the four partners, and the viability of the business. One partner sold his stock and left the business, another partner sought part-time work with an agency. One year later another partner left due to medical, personal, and professional reasons and concerns about what the professional community would think about the capacity of the partners to manage and lead an organization such as PPN.

Bowen theory defined chronic anxiety as the response to imagined threats or to the fear of what might be. This anxiety originates from disturbances within the relationship system. The CEO's fears of "what might be" included the loss of financial security which might increase his dependence on his wife financially, which, in turn, triggered worries about the possibil-

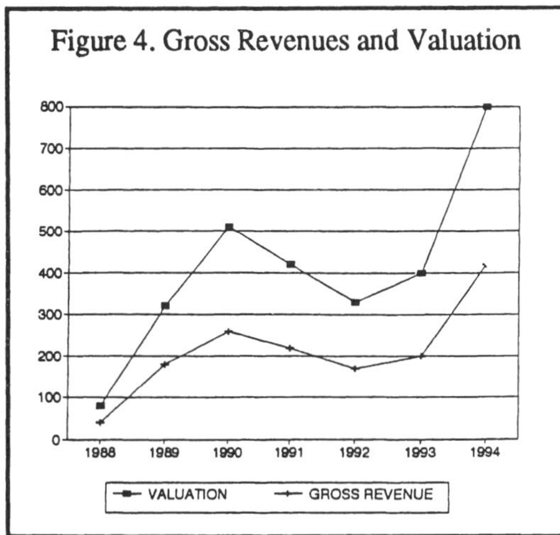

Figure 4. Gross Revenues and Valuation

ity of not fulfilling his family responsibilities; the loss of self-esteem; and the loss of approval. He also questioned and doubted his ability to lead or manage a business.

The CEO observed and experienced the highest levels of reactivity to the loss of the contract from 1991-1994. To him, it was as if the acute anxiety of losing business set off and tapped into chronic anxiety and then the chronic anxiety increased reactivity to the acute anxiety. Bowen theory would describe this phenomenon as a systems reaction. (Theoretically, the above scenario may not always occur. It may be as if there are "shut off" valves attached to the "containers" of acute and chronic anxiety. For example, acute anxiety, which individuals often experience at times of natural disasters, may even enhance and not negatively effect the functioning of an individual at the moment so that the chronic anxiety of the individual does not emerge and intensify the process).

The CEO's emotional reactivity to the loss was significant. To him, the experience compared to the reactivity he experienced at the time his first wife and his father died. He became more aware of chronic anxiety within himself during the months following the contract termination. He was aware that this was the type of reaction that might trigger emotional symptoms, such as depression or physical problems. In other words, it was a both a personal and business vortex at which he could either stand up and move forward or lie down and die. The CEO made the decision to move forward and use the experience as an opportunity to strengthen himself and the business as well.

The past several years have presented the CEO with challenges and opportunities. The question the CEO posed to himself throughout this time was, "In the face of adversity, what does one do to land on one's feet?" Several ideas surfaced as variables for a successful landing: working to be prepared to accept a loss prior to losing whatever "it" may be; to work at decreasing one's emotional, financial, or professional dependence on others or things; to work at increasing one's level of functioning as it relates to family and business relationship systems using the concept of differentiation of self as a guide; to understand one's level of differentiation on the scale which will give one a more accurate perspective about the ways he/she may respond to acute and chronic anxiety; and lastly, to work towards the acceptance of "what is" related to one's level of differentiation. To work toward acceptance does not mean being complacent or pessimistic, but rather knowing the predictors that can assist in charting and navigating the choppy waters that lie ahead.

While the CEO has been addressing these ideas, the organization has mobilized itself and has initially recovered and progressed from the loss of business in 1991. The number of covered lives serviced by PPN has increased from 20,000 in 1992 to 60,000 in 1994. The gross revenues grew from $180,000 in 1992 to $450,000 in 1994. The valuation of PPN increased from $325,000 in 1992 to $800,000 at the close of 1994. (Figures 3. and 4.) At a more personal level, the CEO did not develop any significant physical or emotional problems either within himself or within his family relationship system.

REFERENCES

Bowen, Murray. 1978. *Family Therapy in Clinical Practice.* New York: Jason Aronson, Inc.

Kerr, Michael E. and Bowen, Murray. 1988. *Family Evaluation: An Approach Based on Bowen Theory.* New York: W. W. Norton & Company.

BOWEN FAMILY SYSTEMS THEORY AS A FRAMEWORK FOR CONSULTANTS

Leslie Ann Fox, MA, RRA

Bowen family systems theory is an important theoretical framework for consultants who recognize that bringing knowledge of relationship systems and emotional process to client organizations is as important as bringing them expertise and knowledge of management theories. Consultants want to use their knowledge, experience or competence to help clients solve problems or improve the performance of their organizations. However, just as mastering content does not necessarily make one a good teacher, nor does it necessarily make one a good consultant. Consultants need to develop skills and models for effective consulting. I believe these skills and models should be based on understanding how people behave in relationship systems. Bowen theory provides such a basis.

Bowen family systems theory is a theory of human behavior that has served as a sound theoretical framework for family therapists for more than thirty years. In the late 1950s, Dr. Murray Bowen began developing a series of concepts about emotional process that describe how humans function in their families, their primary relationship system. These concepts are just as apt in describing other relationship systems in which humans must function, such as the workplace, schools, religious institutions, or social organizations.

Bowen theory differs from other well-known theories in the behavioral sciences. Rather than focusing on the individual, as Freud did for example, Bowen theory focuses on the family as a functional unit, addressing the process of mutual influencing and interdependency within the unit. An organization can also be viewed as a functional unit, as can the divisions, departments, and work teams within the organization. Bowen theory also differs from general systems theory, which is widely applied in the management literature. Bowen theory is a theory of natural systems based on observations of the human family to describe the orderly processes that govern human behavior. It views humans as part of nature and human behavior as consistent with behavior in all living systems.

Emotional Process

Emotional refers to behavior that is an automatic response to a stimulus rather than a conscious choice. Responses are affected by the level of anxiety being experienced by the system and the ability of the system to tolerate anxiety. Anxiety means "the arousal of the organism upon perceiving a real or imagined threat" (Papero 1990). When people are in life threatening situations or when they perceive that they are, their behavior is guided more by an automatic (emotional) response system than by a cognitive system. Emotional process is how the organization, its functional units and individuals behave in response to anxiety-provoking factors in the environment.

Papero explains that the intensity of anxiety in the organism and the group is a significant variable influencing whether behavior is emotionally or intellectually driven. Higher anxiety results in more emotionally driven behavior in an organization. Excessive gossiping, cliques, absenteeism, tardiness, blaming, scapegoating, over/underfunctioning, bickering, and conflicts are examples of anxiety-driven behaviors we can observe in the workplace.

Two Consulting Models

A consulting model refers to the general approach and specific methods consultants use to meet the requirements of their clients. Two commonly used consulting models are "content" and "process." In the "content" model, the consultant is viewed primarily as an expert on subject matter. Either the client or the consultant may determine the organization's problems or needs, but the consultant is expected to propose solutions, teach skills or content to client staff, or perform the work required to implement the solution. Or, a senior manager may view a consultant like a "doctor" and call her in to diagnose and treat a problem division, department, or team.

The "process" model, as described by Edgar Schein in *Process Consultation* (1988), offers a different approach. Describing it as an attitude or philosophy, he states that "the main goal of the process consultant is to help the manager (client) to make a diagnosis and to develop a valid action plan for himself." (Schein 1988)

Either model can be used to provide help to clients. They may also be used in combination. However, neither of these models provides the consultant with a broad, underlying theory of human behavior that brings awareness of emotional process in human systems into the model. Bowen family systems theory fills that void.

In Search of a Better Model

I provide consulting services to hospital medical record departments. These services usually include a review of the department's organizational structure, management, staffing, systems, work flow, and procedures. In short, I conduct an operations review and analysis. When I started consulting twenty-three years ago, I saw myself as a content expert. I did not know enough about consulting to even wonder about the process. I had never even had the experience of working with a consultant when I was the director of a medical record department. I only knew that I was knowledgeable about medical record systems and procedures and the people that hired me wanted my help. I suspect that I am not the only consultant that has started so naively. I walked into my first client's medical record department and saw that the records were filed in plastic bags instead of folders. Immediately I knew that there was nothing I could say that wouldn't be helpful. The department had no one with professional training in medical records administration. I was the expert. I looked at how the employees did their work, and told the manager how she could improve the systems and procedures in the department. Sometimes she made the changes I suggested, but often she did not. At the time, I did not recognize her "excuses" as symptomatic of anxiety in the organization. Thus, I usually addressed the issues, oblivious to the underlying emotional process and its impact on my client and on my effectiveness as a consultant.

Over the years, I consulted with medical record departments in hospitals all over the United States. I came, I saw, I submitted a report. Sometimes I succeeded in teaching clients how to do something they didn't already know, or to implement a new way of doing things. But, often the report was left to gather dust. As the 1970s gave way to the 1980s, I began to realize that more and more I was asked to consult in departments where the staff had as much knowledge and experience in medical records as I had. Their departments weren't functioning well, but they needed more than someone to tell them what to do.

That's when I realized I needed to learn more about "how to consult." I began experimenting with more formal diagnostic and intervention strategies. I gathered information more systematically. I interviewed more people in the departments. I drew flow charts, conducted time studies, analyzed fluctuations in work load volume, turnaround time and productivity. I helped the clients establish quality indicators and methods to measure and improve quality. Still, I struggled to effect change and find satisfaction as a consultant. I read about process consulting, and began to facilitate action planning sessions in which the clients participated, hoping for more response to my final recommendations. That helped but I still was missing something important.

Bowen Theory and Health Information Management

In the late 1980s, I learned about Bowen family systems theory. The concepts gave me new insights into the relationships within my family. They changed how I think about relationship systems and soon influenced my thinking about my own company. Finally, as I changed, my approach to consulting changed.

Bowen theory can help consultants observe and think about patterns of behavior in organizations in the same ways that family systems therapists observe and think about relationships in families. These concepts also can help consultants better understand their own relationships with clients and provide a basis for them to manage their own behavior in those relationships. I believe that no matter what method, technique, attitude, or philosophy consultants choose, if they do not understand their client organizations in the context of emotional process, their success and the success of their clients will be compromised.

I still hear excuses about poor performance from clients. They are often in the form of blaming others in the organization. For example, not being able to complete records is blamed on (1) doctors who don't change how their incomplete records are filed; (2) nurses hold the discharged patient records too long, delaying processing, record completion, and consequently billing; or, (3) hospital administrators will not approve funding for more modern equipment. Excessive turnover in the department is blamed on salaries being lower than at other hospitals in the community. Records for clinic visits cannot be retrieved because clinic personnel submit pull lists that are incomplete, illegible and often disorganized. And the list of complaints about others goes on and on.

Although these statements may be factual, they are also what I call "relationship anxiety noise." And, I know that the "noisier" the environment, the more I need to manage my own anxiety. As I do my fact finding, I try to distinguish the facts from the noise, and I try to present those facts in as calm and neutral a manner as possible.

A business consultation model derived from Bowen theory recognizes the importance of the emotional process in the client organization. Principles of this model include:

• Being aware of the organizational anxiety and its sources and trying to avoid absorbing it.
• Reducing anxiety in the system by gathering and focusing on facts rather than feelings.
• Recognizing anxiety in self and choosing responses rather than reacting automatically.
• Avoiding overfunctioning for clients. Being a resource, but allowing clients to be responsible for diagnosing and solving their own problems.
• Observing the triangles and avoiding taking sides. When necessary to take a position, stating one's own position based on facts.
• Continually striving to sharpen ability to observe behavior rather than reacting to it.
• Identifying the better differentiated leaders, or those individuals who have the potential to become better differentiated and assume more of a leadership role.

Combining the principles derived from Bowen theory with my knowledge of content and process consulting methods, resulted in the following steps which describe the consulting model I use in my work with medical record departments. It is a model that I believe can be applied to organizations and departments within organizations regardless of content area.

Defining Self to Client

• Define the role of the consultant to the client organization. *Clients* includes the administrator that hires the consultant as well as the department director or manager. (Consultants who are hired by senior administrators to consult to an individual department find themselves in a triangle with the administrator and the department director before they even begin).

• Agree on the goals and describe the process to the clients that will be used in the consultation before starting the engagement.

• Obtain a commitment from the department director to establish a planning team to spend one or two days at the conclusion of the on-site visit to hear the consultant's findings and participate in developing a departmental action plan. Encourage the administrator to participate in the feedback and action planning session. The administrator learns a lot and the director gets more consistent support for the actions being implemented.

Data Collection and Review

• Obtain a copy of the organization's stated values, mission, goals and strategic direction prior to the visit or as soon as they are available.

• Review the department's organizational chart, job descriptions, policies and procedures, budget, staffing, productivity and quality assurance data prior to the first visit to establish baseline knowledge of the department's performance with as little "emotional noise" as possible. Review customer and employee satisfaction questionnaires.

On-Site Data Collection and Review

• Gather historical facts about the functioning of the organization, its units, and positions within the units early in the on-site visit.
• Identify the anxiety-provoking factors in the environment throughout the visit.
• Seek to discern patterns of behavior and the ways anxiety are managed in the organization throughout the information gathering and during the planning session.
• Interview all of the department's employees, or as many people as possible, individually or in groups. Gather facts about how they do their jobs and listen to their opinions on how they believe they can do them better.
• Interview as many customers of the department as possible to determine how well they perceive their needs are being met.
• Observe how staff perform tasks.
• Observe the work environment. Observe how staff, supervisors, customers, and administration interact throughout the visit.

Analysis and Feedback

• Analyze information. Compare departmental performance to industry standards. Identify contradictions in information reported by those interviewed. Determine to what extent successful change is likely to be limited by anxiety and lack of differentiated leaders in the relationship system.
• Organize information to be reported back to the administrator, department director, planning team, and staff.
• Report findings to the department's planning group.

Collaborate with Client on Development of Change Plan

• Facilitate developing an action plan, including review and revision of the department's mission and vision statements.
• Serve as a resource as the planning group establishes goals, and determines action, target dates, and accountability.

Followup and Evaluation

• Prepare and submit a written report as required. Follow-up with periodic telephone calls or on-site visits as requested to evaluate the effectiveness of the process.

Case Study

The Combined Medical Care Facility (CMCF) is located in a rural area. Two years prior to the involvement of the health information management consultant, the CMCF was created by the Boards of Directors of two sole community public hospitals located in towns about ten miles apart. The directors determined that the continued financial viability of their hospitals would be served best by joining forces to operate as one organization. However, they did not merge the two hospitals into one legal entity. They agreed only to combine all services to eliminate duplication and reduce operating costs for both. They continue to maintain two Boards of Directors, but have one administration and one set of combined clinical and support departments.

Operations were streamlined by consolidating inpatient and emergency services at one location, and by offering the majority of outpatient and urgent care services at the other. All clinical and support departments at the two locations were merged, eliminating many managerial and staff positions. They developed a more efficient health care delivery system for their communities, but all parties involved in or affected by the restructuring of the organizations have been unhappy with the process and the outcome.

Citizens in one of the two communities perceived that they had lost their hospital because they now must travel to the other town for inpatient services. Many citizens were so angry about this change that they boycotted the hospital and started traveling to another hospital about thirty miles further away. They lobbied so intensely against the concept of the combined facility they were able to force a public referendum on its future. The future of the combined facility remains unsettled.

Hospital administrators were under intense pressure from the unanticipated financial difficulties caused by the boycott and from the constant publicity in the local media about the community's dissatisfaction.

As departments were combined, they each lost at least one of the two previous managers and often several staff members. The remaining manager and staff in a newly combined department had to redesign their work. The managers had to determine the most cost effective way to restructure the delivery of services and negotiate with staff each step of the way as to whether things would be done "our way", "their way", or some "new way." The stress was high as staff tried to cope with the ongoing changes and an uncertain future.

The Director of Information Services (IS) initially contacted the Health Information Management (HIM) consultant to request an operations review of the medical record department. The consultant asked for background information and about the purpose of the review. The IS director had been assigned administrative responsibility for the medical record department a few months earlier following the resignation of the chief financial officer. He was concerned about the medical record department because he received numerous complaints about its performance from other departments and medical staff. The department had backlogs in key processing areas that compromised billing and collections up to several million dollars. Physicians complained that dictated reports were regularly delayed in getting to the patients' records due to backlogs in the medical transcription area of the department. He was also concerned because morale in the department was very low. Knowledge of the organization's recent history helped the consultant understand the context in which the department was functioning and to determine the level of service she needed to provide.

The consultant described the process of conducting the operations review and recommended following the review immediately with an action planning workshop for the administrator and/or director responsible for the department, the department manager, supervisors, and representatives of the staff. The IS director indicated he was in favor of this approach because it would provide the medical record manager with the support he believed she needed to improve the functioning of the department. He expressed high expectations of what the consultation could accomplish.

Prior to the on-site visit, the consultant spoke with the medical record department manager, who seemed receptive to the consultation. She believed that her problems were due to staffing shortages and was sure the consultant would support her in this view after seeing the department. She too had very high expectations for the consultation.

Two days before the health information management consultant was to make the initial visit to the hospital, she received a telephone call from another consultant who was working with the organization's business office. He wanted to alert her to the problems that the medical record department was causing the business office in billing and collections. He had very high expectations as well and indicated that he hoped that the health information management consultant would be able to "straighten out" the medical record department.

Before the visit, to survey customer and employee satisfaction, questionnaires had been sent to the IS director to distribute to users and staff. The completed questionnaires were sent to the consultant a few days prior to the initial on-site visit. They were extreme in their criticism of the effectiveness of the department and of the manager specifically. Some of the employees attached lengthy letters describing their dissatisfaction.

The anxiety in this system was so high and so contagious that the consultant's anxiety was soaring before even setting a foot in the door. Fortunately, she had consultation class on Bowen family systems theory the day before she was to leave for the first visit. Discussing systems theory in class helped her get her own anxiety under control so she could start to think about and plan for the upcoming visit more calmly.

With some coaching, she determined that first she had to stop feeling like she was responsible for solving all their problems. She would have to lower expectations and return their anxiety back to them. Then, as always, she would have to rely on her own expertise in medical records to determine what would be the relevant information to collect to be able to judge the seriousness of the problems and to identify possible solutions. She decided to rely on a process of calm fact-finding, making a conscious decision not to judge or be reactive to any of the participants during the consultation process. Everyone would be given an opportunity to tell their story, but the consultant would use only verifiable facts about the department's functioning to set the action planning session in motion. For example, if backlogs are delaying up two million dollars in billing, that is a verifiable fact to be addressed. That backlog, along with several others, has been eliminated.

The consultant conducted the interviews and reviews over three days. She presented the facts as she saw them to the IS director, the medical record manager, and a team the manager had selected to help develop the plan. She served as a resource to the planning group as they developed measurable goals, actions, target dates and a responsible person for each problem identified by the consultant during the review, observation, and interview process. After working on implementation of the plan for six months, the staff has implemented the majority of actions. Overall functioning of the department is much improved.

Their success has not been without considerable work and pain. The manager is no longer the manager, but has remained in the department as a member of the staff. Her lack of management skills was obvious, but her knowledge of medical record procedures is acceptable. The IS director decided to move her into a more suitable position for her talents. The manager's position has been left vacant. Staff have been divided into three teams around the three key work processes performed by the department. A supervisor or team leader has been selected for each team, and these supervisors now comprise a management team. They report directly to the Director of Information Services. It took the IS director about six months to make these organizational changes. The consultant's company continues to provide expertise through a monthly visit to answer technical questions and to facilitate continued planning and implementation.

Knowledge of family systems theory continued to be important for the consultant. Conflict between the IS director and the hospital administrator created confusion for the consultant and the staff following the initial on-site assessment and action planning session. Though the IS director had hired the consultant, the hospital's assistant administrator had made all contacts for further assistance. The consultant perceived herself being caught in an anxious triangle and had to be cautious about relating to the IS director and the assistant administrator without appearing to take sides. The consultant continues to make appointments for visits with the IS director, and responds to the assistant administrator only when contacted.

Decisions regarding the implementation of the action plan that needed to be made by the IS director were slow. Employees in the medical record department were often unclear as to who was in charge of the department, because they were informed that the manager's position would be eliminated and replaced with the three supervisory positions, but they did not know for several months when that change would become official. Also, the assistant administrator started dropping by the department more frequently to make sure that actions were being implemented, while the IS director continued to keep a rather low profile with the staff.

The department still suffers considerable angst due to a perceived lack of leadership in the department and apparent conflict between the IS director and the assistant administrator. The department's management team has progressed with improving internal operations but is inexperienced and ill-prepared to interact effectively externally. Their remaining challenges require both technical expertise and political savvy to meet their objectives. The IS director is remote, geographically, professionally, and philosophically from the medical record department. He reports to a new chief financial officer who is not yet knowledgeable about the needs of the medical record department. The assistant administrator does not want to bring in an experienced medical record director, even on an interim basis, to help develop the skills of the new supervisors. It remains to be seen whether a monthly visit from a consultant, and continued development of the change management process, will be sufficient support to allow any of the new supervisors to emerge as effective leaders.

The consultant's knowledge of Bowen family systems theory is evident in several ways in this case study. The consultant recognized from the outset that the system was highly anxious; developed a plan for managing her own anxiety; presented a calm presence to staff, manager, director and administrators, keeping all parties focused on facts; recognized that the pull of triangles would be intense because of the high anxiety and worked hard to be a neutralizer rather than an intensifier; recognizes conflicts at a higher level in the organization have slowed the reorganization and continue to impede progress on the plan; recognizes that the absence of well-differentiated leadership throughout the organization is an inhibitor to more rapid progress; and recognizes that it is important to be on guard against overfunctioning for this organization.

Conclusion

Knowledge of Bowen theory provides this consultant with a new way of thinking about organizations, but it also provides a way of thinking about the larger health care delivery system in the United States. The changes in the financial structure, as well as the astounding advances in medical and information technologies, have hospital administration and staff coping with more than gradual changes in their organizations. Their work systems are changing within the larger health care delivery system which is also changing. As a result, many health care professionals are being dislocated. As inpatient care diminishes and outpatient care increases, as paper records evolve into electronic ones, as patient focused care centers emerge with multi-skilled health care professionals, the work processes of all health care professionals will change radically. Medical record professionals are even confronting possible extinction if they do not redefine their role quickly. To this consultant, the anxiety in all health care organizations seems higher than ever. Using Bowen theory as a framework helps me think about rather than react to the events in my field. It provides me with a broader perspective and keeps me open to many options.

REFERENCES

Kerr, Michael E. and Murray Bowen. 1988. *Family Evaluation: An Approach Based on Bowen Theory*. New York: W. W. Norton & Company.

Papero, Daniel V. 1990. *Bowen Family Systems Theory*. Boston, Massachusetts: Allyn and Bacon.

Schein, E. 1988. *Process Consultation, Volume I: Its Role in Organization Development*. Reading, Massachusetts: Addison-Wesley Publishing Company.

THE SCHOOL AS AN EMOTIONAL SYSTEM

Roger Dillow, MA, MSW

Cooperative care-taking and education of the young have a long and important history in mammalian species (Napier and Napier 1985, Wilson 1975).[1] Formal human schools date back at least to the time of ancient Greece. While acknowledging these histories as the large, multigenerational context for the development of the institution of the school, this paper focuses on the schools we know today. These schools, the purposes they serve, and the emotional intensity in and around them are all, in many ways, relatively new phenomena. Nearly universal compulsory education and the perceived importance of schools in this country have been established mainly in the twentieth-century (Cremin 1988). A paper with a somewhat different focus could identify elements of societal emotional process in, among other things, the urbanization of the population in the United States. This shift toward not only increased but dense, localized populations may contribute to increased anxiety,[2] which may be associated with the escalating expectations of social institutions.

The focus of this paper is on the individual American school as an emotional system of human relationships. The school as we know it today operates as an emotional unit second to the family, in its direct influence on the development of children. The school parallels the family in providing child-rearing functions in the context of ongoing and relatively intense adult-child or adult-adolescent relationships.[3]

Identifying emotional processes in family, work, and other social systems, Bowen theory offers a perspective that accounts for variability in organizations' functioning and fulfillment of mission (Bowen 1978a, Gilbert 1992, K. Kerr 1982, Wiseman 1982). The purpose of this paper is to identify some processes that characterize emotional systems and to illustrate how they manifest themselves in schools whether they be elementary or secondary, rural or urban. Experience is the high road to understanding emotional systems when it is based as much as possible on systems thinking and includes relatively objective observation of not only the behavior of others in the social system but also one's own patterns of emotional reactivity.

This descriptive analysis represents a step in the direction of understanding human functioning in educational institutions and suggests further applications of Bowen theory to nonfamily, human systems. Some elements of individual student progress and, particularly, staff performance are discussed here as being influenced by and reflective of the school's emotional atmosphere. Central to this perspective is understanding the school as an emotional system. Gilbert defines the emotional system as

> The emotional unit, a group of individuals who, by virtue of time spent together are involved in meaningful relationships. This might be a herd of animals, a human family, or a workplace system. (1992, 182)

The stated mission of most schools is the education of its students. How schools vary in defining "education" and in adhering to and fulfilling their educational missions can be accounted for in terms of emotional process.

As an emotional relationship system, a school is greatly influenced by several factors: level of differentiation of administrators and others in key leadership positions; level of chronic anxiety in the system; and staff members' emotional cutoff from own family. There are several identifiable expressions of the interplay of these variables.

Differentiation

The concept of differentiation of self is central to Bowen theory, is discussed in detail in the literature (see particularly Bowen 1978a and Kerr and Bowen 1988), and "is the concept most vulnerable to misinterpretation" (Bowen 1982, x). Differentiation of self "addresses how people differ from one another in terms of their sensitivity to one another and their varying abilities to preserve a degree of autonomy in the face of pressures for togetherness" (Papero 1990, 45). As applied here, the basic level of differentiation describes "functioning that is ***"not dependent on the relationship process"*** and is not influenced by chronic anxiety in the emotional system (Kerr and Bowen 1988, 98). A relatively well-differentiated educational leader has been drawn to the profession less by relationship needs and more by thoughtful assessment of the institution of school and an interest in the development of young people and their potential abilities. He/she would tend to be outside the "wide spectrum of people [who] find work relationships to be more useful than social relationships for fulfilling emotional 'needs'." (Bowen 1978, 462). He/she is more likely to see the behavior of others at school objectively, to operate on the basis of fact rather than on subjective perceptions of people and interpretations of their motives, and to have a "built-in" long-range perspective on the growth and development of both individuals and institutions as well as an objective understanding of the history of the school and its larger social context.

An administrator's level of differentiation is reflected in his/her ability to maintain emotional flexibility in staying in contact with important constituencies in and outside school. This contact includes hearing points of view without automatic side-taking, defensiveness, accommodation, or retaliation.

In the emotional system of a school, level of differentiation is a critical element in determining focus on mission. Under uncertain leadership, educational focus becomes blurred as staff react to an array of complaints or "demands" on a variety of issues. Oftentimes the demand is to "do more." Anticipation of the threat of new issues can contribute to anxiety in the system and further distract people from the mission.

Level of differentiation also determines an administrator's ability to see objectively his or her own part in emotional process and to assume responsibility for managing his/her reactivity while maintaining awareness of his/her own emotional influence on people. Such an administrator maintains internal awareness of his/her own emotional vulnerabilities and external awareness of the wide variability in reactivity among staff. A particularly "sore point" in schools is staff evaluation and general sensitivity about "bosses" or "authority figures." The differentiated administrator has the ability to see reactivity for what it is. Such awareness may be particularly important in the process of evaluating professional staff.

Anxiety

The emotional variable closely related to differentiation is anxiety (Bowen 1978a, Kerr and Bowen 1988). Kerr defines anxiety as "the response of an organism to a threat, real or imagined." (Kerr and Bowen 1988, 112) Acute anxiety is a time-limited response to actual threat, while chronic anxiety is a response to imagined threat, to what "might be." The concept of chronic anxiety is so essential to understanding emotional process that it merits more formalized definition:

> [Chronic anxiety] . . . is most accurately conceptualized as a system or process of actions and reactions that, once triggered, quickly provides its own momentum and becomes largely independent of the initial triggering stimuli . . . the principal generation of chronic anxiety are people's reactions to a disturbance in the balance of a relationship system. . . . [Chronic anxiety is] propagated more by people's reactions to the disturbance than by reactions to the event itself. (Kerr and Bowen 1988, 113-4)

In the dense, physically contained environment of a school, staff and students are naturally and regularly reactive to the uncertainty of others' behavior. Schools experiencing high levels of chronic anxiety are very often characterized by investments of energy in reaction to and apprehension about relationships. It is the transmission of this anxiety in the system that fuels symptom development. Under conditions of relatively high chronic anxiety (often coexisting with crisis-precipitated acute anxiety) teacher or student may spend a particular day at school with relatively little attention to mission-based, educational processes.[4]

Individual schools are vulnerable to infusions of anxiety from a variety of directions—families, school boards, taxpayers, governments, media—and can themselves "pass on" anxiety through interlocking triangles. "The spreading through interlocking triangles is dependent on the amount of anxiety in the system" (M. Kerr 1982, 124). All schools are chronically anxious environments—the issue is not the presence or absence of anxiety but rather the relative level of chronic anxiety in the system. M. Kerr (1982, 121) observes

> When anxiety increases in an emotional system, the functioning of the system's members is increasingly determined by the dictates of the emotional system. This is true in a family, in a work situation, or in a social system.

Emotional Cutoff

Teachers strongly influence the emotional field of their classrooms and frequently develop unacknowledged, intense, emotional relationships with students or with other adults at school. A factor that is rarely considered in conventional understanding of this intensity is the individual teacher's emotional cutoff from his/her own family and the implications of this cutoff for school relationships. The essence of emotional cutoff is

> the manner in which people attempt to manage the emotional attachment to their parents and important other individuals. . . . Although the cutoff appears to handle the relationship to parents, the individual remains vulnerable to other intense relationships. (Papero 1990, 62-3).

Bowen makes the general observation that people "who use distance in 'cutting off' from the parents tend to have the most intense relationships with those outside the family." (1978a, 462)

The greater the degree of a teacher's emotional cutoff from original family or from his/her own children, the greater the likelihood of emotional importance and sensitivity in relationships at school. This importance may be reflected in several ways: "taking personally" the progress or problems of individual students; preoccupation with "being liked" by some students or "disliked" by others; preoccupation with "liking" and "disliking" certain students or other staff members; preoccupation with fearing certain students or their parents; seeing oneself as a better parent than a student's own parents; forming most or all of one's personal, primary relationships among colleagues; chronic conflict with some colleagues; and "not talking" to certain colleagues.

In many social systems sustained higher levels of anxiety will contribute to the "not talking" phenomenon or to other forms of cutoff. In schools, the end of one academic year and the beginning of a new one provide something like annual cycles of increasing intensity followed by built-in, end-of-year release of relationship tension.

Differentiation, chronic anxiety, and cutoff are all "parallel" concepts in that they derive from a process of emotional sensitivity in relationships across generations in a family and are manifest in current relationship systems. When differentiation, chronic anxiety, and cutoff variables are favorable in a particular school, emotional process fosters relatively few and transitory symptoms that impede fulfillment of the mission. With lower levels of differentiation in key positions, higher levels of chronic anxiety in the system, and more intense emotional cutoff in the personal lives of staff, symptoms are likely to be multiple, chronic, and debilitating to the functioning of the school.

Emotional Process

Bowen theory identifies several expressions of emotional process in the nuclear family (Bowen 1978a). Bowen notes that "the basic patterns in social and work relationships are identical to relationship patterns in the family, except in intensity." (1978a, 462) Gilbert describes "relationship patterns," which "form to 'solve' the problem of relationship anxiety." (1992, 41) Papero in discussing emotional process in the nuclear family, refers to these patterns as "mechanisms." (1990, 51) Among these "patterns" or "mechanisms" of the expression of emotional process are triangling, conflict and distance, physical and emotional illness in individuals, and over/underfunctioning. Several forms of expression may coexist. A discussion of triangles in schools could itself form the basis for an entire paper.

> The patterns of triangle functioning are the same in all emotional systems. . . A two-person emotional system is unstable in that it forms itself into a three-person system or triangle under stress. (Bowen 1978a, 478)

As a process, triangling ranges from subtle to explicit and emphatic side-taking. Petition-signing is a frequently seen, hallmark example of the latter. Other representative examples are teachers complaining to students about the perceived wrongdoings of administration or board, parents passing on judgments about certain teachers, teachers passing on judgments about certain parents, teachers siding with or against a department chair.

Chronic interlocking triangles tend to trap individuals within an established perspective of subjectivities about the "way" other people "are." In a sense they absorb anxiety by simplifying the task of "understanding" so many "different" personalities. Given the varying levels of emotional maturity—among students and staff—some in schools may regularly function in particularly active triangles and regularly operate on the basis of a caricatured perspective of others.

As anxiety rises in the emotional system of the school, one expression of reactivity may be conflict or distancing among emotionally vulnerable people. Under sufficient anxiety and in close quarters, disagreement escalates into conflict, verbal exchanges in person or in print, and sometimes into physical violence. Well-meaning efforts to address the "issues" over which conflict arises or to "talk out" the problems tend to miss the essential factors of anxiety and, oftentimes, unclear positions by those in authority. The assignment of blame is a frequent phenomenon in conflicts at school. Fingers are literally and figuratively pointed. As with the emotional system of the family, it is most helpful to understand conflict as a natural property of relationships that, on a fundamental level, may be accounted for in terms of differentiation and anxiety.[5]

Another "solution" to relationship tension is emotional distance, which "can be achieved by physically avoiding others and by various forms of internally withdrawing." (Kerr and Bowen 1988 81) Manifestations of this are numerous in schools and range from subtle avoidance to more extreme cutoff. One challenge of systems thinking is to see the broader implications of a particular process. "The more people use emotional distance to reduce anxiety in their relationship, for example, the more likely it is that one or both people invest energy in another relationship or project that has emotional significance" (Kerr and Bowen 1988, 81). This distancing process, then, relates to the chronic triangling referred to above. In thinking in terms of emotional systems, one may view, for example, "loyalty" (to a social clique, a team, a gang, a union, a department or committee) in terms of these interrelated processes of distancing or conflict and of triangling.

Like other emotional relationship systems, a school may also be the anxious breeding ground for emotional and physical symptoms.[6] Sustained high levels of chronic anxiety in some schools may be expressed in chronic health problems among some students and staff, particularly, perhaps, among those whose genetic and original family emotional programming incline them to these types of symptoms.[7] Some schools with disproportionately high levels of student or staff absenteeism because of illness or with disproportionately frequent deaths from cancer or other diseases may be further characterized by frequent conversation or speculation about being "sick schools" or "carcinogenic" environments. Chronic worry about environmental toxins, overwork, stress, and health insurance benefits may be seen as both "cause" and "effect" in some developing some symptoms.

Given the hierarchical structure of most schools and the implicit responsibility differentials between adult staff and child/adolescent student, patterns of over- and under-responsibility evolve in a number of ways. Undifferentiation, anxiety and cutoff contribute to functional imbalances. Given the varying dependency needs of individual students and the challenge of managing large numbers of students in an enclosed space, it is a particular challenge for staff to maintain a responsible posture in relation to individual students and to groups of students. Patterns of over- and underfunctioning tend to reflect anxiety-driven distraction from the actual developmental needs of students.

Underfunctioning of staff may be reflected in not holding students accountable for academic work or misconduct, literally or figuratively "looking the other way," taking a self-centered perspective on work load (i.e., finding the easy way out), and, in general, chronically deviating from the mission and job description. Overfunctioning may be reflected in taking over responsibility for students' belongings, filling-in periods of reflective classroom silence, and making frequent expressions of "concern" about a student's future. Students play out the other sides of these patterns.

On a broader level, schools in general have increasingly taken on an arguably overfunctioning position to students and their families in the form of increased responsibility for services like serving meals to students, sponsoring athletic teams; teaching students about sex, driving automobiles, social skills, and community volunteerism, sponsoring after-school child care, recreational activities, or "homework" centers, and providing peer discussion groups for students with family problems like death, divorce, and alcoholism.

In a particularly child-focused school, many students may underfunction in relation to overprotective, overworried, and otherwise over-vigilant staff and may be said to overfunction in relation to other kinds of adult uncertainty. These processes may contribute to the educational and behavioral impairment of students, especially those identified as having special needs. The balance can tip in the direction of fueling the very impairment the efforts are designed to be remediating.[8]

The successfully functioning school is led by differentiated people in administrative positions. It is staffed by people with generally viable relationships in their own family. It is not positioned in an anxious larger environment nor is it markedly internally reactive to perceived threat. Such schools have relatively few staff problems and have students who assume a generally high level of responsibility for their own education. Focus on educational mission is maintained.

The degree of success is further influenced by other emotional factors not addressed in this paper, particularly, differentiation in students' families and intensity of societal emotional process. Among the concepts of Bowen theory not directly addressed in this paper, two others are particularly relevant to understanding the school as an emotional system: sibling position and the projection process. Research and further analysis will refine and revise some of the ideas offered here.

Notes

1. Wilson (1975 207) comments that "cooperative nursery groups. . . constitute the building blocks of mammalian society."

2. Bowen (1978a 272), in a paper on societal regression, identifies a hypothesis that human anxiety is a product of the explosion of the population. "Man is a territorial animal who reacts to being 'hemmed in' with the same basic patterns as lower forms of life."

3. Friedman (1985 197), in discussing family process and organizational life, asserts that "Family theory can be applied to all work systems, depending primarily on two factors: (1) the degree of emotional interdependency in that relationship and (2) the extent to which its business is 'life'," which would include, for example, religious and educational institutions.

4. A school board's announcement of likely staff cuts at a district high school precipitated not only acute anxiety but a heightening of chronic anxiety, which is more related to the system of relationships than to the actual issues. For several days, some faculty openly discussed these budgetary and staffing issues in class, some students met to plan boycotts and "demonstrations," and administrators had to make decisions about how tolerant to be with the students' "anger."

5. deWaal (1989 236), in discussing the phenomenon of aggression, comments "It is time that we learn how people use aggressive behavior to reach their goals, and how they subsequently deal with the consequences. Insight into these processes will undoubtedly blur the distinction between positive and negative acts, for all acts are fused in the relationship and it is only the end result that counts." With reference to the issue of crowding and conflict, deWaal comments that human societies vary in their adaptations to limitations of physical space (263-4).

6. Bowen (1978a 361-2) on anxiety and symptom development: "When anxiety increases and remains chronic for a certain period, the organism develops tension, either within itself or in the relationship system, and the tension results in symptoms or dysfunction or sickness. The tension may result in physiological symptoms or physical illness, in emotional dysfunction, in social illness . . ."

7. Bowen (1978b) describes this inclination as an "indoctrination" toward physical symptoms in some families of origin through a prevailing attention to bodily functioning and sees anxiety, in such families, as "lighting up" the chronic symptom and making it acute or as "triggering" the development of a physical illness.

8. The issue of "child-focus" may be considered through the following statement by Kerr and by substituting the words "teacher" for "parent" and "student" for "child:"

> The development of differentiation in a child is fostered (not caused) by the ability of parents to focus on their own functioning (individuality) rather than on the functioning of the child (togetherness). [One illustration of variability in development of differentiation] is the characteristics of the interaction between parents and a child that influence the degree to which a child accepts responsibility for his own actions. When children are not accepting responsibility for their own actions, this indicates that their parents are not accepting responsibility for their own actions. (Kerr and Bowen 1988 202)

In a child-focused school, adult behavior is influenced more by perceived behavior and feelings of students than by this kind of responsibility for self and by guidance by principle.

REFERENCES

Bowen, Murray. 1978a. *Family Therapy in Clinical Practice.* New York: Jason Aronson.

——1978b. "Symptom Development in the Nuclear Family." Lecture Videotape: The Basic Series. The Georgetown Family Center.

——"Introduction." 1982. In *Understanding Organizations: Applications of Bowen Family Systems Theory.* Ruth R. Sagar and Kathleen K. Wiseman. Washington, DC: Georgetown University Family Center.

Cremin, Lawrence A. 1988. *American Education: The Metropolitan Experience, 1876-1980.* New York: Harper & Row.

deWaal, Frans. 1989. *Peacemaking Among Primates.* Cambridge: Harvard University Press.

Friedman, Edwin H. 1985. *Generation to Generation: Family Process in Church and Synagogue.* New York: Guilford Press.

Gilbert, Roberta. 1992. *Extraordinary Relationships.* Minneapolis: Chronimed.

Kerr, Kathleen. 1982. "An Overview of Bowen Theory and Organizations." In *Understanding Organizations: Applications of Bowen Family Systems Theory*, eds. Ruth R. Sagar and Kathleen K. Wiseman. Washington, DC: Georgetown University Family Center.

Kerr, Michael E. 1982. "Application of Family Systems Theory to a Work Place." In *Understanding Organizations: Applications of Bowen Family Systems Theory.* Ruth R. Sagar and Kathleen K. Wiseman, eds. Washington, DC: Georgetown University Family Center.

Kerr, Michael E. and Murray Bowen. 1988. *Family Evaluation.* New York: W. W. Norton.

Napier, J. R. and P. H. Napier. 1985. *The Natural History of Primates.* Cambridge, Massachusetts: The MIT Press.

Papero, Daniel V. 1990. *Bowen Family Systems Theory.* Boston, Massachusetts: Allyn and Bacon.

Wilson, Edward O. 1975. *Sociobiology (The Abridged Edition).* Cambridge: The Belknap Press of Harvard University.

Wiseman, Kathleen K. 1982. "Emotional Process in Organizations." In *Understanding Organizations: Applications of Bowen Family Systems Theory.* Ruth R. Sagar and Kathleen K. Wiseman, eds. Washington, DC: Georgetown University Family Center.

6

PRACTITIONERS

PRACTITIONERS

Introduction

In this section, six practitioners present their ideas about consulting or the training of consultants. Five of the individuals employ Bowen family systems theory concepts in their practices. The sixth, Robert Cahill of Arlington, VA, brings a general systems perspective to his consulting practice. The conference co-organizers invited Mr. Cahill's participation so that he might ground the conference with a presentation about contemporary consulting practice which does not rely on Bowen family systems theory.

The five practitioners who employ Bowen family systems theory practice in a variety of settings and with different emphases. Drs. Peter Norlin and Richard Olson head independent consulting practices in Ann Arbor, MI and Minneapolis, MN, respectively. Dr. Morley Segal is a professor of public administration at The American University in Washington, DC who has brought Bowen theory to the classroom. Dr. Sue Zabel is a professor at Wesley Theological Seminary in Washington, DC who has worked extensively with members of the clergy on a variety of emotional issues facing the contemporary church. Mr. Norman Leigh Jones of Silver Spring, MD, consults to organizations concerning diversity issues in the American workplace. Much of the interview between Dr. Bowen and Kathleen Wiseman has relevance for practitioners. Before presenting the papers for this section, the editors present excerpts from the interview which practitioners may find useful.

Coaching

I've always thought that if somebody coaching a family business could begin to think about emotional process, or the way that family has functioned over generations, that even that is an additional resource to the family. It might not be a total appreciation of the theory. I tried to be aware of this back in the beginning, and I tried never to program anybody else's thinking. I let them think what they wanted to think.

I don't think that [people who work with family businesses] can touch [such systems] before they deal with their own families.

[Principles that have worked for family businesses and their successes appear to have been] related to the level of differentiation of the person who runs it and their family. [It] has to do with people who would have a better understanding of the forces that go into it and the relationship system that supports the administrative system.

Leadership

What is a leader? I don't know what a leader is. The average person doesn't see leadership as being within themselves. They see it as being in someone else. They see themselves as being in an inferior position to the leader. So what do you use? I've tried to use the idea of responsible self. What is a responsible self? How responsible are you for yourself or for others? I would say your responsible self is responsible for certain important others, not all others. I'd say that's built into the family phenomenon.

A leader encourages responsible leadership in others by doing it, not by preaching.

[I am] allergic to that term leader. If a responsible person leads by being a responsible person, then he also has to be responsible to the people on whom he is dependent.

Working on Self

I started out with a working proposition which said that if any disharmony occurs within the outfit, I played a part in it. And if I don't get critical of things and I try to fix my part in it, the business will give back. And it has.
That means if somebody in your outfit is not doing well the problem is partly within you. I can fix that but I'm not going to fuss at them. I believe they know what they want to do and will do it if they can.

My notion is that theory determines every decision. It is not determined by your head. That's determined by theory. And if your theory is good, it does a good job. The thing you've got to watch out for is putting yourself out as a model because as soon as you do, somebody says, "I understand completely and now I'm going to be like you." They've got to be themselves, not me. That's the problem with using self as a model. It is essential in some things, but there is a pitfall.

Characteristics of Family Business

[Thirty years ago I put into the theory that] people are moving up on the scale [of differentiation] and people are moving down the scale always. Generally, a family business picks up a preponderance of people when moving down the scale. That's one of the points of a family business. You just give enough generations and they'll go off the bottom of the scale. That puts family businesses in jeopardy. The family business might go up the scale if it stays within the family. The chances of it phasing out of a family and into a corporation are pretty high.

And it goes that when one person can focus on self and not focus on what's wrong with others, he can serve as a working model for others, then another, then another, and then others will pull up a little bit. And over time they will pull up a fair amount. That is true for the future of the family business, any business. That is so in families, in other words if they can focus on self and not on others.

You see a family business generally accumulates the family failures and the parents feel sorry for these people and then these people are either hanger-oners or if they get in any kind of administrative positions they are adaptive. And then the head of the business feels sorry for them and keeps them on any way, which he might not do with a nonfamily member. Anyway, the important thing is to work on self.

"I" OPENINGS: BOWEN THEORY AS A FRAMEWORK TO SUSTAIN PLANNED CHANGE

Peter F. Norlin, PhD

Kurt Lewin, the distinguished psychologist who is often credited with creating the profession now called "organization development," used to say that "nothing is as practical as a good theory." The challenge, for those of us who struggle to work effectively as applied behavioral scientists, is *finding* that good theory. Over the past fifteen years, as I first read about Bowen family systems theory (Bowen 1978) and later began to use it to guide my own process of differentiation, I have begun to wonder about the relevance of Bowen family systems theory for understanding human systems beyond the family boundary.

For a number of years I rarely encountered anyone else with an interest in both Bowen theory and organizational behavior, so I simply watched, waited, and thought hard about possible applications of Bowen concepts in organizational environments. Then, in 1982, the Georgetown Family Center sponsored a conference on organizations and Bowen theory and for the first time I found a cluster of people who had been exploring similar questions, and who suggested a number of provocative and energizing possibilities for further application that I have continued to pursue.

The following report is a "telegram from the trenches," a report on my own efforts to experiment with using Bowen theory in organizational contexts and a statement of my growing conviction that, far from being merely an interesting alternative theoretical stance for thinking about organizational dynamics, the theory in fact fills a gap in (at least) my understanding of how to think about organizational change and how to design and guide change efforts that have integrity and impact.

As an independent organizational development consultant, I have been noticing two things with greater frequency in the last few years. First, of course, is that most organizations are experiencing change with increasing speed and at increasing orders of magnitude and second, is that an industry has been mushrooming to support the process of "change management."

As the pressure for change intensifies in most organizations in response to turbulence in the marketplace, business leaders who must manage change now face a bewildering array of models and strategies for redesigning and "re-engineering" the "whole system." Leaders and consulting professionals now find themselves buried under an avalanche of marketing materials describing model after model, program after program, and approach after approach for managing organizational change. And, just as typically, most of these models, programs, and approaches make conceptual sense and seem thoughtfully designed. However, in my experience they almost all share the same level of focus.

When organization development professionals think about change in human systems, they often identify three levels for intervention: the *whole-system*; the *group or team*; and the *individual* levels. The change management industry has targeted the first two levels almost exclusively in the theories, models, and materials it currently markets to leaders and consultants. In general, it appears that almost no approaches to organizational change recognize the need to link the individual level with either the group or the large-system levels to ensure a successful change process. The costs and implications of such a disconnection are significant.

For instance, planning and guiding complicated, large-system change in organizations typically involves "thinking big" and conceptualizing the process as a logical, carefully-orchestrated sequence of action steps. Though clearly necessary as road maps, such macro-level, "rational" plans for change are not sufficient to help the people who must actually implement them also cope with the personal, day-to-day emotional consequences. During profound, system-wide change, the anxiety that rises at the individual level often makes the most elegant, logical plans go mysteriously awry. In the confusion, planned outcomes are never achieved, and large amounts of money and human energy are lost.

Similarly, many businesses and organizations are working diligently to make a transition to a "team-based" environment. This shift, from individual performance and accountability to collective, interdependent effort, involves not only reorganization into an entirely new work structure but even more significantly, an about-face in core values from competition to collaboration that many people find disorienting. Unfortunately, because collaboration and competition are mutually-exclusive, and because our society is so committed to a competitive approach to human motivation, the very effort to eliminate personal competition from team process often creates a sense of cognitive dissonance among members who can't imagine *not* trying to pit themselves against their colleagues.

Also, when groups of people work together, personal differences soon become apparent. Whether these differences become a source of team success or failure depends on what happens when conflict surfaces. To manage conflict openly and successfully, individual team members must have the capacity to respond to personal challenges from their colleagues without either "fight or flight." If people on teams are not working on their own differentiation, they will find it difficult to take an "I"-position during problem-solving and decision-making, to avoid fusion during moments of direct conflict, and to avoid triangling when pressure for team accountability rises. Not surprisingly, then, when trying to work in collaboration with others, people often experience increased anxiety and stress, and this in turn will often cause teams to stall, derail, or explode.

To help organizations achieve successful, whole-system change, or to help groups make a successful transition to teamwork, consultants must also focus on supporting critical change at the individual level. A lack of such support accounts for much of what goes wrong in the implementation of strategies for managing change on the organization and team levels.

Organization development professionals are not entirely ignoring the needs for personal development and change in the workplace. Individual change is supported, of course, in most businesses and organizations through extensive training and development curricula that help people acquire technical job skills, interpersonal skills needed at work, and specific problem-solving skills. However, I do believe that, as a profession, we have failed to recognize that individuals must also develop their capacity to cope successfully with the speed and pressure of ongoing change. What seems to be missing are specific methods to help people manage and resolve the anxiety, uncertainty, and ambivalence that most people experience internally during periods of transition. This blind spot may exist because consultants believe that this type of individual change is more properly handled by psychotherapists, or consultants may not have a compelling theory to deal with the interaction and relationship between individual experience and collective experience.

This is precisely where Bowen family systems theory is most powerful. It provides a lens for understanding the emotional process in large human systems that helps explain why "the best laid plans" often remain just that. Integrating the theory into internal models, creates a unified model of change management that acknowledges the importance of intervening at the individual level, as the most critical variable in the process.

If plans for organization-wide change are to succeed with Bowen theory as a guide, a consultant/coach should also design and use strategies that encourage people who must implement and live with these changes to become more differentiated. Without supporting such differentiation at the individual level, system-wide change is likely to be derailed by anxious, vacillating leaders and terrified, confused followers. However, while this goal represents a natural extension of Bowen theory to the workplace, the shift in context from family to organization also raises concerns about whether the approaches that work so successfully in the therapy room can (or should) be used in the boardroom.

Since using Bowen theory overtly as a coaching and teaching tool in the workplace is largely uncharted territory, I have focused on these questions: (1) Can I raise the issue of individual differentiation in organizational environments? (2) How might I so that people respond to it positively and are able to begin to use it successfully?

Just as important, as a corollary, is the question of the consultant's role in this situation. How should a consultant practice evolving his own differentiation? Specifically, does the consultant communicate Bowen theory to clients and coach them to take a more differentiated position in their key work relationships, while the consultant's own efforts at differentiation are beginning to evolve?

Over the past three years, I have been actively working to answer these questions during my consulting engagements, and I offer two examples of my learning-in-progress. In both situations, I introduced two concepts of differentiation—the act of taking an "I"-position and the process of triangling—to an entire management team, but with a different intent in each situation. By taking an "I"-position, I mean a person's ability to maintain a clear commitment to his or her intention, belief, or idea in a calm, non-reactive way, despite challenge or disagreement from others.

Building leadership: communicating Bowen theory to a family business. The goal here was to assist the family business leaders to develop a more differentiated position. When contracts were renewed, a key customer typically triangled the CEO and raised anxiety in the system. By report, in addition to being loud and abrasive in style, the customer always requested that the CEO accompany him to another room for personal negotiations when a conflict emerged during the interaction with the company's leadership team. Other team members described how frustrating it was to see this happen, knowing that after a time the CEO and the customer would come back to the room and announce a resolution of the conflict and a new contract for the coming year.

After defining and describing key Bowen theory concepts, I worked with the leadership team —three family members and three unrelated managers—to frame the company's "I"-position for their impending contract negotiations, as well as to create strategy to help the company's founder and CEO remain detriangled. The CEO expressed his desire for this support, since he had always felt uncomfortable with the situation yet had never felt able to find a way to refuse to comply with his customer's demands. During the actual negotiation process, the leadership team held its position firmly, maintained a calm demeanor collectively, and established a mutually-satisfactory contract with clearer guidelines.

Building teamwork: communicating Bowen theory to a division of a larger organization. In this context, I introduced Bowen theory to managers during a series of workshops held prior to a division-wide reorganization from hierarchy and functional work units into self-managing, cross-functional teams. The goal of these workshops was to identify and explore behavior required for successful collaboration and teamwork. Because I believe that people can work *inter*dependently only if they can work autonomously and *in*dependently, I reviewed and illustrated the key concepts of differentiation and linked the ability to take and maintain an "I" position with the key elements of teamwork: conflict resolution, participative decision-making, and mutual accountability. Participants were then invited to brainstorm ways to practice differentiation and to support each other's efforts. Somewhat to my surprise, people's questions and responses during this discussion indicated that they understood the concepts and found the rationale for differentiation as a condition for collaboration both logical and persuasive.

During a series of follow-up meetings with each intact management team, we continued to explore actual behaviors and approaches that people could use to manage their anxiety, maintain a calm "I" position during moments of conflict, and avoid triangling between team meetings. Managers brainstormed a series of typical scenarios that they had experienced, and then they took turns role-playing in these situations, practicing the use of the calm, non-reactive alternative responses they had developed earlier. Over the course of several months, these strategies and the concepts became part of the managers' behavior, and they became able to pinpoint examples of differentiation with greater and greater precision. By report, they also began to coach one another openly during team meetings, pointing out more or less successful attempts to take and hold an "I" position, and they indicated that moments of conflict seemed to be resolved more productively.

In neither of these situations did I provide personal, one-to-one coaching. However, based on these two examples and on several other similar experiences, I now have preliminary evidence that I can introduce and explain Bowen theory explicitly at specific, appropriate moments in my consulting projects with clients. People in business settings who are struggling to find concrete ways to navigate and survive the whitewater of organizational change also perceive the theory as a powerful, personal resource.

As I continue to experiment with the Bowen theory to strengthen and sustain key organizational changes, I now have three priorities. First, I am developing a strategy and materials to use when I talk with senior leaders at the beginning of a system-wide project that raises the issue of individual anxiety and describes its possible impact on the success of the project. My goal is influencing senior decision-makers to recognize the need to add a parallel track to the change design that promotes individual differentiation.

To build this track, as a second priority, I am beginning to design coaching methods and approaches to help individual leaders and team members become more differentiated while they make organizational changes. The challenge here, of course, is to maintain the integrity of the theory while embedding it in language and activities that feel logical and relevant in the workplace.

My third priority is taking every opportunity to define myself as I work as a consultant, holding myself accountable for my own differentiation during this process. From my earliest experiences as an independent consultant, I became aware of the specific, personal challenges that this role presented. Based on the emotional process in my family of origin, I learned that when I defined an "I"-position with a customer, I often tended to feel anxious because I feared that I could lose my relationship with that person, and because I might also potentially jeopardize my livelihood. I always encounter this "moment of truth" at some point in every consulting relationship I have, so that I must be vigilant for chances to practice being a calm, clear, non-reactive presence, and creating a context for further differentiation. Fortunately, given the "I"-position I am now taking about the importance of Bowen theory in the process of planned change, I should have more than enough opportunities to respond to the ongoing challenge of defining myself.

REFERENCES

Bowen, Murray. 1978. *Family Therapy in Clinical Practice.* New York: Jason Aronson.

BRINGING BOWEN THEORY TO THE ORGANIZATION BEHAVIOR CLASSROOM

Morley Segal, PhD

The very qualities of Bowen family systems theory that make it attractive as a way to work with future managers also make it hard to introduce in the current Organizational Behavior (OB) classroom. Family systems can make a valuable contribution to OB because it is different (differentiated). But, in order to get a fair hearing and to be *heard* and *understood* by practitioners in OB, a minimal common ground of communication and integration needs to be built between the two fields.

The basic framework and *intellectual roots* of family systems theory are very different than those of OB. It also draws a quite different *boundary* between *family* and *work* and defines the *triangle* rather than the *small group*—as the configuration for understanding work relationships. Yet, it is a worthwhile effort to bridge this gap.

The required introductory OB class is a part of most Masters of Business Administration (MBA) and Masters of Public Administration (MPA) programs. It is the vehicle by which significant numbers of future managers can be exposed to Bowen family systems theory.

This paper explores these differences from a vantage point of academic and experiential familiarity with both areas and describes areas in which mutual adjustment can be made without damaging either field's integrity.

The research tradition of OB focuses on discrete behavior in the workplace such as job attitudes, motivation, leadership, job design, individual differences and on outcomes such as absenteeism, turnover, and performance. Macro OB looks at the whole organization but focuses on particular functions or characteristics, such as the dispersion of responsibility, often comparing them to other organizations (O'Reilly 1991, Schneider 1985).

OB instructors often draw upon general systems theory. Typical is the model offered in a widely used OB text, *Effective Behavior in Organizations* (Cohen et al. 1988).

The system takes input from the environment in the form of finances, raw material, and ideas, transforms these inputs, and then sends them back to the environment. The system survives over time by acting as a thermostat and thus preserving an equilibrium between itself and the environment.

The general systems approach helps students and practicing managers view the interrelationship among a wide range of structures, practices, and behaviors. It encourages managers to focus on how apparently dysfunctional practices or behaviors *function* to preserve the system.

The limitation of general systems theory as an image of the organization is that it describes families and organizations based on principles taken from physics and engineering. General systems theory is a human blend of principles from a wide range of scientific theories (Caskie 1994). It presents an operational adaptation to the environment based on an assumed purpose for the organization rather than an evolution and change of the organism itself as found in living systems. For example, it is hard to find a place in the image of a thermostat for powerful instinctive drives. Bowen theory, in contrast, draws upon the image of a *natural* system, one modeled after the process described by Charles Darwin. This process pays considerable attention to instinctive behavior and the processes that govern the life processes in all living things (Bowen 1976).

Bowen family systems theory first developed from clinical experience, and has been described a natural systems theory (Caskie 1994). In a 1976 interview, Murray Bowen described basing his theory in evolutionary biology and the natural sciences. At the time, the custom was to describe disturbed behavior as *mental* illness, emphasizing the aspect of development in which humans were most different from other forms of life. Bowen chose to describe *emotional* illness, likening emotions to that range of instinctive behavior that is the "part of man that he shares with other forms of life" (Bowen 1978). In this phrase Bowen used the term *emotion*, which is used synonymously with *feeling* in OB to describe a deeper, more fundamental range of experience. In Bowen theory, emotion includes "the forces that biology defines as *instinct*, reproduction, the automatic activity controlled by the automatic nervous system, subjective emotional and feeling states, and *the forces that govern relationship systems* " (emphasis mine) (Bowen 1975). The definition of emotionally based behavior in Bowen family systems theory includes the relationship system at work and at home.

Emotions, however, are not synonymous with feelings, as they are in OB. In Bowen family systems theory, feelings derive from an emotional state. The view in Bowen family systems theory, is that although open expression of feelings may help some individuals *feel* better, for others the process is followed by increased disharmony, and the process is antithetical to the efforts of a majority of family therapists. (Bowen 1975).

In addition, in Bowen family systems theory, emotional illness and emotional functioning result from a *multigenerational process*. The process of understanding and changing requires dealing with one's multigenerational past.

Teaching Family Systems Theory in an OB Setting

General systems theory has received wide acceptance in OB. The distinctions made by writers in the family field between general and natural systems would be helpful as they would encourage practitioners in OB to have a better understanding of their own theoretical framework. Bowen family systems theory's unique contribution to understanding behavior in organizations is to demonstrate the impact of instinctually based social behavior, particularly its multigenerational origin. In OB, emotions are synonymous with feelings. In Bowen family systems theory, feelings are expressions of emotions and are not usually regarded as a useful avenue for learning about emotions. One of the significant contributions that family systems theory can make to OB is to identify what Bowen terms the automatic and emotional (instinctive?) basis of behavior. The term "emotion" as it is used in OB and in everyday usage refers to a reaction that includes the experience of "strong feeling" (Webster 1986). Bowen also acknowledged this common usage (Bowen, 1976b). With this connotation the importance of Bowen's message can be lost. Given Bowen's own definition, cited previously, that *includes* "instinct," I offer that term as a substitute.

With the caveat that Bowen's definition of the emotional system is broader than MacLean's view of that section of the brain, Paul MacLean's (1978) theory of the *triune brain* can also be used as a broad framework to clarify the difference between emotions, feelings, and thinking, and bridge the gap between OB and Bowen family systems theory.

According to MacLean, the three sections of our brain developed at different times in the evolutionary process. These three sections correspond to three distinct aspects of functioning. The first section corresponds to emotions or, in my terms, instinct. The second section corresponds to feelings. The third section corresponds to intellect. In OB, intrapersonal awareness is used first to understand the second or feeling level of the brain and secondarily to gain clues about the emotional or first level. In OB, however, the emotional level does not receive direct attention. Similarly, in family systems theory I find little attention to the second or feeling level. The third level of intellect, however, is used to observe and understand the previously obscured first level of emotions or instinct.

The framework of the triune brain can help those in OB understand the instinctive basis of the emotional system, which is one of the significant contributions of family systems theory. It can alert those in family systems theory to the possible contribution of paying attention to feelings which is the contribution of OB.

The Family and Work Boundary

OB pays little attention to the family and the domain of family life. Family life is not studied as a premise for understanding workplace behavior. OB draws on approaches that place the source of dysfunctional behavior in the family of origin. OB focuses on understanding the origins of this behavior in order to limit its impact on the workplace. In OB classes, individuals study and report on their efforts at work, but they generally do not report on their life at home or on their family of origin.

Family systems theory takes a different approach to linking family and work behavior. The individual is viewed as forming a level of basic differentiation of self in the family of origin. This level follows that individual to the workplace. The family of origin is viewed as the *source* of emotional fusion and as a potential arena for the differentiation of self. In the process of defining a self, individuals are encouraged to return to the family of origin for periodic visits. With a systematic coaching of behavior, they slowly increase the level of differentiation of self so that they can become objective observers of themselves in relation to their families of origin (Bowen 1974b). Bowen found that psychiatric residents who began to explore their own families of origin seemed almost automatically to start doing better clinical work as family therapists (Bowen 1974b). The family of origin, rather than being a negative force, is viewed as a source of change that can have an automatic payoff in the workplace. Bowen family systems theory, however, does not include range of structures, and norms, such as the self-managed team, that are unique to the workplace.

That psychiatrists who returned to their family of origin automatically become more effective clinicians has important implications for OB, for it could also be used to help prospective managers increase their ability to keep thinking, while being relatively free of the instinctive forces that prevail in both family and work systems. This method would involve coaching and systematic visits to one's family of origin. Having people return for periodic visits to their families of origin, particularly if they were to attempt efforts at differentiation of self (Bowen 1972), would be a radical departure from the present norms of OB classes. This prospect is promising, but the case for such a process would be stronger in the OB realm if there were some empirical research to back up Bowen's observations about psychiatric residents. Are managers who have made efforts at differentiation of self more effective in their relationships at work than those who have not? This is not an easy question, but it is testable and is promising enough to warrant the effort of testing it.

Individual and Group Behavior

OB deals with behavior in a number of configurations: individual, dyad, group, and total organization. At the individual and dyadic level, the individual is conceived as a contained system reacting with other individuals (systems). As a composite applied discipline, OB pulls from a variety of psychological and personality theories to explain such individual behavior: psychoanalytic, object relations, humanistic, and behavioral theories. In varying degrees, each approach acknowledges individuals as part of a system of relationships, but each starts with a notion of the individual as the basic unit.

Groups and behavior in groups play a large part in OB because groups play a prominent role in influencing work behavior. The early accounts of Frederick Winslow Taylor in the nineteenth century identified the importance of the work group (Taylor 1915). The importance of group sentiment or feelings was introduced in the Hawthorne studies of the 1920s (Mayo 1945; Roethlisberger and Dickson 1939). Groups remain important with today's emphasis on self-directed teams.

In OB, considerable attention is paid to the integrative aspects of group development. The goal is a group synergy in which the combination of individual efforts yields a product greater than either that of any individual or even that of all individuals in the group. In my experience, *OB emphasizes collective effort over individual performance.*

OB in the classroom reflects this focus on groups. Team task forces and group projects play a prominent role in many OB classes. In OB classes, the small group is both an object and a method of study. Students learn how the small group is the basic building block of most work situations, and they prepare reports and presentations about small groups while working in small groups. OB emphasizes learning to work cooperatively in a variety of collective arrangements.

When OB considers the entire organization or system, that system is derived from general systems theory. Family systems theory, in contrast, focuses on the multigenerational family, but practitioners who apply the theory in organizations do not necessarily call the organization a family. Instead, they conceptualize an emotional or, in my terms, an instinctive system that heavily influences both family and work behavior. The family is conceptualized as an emotional system, and so are individuals in the workplace. In my view, this emotional system *transcends* the OB focus on the individual, the group, and the organization.

The emotional triangle is to Bowen family systems theory what the group is to OB—a basic configuration. The dyad or two-person relationship is considered inherently unstable. It becomes stable only when a third person is "triangled" in to carry some of the tension between the other two. The roles of insider and outsider shift within triangles as tension increases and decreases. Families and work systems can also become a series of interlocking triangles (Bowen 1972). Triangles, like the emotional system itself, cut across the individual and group structures that are part of OB. Family systems theory makes a valuable contribution in identifying relationships that cut across the boundary of these structures.

The role of the therapist in Bowen family systems theory is to relate actively to the other corners of a triangle while remaining free of the pull of forces in the emotional field of the triangle (Bowen 1971b). This also is the position Bowen defines for the successful administrator—an individual who focuses on "maintaining a self" while actively relating to the members of the system and giving them as much latitude as possible to solve their own problems (Bowen 1974a, 461-465). As in the case of the psychiatric residents who performed more effectively when they began relating to members of their family of origin, this is an automatic process. When an individual is able to remain free of the emotional field, the path is open for clear thought to prevail over instincts, and individuals will perform more effectively. Here Bowen family systems theory suggests a new dimension of competent managerial behavior.

In Bowen family systems theory, the small group is not mentioned. From this omission I conclude that it is not regarded as a basic building block of either the family or work systems. Bowen theory instead focuses on differentiation in individual development. The first step is a process in which individuals "differentiate a self" from the emotional system. Bowen theory emphasizes *differentiation* of a self, stating that those with a higher level of differentiation cope better with life stress, have a more successful and orderly life course, and are remarkably free of human problems (Bowen 1976b).

This differentiation or separation is both internal and external: "the greater the fusion between the emotion and the intellect, the more the individual is fused into the emotional fusions of people around him." (Bowen 1975, 305) One differentiates internally by learning to remain thinking under greater degrees of external stress. This *internal* differentiation leads one to keep separate from the collective emotional (instinctive) system that which is *external. The emphasis in Bowen theory is upon differentiation of self.*

There is no discussion of the kind of group—or organization building—that is such a prominent part of OB. Similarly, OB largely ignores the instinctual aspects of humans and focuses on harnessing feelings so that work in existing or evolving structures can be productive. The emphasis is on *integration* with the various organizational structures of work.

Bowen Theory in the OB Classroom

OB and Bowen family systems theory have different messages and different ways of learning. Much of OB teaching is built upon the assumption that the classroom is a microcosm of the rest of the world. It assumes that behavior, reactions and feelings in the classroom are all representations of the world outside. The intellectual roots of this style of learning go back to the "here and now" learning that emerged from early T group and sensitivity sessions (French and Bell 1972). If Bowen theory is to become part of OB teaching, then students must learn to understand and value differentiation of self as they now understand and value expression of feelings and cooperative behavior. In the classroom, OB teaches how to *work within* as well as change those structures. The message of Bowen family systems theory, in contrast, appears to be how to *transcend* existing and future structures by differentiating the self from the emotional system of one's family of origin and work.

The question for me is whether OB can use one of its strengths—the methods of experiential learning—to help individuals learn some of the strengths of Bowen theory, the process of triangles, and what it means to engage in a process of differentiation of self.

Conclusion

Can Bowen family systems theory be understood in a different but potentially valuable arena without losing the qualities of difference that give it its identity and value? The notion of a natural system lends a great deal of clarity. To those in OB who are used to seeing system theory as synonymous with general system theory this is a plus. I suggest that the term "emotion" is easily confused with feeling, both in the OB field and in general usage, and that the term "instincts" is more clear and has some basis in Bowen's own writing. MacLean's theory of the triune brain offers a solid physiological explanation of the difference between feelings and emotions and would be a good place to start with OB students. Bowen's notion that the process of working with one's family of origin has an automatic payoff in the world of work is very exciting and could and should be tested empirically. Finally, I note that the triangle and the ability to remain free of the forces of the emotional field are also exciting ideas for the fledgling administrator, and I wonder if these concepts can be experienced in the classroom using the experiential methods of OB.

REFERENCES

Bowen, Murray. 1961. "Family Psychotherapy." *The American Journal of Orthopsychiatry*, 31 (1), 40-60. In M. Bowen, *Family Therapy in Clinical Practice*. New York: Jason Aronson, 1978, pp. 71-90.

———. 1971a. "Family Therapy and Family Group Therapy." In H. Kaplan and B. Sadock (Eds.), *Comprehensive Group Psychotherapy*. Baltimore: Williams and Wilkins. In M. Bowen,

Family Therapy in Clinical Practice. New York: Jason Aronson, 1978, pp. 183-240.

———. 1971b. "Principles and Techniques of Multiple Family Therapy." In J. Bradt and C. Moynihan, eds., *Systems Theory.* Washington, D.C., pp. 388-404. In M. Bowen, *Family Therapy in Clinical Practice.* New York: Jason Aronson, 1978, pp. 241-257.

———. 1972. "On the Differentiation of the Self." *Family Interaction: A Dialogue Between Family Researchers and Family Therapists.* New York: Springer, pp. 111-173. In M. Bowen, *Family Therapy in Clinical Practice.* New York: Jason Aronson, 1978, pp. 467-528.

———. 1974a. "Toward the Differentiation of Self in Administrative Systems." In F. Andres and J. Lorio (Eds.), *Georgetown Family Symposia* Vol. 1. Washington, DC: Georgetown University Medical Center. In M. Bowen, *Family Therapy in Clinical Practice.* New York: Jason Aronson, 1978, pp. 461-465.

———. 1974b. "Toward the Differentiation of Self in One's Family of Origin." In F. Andres and J. Lorio (Eds.), *Georgetown Family Symposia* Vol. 1. Washington, DC: Georgetown University Medical Center. In M. Bowen, *Family Therapy in Clinical Practice.* New York: Jason Aronson, 1978, pp. 529-547.

———. 1975. "Family Therapy After Twenty Years." In A. Silvano (Ed.), *American Handbook of Psychiatry,* 2nd ed., Vol. 5. New York: Basic Books. In M. Bowen, *Family Therapy in Clinical Practice.* New York: Jason Aronson, 1978, pp. 285-320.

———. 1976a. "An Interview with Murray Bowen." *The Family,* 3, 50-62. In M. Bowen, *Family Therapy in Clinical Practice.* New York: Jason Aronson, 1978, pp. 390-411.

———. 1976b. "Theory in the Practice of Psychotherapy." In P. Guerin (Ed.), *Family Therapy.* New York: Gardner Press, pp. 42-90. In M. Bowen, *Family Therapy in Clinical Practice.* New York: Jason Aronson, 1978, pp. 337-387.

———. 1982. "Introduction." In R. Sagar and K. Wiseman (Eds.), *Understanding Organizations: Applications of Bowen Family System Theory.* Washington, DC: Georgetown University Medical Center.

Caskie, Polly D. 1994. "What Kind of System Is the Family?" *Family Systems,* 1 (1), 7-19.

Cohen, A. R. et al. 1988. *Effective Behavior in Organizations: Learning From the Interplay of Cases, Concepts, and Student Experiences.* Homewood, IL: Irwin.

French, W. L., & C. H. Bell. 1972. "A Brief History of Organization Development." *Journal of Contemporary Business,* 1-8. In W. L. French et al. (Eds.), *Organization Development: Theory, Practice, and Research.* Dallas: Business Publications, 1978, pp. 15-19.

Lindsay, C. 1992. "Learning Through Emotion: An Approach for Integrating Student and Teacher Emotions Into the Classroom." *Journal of Management Education,* 16 (1):25-38.

MacLean, P. 1978. "A Mind of Three Minds." In J. S. Chall and A. F. Mirsky (Eds.), *Education and the Brain.* Chicago: The National Society for the Study of Education, University of Chicago Press.

Mayo, E. 1945. *The Social Problems of an Industrial Civilization.* Boston: School of Business Administration, Harvard University.

O'Reilly, C. A. 1991. "Organizational Behavior: Where We've Been, Where We're Going." *Annual Review of Psychology,* 42:427-458.

Roethlisberger F. J., & W. J. Dickson. (1939). *Management and the Worker,* Cambridge, Massachusetts: Harvard University Press.

Schneider, B. 1985. "Organizational Behavior." *Annual Review of Psychology,* 36:573-611.

Taylor, F. W. 1911. *Principles of Scientific Management.* New York: Harper and Row.

Webster's Third New International Dictionary of the English Language Unabridged, 3d ed., S.V., "emotion."

DIFFERENTIATION AND TRIANGLES IN COACHING EXECUTIVES

Richard D. Olson, PhD

Executive coaching is becoming increasingly popular in organizations. *Fortune* magazine in December of 1993 had an article titled "The Executive's New Coach."

> A decade ago, that title belonged mostly to people who helped the boss pick a hair style or deliver a speech without notes. No longer.
>
> In the stressful 1990s, coaches and outside counselors are assigned to improve an executive's managerial skills and straighten out his personality disorder not his wardrobe. The coaching business is thriving at American Express, AT&T, CitiBank, Colgate, Levi Straus, Northern Telecom, Proctor and Gamble, and many other major companies. (Smith 1993, 126-134)

While these executive coaching programs certainly have a positive side, they are often designed to "fix a problem" or to "fix an individual." Much of that which is done under the label of "executive coaching" is often a band-aid. Often quick fixes require a manager to fit into a pre-designed mold, to focus on enhancing one's skills directly related to one's weaknesses and to develop behaviors that are often inconsistent with one's natural style and those motivating factors that energize oneself. This type of fix-it approach does not generally produce lasting results. There is implicit if not explicit manipulation and control of one person by another. Teaching and coaching executives to utilize their strengths more fully and to play to their natural styles has a much bigger payoff and it produces lasting growth and development (and modifies weaknesses). Bowen theory plays a central role in this approach.

Table 1 provides an overview of our approach to executive coaching.

I seldom use the word "differentiation" in the early stages of my work, but keep that concept in mind at all times. I use stories, questions and examples about taking positions for self-definition to help them calm down and gain a stronger perspective and sense of control. I have found generally that people who have stress in their work life also have stress in their home life. I seek to become aware of the "emotional system" in both places.

As industrial psychologists we use a variety of tools to gather information. We

---

NOTE: Each case presented is based on a combination of individuals to protect confidentiality.

ACKNOWLEDGMENT: Thanks to Mary Bourne of the Minnesota Institute of Family Dynamics for her input on a draft of this article.

TABLE 1: OVERVIEW OF OUR APPROACH TO EXECUTIVE COACHING

I. We find out how the client sees the problem. This is often related to the question,"Where is the anxiety?" If someone isn't feeling some discomfort or pain, they are likely not motivated to change. In essence, we begin by listening to the executive.

II. Depending on the scope of our work, we gather information by using multiple sources:
1) Work style interview.
2) System and background interview.
3) Interview with "the boss."
4) Interviewing or surveying others in the workplace.
5) Personality and other inventories.
6) Work simulations.
7) Aptitude and ability tests.

III. We share the information we have gathered and we continue to include the executive as we think through the process.

IV. In dialogue with our client, we work to:
1) Help them understand their strengths, natural styles, motivating factors that energize, and limitations.
2) *Help them understand the nature of the system in which they live and in which they work.*
3) *Coach them in understanding concepts related to triangling and differentiation.*
4) Help them understand key issues and define goals.
5) Coach them in defining specific actions to meet their needs and goals.
6) When necessary, continue to talk with them about specific skills, such as listening, delegating, dealing with conflict, etc.
7) Meet with them periodically to follow up on their understanding and implementation of new ideas and behaviors.

often have our client complete a background/systems and work style interview. We also have them complete a variety of questionnaires and inventories so that we can better understand their work related strengths and style. As a part of this information gathering process, we ask lots of questions about the systems in which the individual operates, including non-work family/emotional system as well as the culture and dynamics within his or her work system.

As I become more experienced and comfortable with Bowen theory, my information gathering focuses more on exploring facts related to the individual's level of reactivity to the system and the overall level of reactivity in the system. As a consultant, I find understanding triangles and learning about my own vulnerability as I come into client situations is an ongoing and difficult challenge.

This paper describes three work situations in which Bowen theory has been useful to me in the executive coaching context. This is not intended to be a detailed description of Bowen theory or of how to do executive coaching. The first case is set in a family business, the second in a professional partnership, and the third in a large, national corporation. I found the theory useful to me in all three contexts.

Why Use a Systems Approach in Executive Coaching?

Recently the president of a small company called me because he had high turnover in one position — four people in a department head position within two years. The presidentt was concerned because this department had an absolutely critical role in the coming six to twelve months. Of the three people who had left that job, one was fired, one quit, and the third, having been promoted to the position from within, demoted himself after only a few months. While no one was really surprised, a number of people, including the president, were extremely frustrated.

In this type of situation, industrial psychologists have traditionally looked at two different sources of the problem: (1) The expectations of the job are not clearly defined or they are too overreaching for one person. (2) The person in the job is not properly qualified, either lacking the necessary aptitude or skill to do the job, or lacking training or motivation.

The approach we took initially was the traditional one: to take a careful look at the role and expectations of the department manager. We reviewed some information and interviewed a number of people and found that job was, in many ways, very similar to ones in other organizations. We looked at the qualifications of the department manager, the capabilities, and the skills and found her to be highly qualified. In fact we had done a pre-employment management evaluation of her and had given her a strong recommendation.

She told me this story. The organization had a large new information system coming on-line. One of her staff needed to obtain some crucial training in advance of going on-line, and she had asked her boss for authorization. There was no response. The program was expensive but absolutely critical. She began to send follow-up memos, talk to her boss, and to do everything possible in an attempt to get approval. There were apparently some "bureaucratic budgetary problems." She talked about how anxiety went up *within the department* and *within her*. I began to understand that her boss had difficulty taking responsibility and making things happen.

She was a person who had a tendency to be overly responsible. Her boss was calm and charming, a "nice guy." Meanwhile she was becoming increasingly anxious, frenetic and stressed. She was obviously under pressure from the person who was to attend the seminar to get it approved. Her work system was highly anxious and, more importantly, her level of reactivity was high.

To make a long story short, I talked about triangles, and helped her to see how to keep responsibility where it belongs, and to not take on other people's anxiety. By the way, her subordinate did not go to the "required" training seminar, the system was effectively implemented, and her boss (the vice president) was eventually terminated. This all happened within four months. To depart from her normal role looked risky to her at first but, in a very real way, with her three predecessors already gone, she was at risk anyway. The shift in her role paid off for her. So more traditional approaches which look at job and role expectations and managerial competencies, while important, are just not enough. One must also understand the dynamics of the system and the situation, and Bowen theory provides an excellent framework.

Three Case Studies

Case One: Coaching in a Family Business. A number of years ago, I was asked to work with a family-owned business to help the three brothers take over the management from their parents. The family requested consultation since one son had always had an antagonistic relationship with the father and they were concerned that the process proceed in an orderly and effective way.

The family expected me to get them together as a group for a "family meeting or family workshop." Instead I met with each of the three brothers (partners) individually to talk about the triangle that existed with the three of them. Animosity and stress that existed between the oldest and the youngest brothers surfaced, and the son in the middle had taken on the responsibility for keeping that relationship harmonious. While doing it, he seemed to create even more animosity between them as well as feeling frustrated and helpless himself.

I coached the middle brother on the nature of triangles. Eventually he began to consider and ultimately tried some different approaches so that each of his brothers would be more responsible for his own problem-solving. At the same time, he did not run away from their conflict but rather would talk with each of them briefly about it and acknowledge that each was responsible for solving the difficulties with the other. He stayed connected with his brothers but rather than taking responsibility (and anxiety), he remained a neutral presence while acknowledging their responsibilities related to the issues.

In working with each of the other brothers, I not only coached them around some of the theory related to triangling but also eventually helped them develop some skills in effectively taking responsibility for conflict. We never did get the whole family together for a "family meeting." In fact, those skeletons in the closet that supposedly existed in the relationship between the father and the son did not seem to require a lot of attention. In many respects, the parents were working hard to move away from the business and allowing their sons to be responsible.

In this story, the theory was helpful in working with family members who also were in business together. They were experiencing conflict which influenced their relationship and which interfered with the success of their business.

Case Two: A Partner in a Professional Association. Many managers are overly responsible. And, of course, over- responsibility does just the opposite of promoting responsibility. It actually promotes irresponsibility. It is not unusual to find that people who are overly responsible in the workplace are often overly responsible at home as well.

Ron was a 52 year-old partner in an accounting firm. He had been asked, at least temporarily, to move into the position of a non-equity partner. In the accounting world, this is like being demoted to a second class citizen.

I learned that he had billable hours that were below expectation, and he was not bringing in nearly as much business as what was expected of a partner. But at the same time he was being asked to do more administrative work and development work with younger people in the organization which he seemed willing to take on. He was heavily into strenuous sports including biking and skiing. He had a strong sense of discipline and exercised with a great deal of regularity and zeal. He had a deep sense of responsibility. Yet he complained that he had no energy for work, seemed unable to meet the expectations, and there seemed to be no energy left for issues at home.

In interviewing him further, I learned that his wife was experiencing some ups and downs, mostly downs, and drank too much. His oldest daughter had received poor grades in college, dropped out, and was living at home. This increased the stress for everyone. His wife and daughter fought and he would take the role of peacemaker. It appeared the daughter was doing very little to find a job and take responsibility for herself and her belongings in the home. His wife would give her use of the family car and often loan her money without expecting it to be paid back.

Ron was to trying to keep his wife from being depressed and to keep her from drinking too much. He tried to keep the peace in the family. He wanted to help his daughter become responsible but was really frustrated with how to do this. Nothing seemed to work, no matter how hard he tried.

I suggested to Ron that he was a very responsible person, and that although this was a strength that he had, in being overly responsible with his family he was not teaching and demonstrating responsibility. In some ways, he believed that being responsible meant making up for their lack of responsibility. It was not easy for him to give up being responsible for them, to give up taking care of them, to give up the peacemaker role, and yet to be present and connected with the family. Yet he knew that the more he tried to fix things the seemingly worse they got.

While he exercised regularly, he seemed to have no energy for work. Yet the tremendous discipline he showed with his physical exercise gave a clue to his ability to follow through on something. Indeed, in talking with people in the workplace, I learned he was known as an exceptionally reliable and dependable person whose integrity was above question.

For a period of time I met with him weekly, coaching him in some of the aspects of staying connected with his wife and daughter without being overly responsible. He began to observe the triangling at home, such as when he refused to loan money to his daughter, his wife would sometimes come and ask him for money so that she could give it to her. The ideas of triangling and of self-definition were extremely helpful to him in living more consistently what he believed to be a responsible life. He started to do things he *enjoyed* with his daughter. He avoided blaming behavior. He started to stay connected emotionally without assuming responsibility for fixing them.

After a number of sessions, Ron began to get his energy for work back. We formed a specific development plan by which he would work on increasing his billable hours as well as become more involved in business development. Not surprisingly, he had served on a number of volunteer commissions and boards and he had a large network of contacts that he could tap for business development. He developed networking skills.

In working with another partner, he landed a large contract with a nationwide manufacturer. But now he had to spend twenty to thirty percent of his time out of town. This left his wife alone at home. This was a real test for him and in many respects for his wife also, as she did her best initially to show that his being out of town left her helpless at home. And the first couple of times she overindulged in alcohol as we had predicted might happen. Eventually this settled down and she sought counseling.

Yes, he had to watch his reactivity to various triangles at work. A great pitfall for him was helping senior managers who had a variety of problems and would come to him for assistance. He began to say no and structure his time to help some of these but not all. He simply did not have time and needed to focus on other aspects of his business. He also had to deal with a number of nay-sayers in the organization who continued to criticize him even after he changed his behavior. He learned to set goals effectively and work toward those goals in a very responsible but not overly responsible way.

In coaching executives about triangles, I am very careful to help them understand that triangles are not negative, they exist everywhere and are a fact of life. They are the building blocks on which interpersonal systems are built. I teach people about triangles, understanding and using triangles effectively. I often talk about what activates triangles and those triangles in which people need to work very hard to not overreact.

This case shows that the ability to maintain a nonreactive presence in one's family system is often the first step toward taking a nonreactive and differentiating stance in one's work situation.

Case Three: An Executive in a Large Corporation. Executive coaching does not always result in a person staying in the same job. The vice president in a large Michigan corporation brought us in to work with a director who reported to him. The director's responsibilities involved supporting five divisions in the company with specific programs but he was not getting the job done, had two bad performance reviews, and something needed to change.

His boss said he did not communicate well with his field people. Yet, when he came into our offices, he seemed to connect with everyone: our administrative assistant, consultants, and even the courier who came into our office to deliver a package. In essence, he was communicating with everyone. I was confused about the problem and sought more information. While he tended to communicate very effectively with the field, he was determined not to play politics in the organization. And he was holding back artificially or resisting using his natural skills.

Through interviews, I learned that the president of the company was questioning why the vice president was keeping the director in the job. The vice president, who had worked at developing a close relationship with the president, described how he thought it was going to be difficult for his subordinate to work effectively in this job or in any other job because of the director's poor relationship with the president. According to him, "The president wanted him out!"

I helped our client understand the nature of the triangle he was in. This is probably the most difficult work triangle one can get into, where one's boss is linked up closely with one's boss's boss, with one's own boss pushing his/her own anxiety down.

The executive we were coaching learned extremely quickly. He decided to resign his position even before finding another and used his new networking skills with his extensive network of colleagues and friends to find a new job. His new job as a vice president is in a difficult environment which many would describe as dysfunctional. There is a lot of change, a lot of stress, and people are feeling overwhelmed. Yet, he displays a gentle smile and talks about his own goals and how he is pursuing them in this environment. As he does so, changes keep happening around him—and both he and his co-workers are becoming more satisfied with their jobs. In this case, unlike the previous ones, as the director began to more clearly understand his work situation, he believed it was important for his growth to resign and move to a new job.

Summary

The changes, competitive pressures, and stress in today's workplace are having detrimental effects on productivity and effectiveness. Organizations are increasingly looking to professional executive coaches with training in psychology.

Traditional industrial/organizational psychology approaches are not enough. A systems approach can be useful in three different situations as described. Helping people understand and deal with group dynamics through the understanding of triangles has proven useful. Coaching people who strive to be more highly differentiated gradually leads to shifts in the workplace and creates a less anxious environment in which people can play to their natural strengths and contribute effectively to organizations.

REFERENCES

Smith, Lee. December 27, 1993. "The Executive's New Coach." *Fortune*.

Suggested Readings

Friedman, Edwin H. 1985. *Generation to Generation, Family Process in Church and Synagogue*. New York: The Guilford Press.

Kerr, Michael E. and Murray Bowen. 1988. *Family Evaluation*. New York: W. W. Norton & Company.

Naj, Amal Kumar. August 29,1994. "Corporate Therapy: The Latest Addition to Executive Suite is Psychologist's Couch." *The Wall Street Journal*.

Papero, Daniel V. 1990. *Bowen Family Systems Theory*. Boston, MA: Allyn and Bacon.

Richardson, Ronald W. 1984. *Family Ties that Bind*. Vancouver: Self Counsel Press.

Sagar, Ruth R. and Kathleen K. Wiseman, eds. 1982. *Understanding Organizations: Applications of Family Systems Theory*. Washington, DC: Georgetown University Family Center.

DIVERSITY AND DIFFERENTIATION

Norman Leigh Jones, MA

This paper is an effort to discuss the relationship between the concept of differentiation of self as developed by Murray Bowen and the notion of diversity as developed by organizational consultants and, more specifically, from a network of consultants and trainers working with Elsie Y. Cross and Associates of Philadelphia. These two concepts have no obvious connection, but I believe they both have critical relevance for how human beings find ways to live and work successfully in groups in an increasingly emotionally confined space known as planet Earth. Although the terms "differentiation" and "diversity" share a common linguistic heritage, very few people who are not explicitly involved with differentiation or diversity could be expected to understand what either is and, furthermore, those involved with differentiation may not see the relevance of diversity while those working in the diversity arena may view differentiation efforts as a "luxury." The basic premise of this paper is that modern organizations of any significant size and of all types will need to find a way to be both diverse and differentiated if they are to be productive into the twenty-first century and beyond. This author would view this as simply a matter of survival of the fittest in a hostile and competitive environment. To begin at the same reference point, both general and esoteric definitions of both differentiation and diversity follow. *Differentiation*: The sum of the processes whereby apparently indifferent cells, tissues, and structures attain their adult form and function (Webster). *Differentiation*: The ability to be in emotional contact with others and yet still be autonomous in one's emotional functioning (Bowen and Kerr 1988). *Diversity:* The quality of being made of many different elements, forms, kinds, or individuals (Webster). *Diversity*: Acknowledging and using the differences of race and gender and other forms of difference and moving towards cultural pluralism (Cross 1985).

In addition to these definitions, I view diversity as describing efforts to acknowledge and use the differences of race, gender, and other categories of group identity to create a mosaic that uses differences positively and acknowledges the contributions of those involved. Diversity, in its most positive sense, looks at the strengths of groups and highlights the process of learning about self as one learns about others. To that end, the most common error made about diversity is that it is about someone else, usually defined as the "minority," when any authentic student of di-

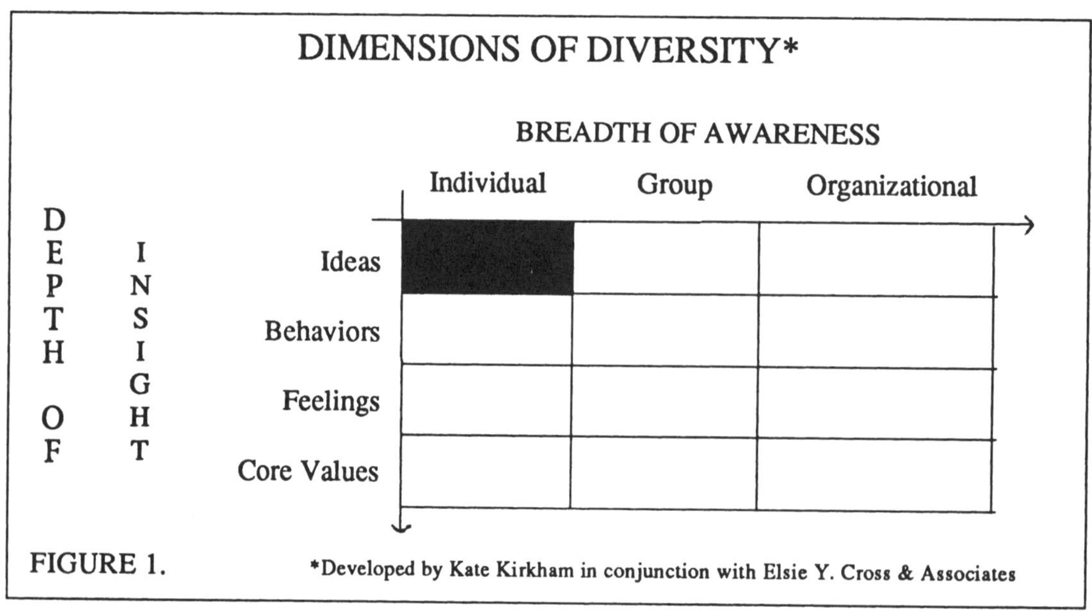

FIGURE 1.

versity will tell you the same thing as any authentic student of Bowen; namely, that the work is about "the self."

To provide some background to those not familiar with diversity training, a diversity concept will be presented that gives some idea about the complexity of the ideas with which diversity trainers grapple in their daily work with organizations. We call it the Dimensions of Diversity (developed by Dr. Kate Kirkham in conjunction with others in Elsie Y. Cross and Associates), and it is a conceptual tool that is used in this work to give the average corporate worker some idea why dealing in diversity feels like "walking through a swamp." (Figure 1.) There are two major axes—horizontally the focus is on breadth of awareness from the individual level to the societal level. This dimension represents the notion that at any moment human beings are operating from several different frames of reference and that the particular frame of reference that one is most aware of at a given time can shape the experience in ways we are conscious of and ways we are not. Vertically, the dimension, depth of insight, deals with internal awareness and congruency from the surface or idea level to the deepest or core value level. These two axes produce a grid which describes the many places from which human beings operate when communicating with others in the context of diversity. Using this conceptual model, it can be expected that most humans will be comfortable at the individual, idea level and not much beyond; but a quick glance at the grid shows that staying there leaves out about 90 percent of the possibilities. One major notion that comes out of this grid is that persons in the dominant position often have the option of primarily experiencing life at and retreat to the individual idea level while members of subordinate groups often experience life based on their membership in a group. A theoretical example follows.

The African-American owner of a major company leaves an office building in a major city shortly after telling his maintenance man, who is white, about a problem he wants taken care of. Both of them leave the building about the same time and go out to catch a cab. The cab driver pulls right past the well-dressed executive to pick up the casually clad maintenance man. The maintenance man casually notes what has happened while the black executive starts to swear before deciding it is not worth it. He thinks, "I'll just go next door to the hotel bell captain and have him call a cab quickly," and he makes a mental note to have a cab called when he is in a hurry, thus avoiding this indignity. In a discussion of this incident, the maintenance man might likely dismiss it as a quirk that just happened, not bringing whiteness into it at all. The black executive having had or heard about such experiences many times knows much better. He knows it is a kind of experience that African-American men have over and over; it is just part of what goes with his group identity and he really cannot afford to forget it when he is in public. In this example, the white male stayed at the individual idea level ("Interesting, that cab passed the boss and picked me up first.") while the black executive started at that level ("Guess I'll get a cab home."), but his feelings about not being picked up led him first to the group feeling level for a moment ("This _____ me off!"), then to the group idea level ("This happens to brothers like me every day. No need to get upset."), and then back to the individual idea level ("I'll remember to call a cab next time I need to leave in a hurry."). This example very briefly illustrates the complexity involved in simple decision-making where potential issues of diversity are involved. Of course, one explanation for what happened to the executive is that the cab driver was a cousin of the maintenance man and recognized him instantly. However, unless the executive and the maintenance man had a relationship where such issues could be easily and routinely discussed, the executive could easily have continued to think he was passed over because of his color.

Another very different kind of diversity example follows. Very recently a colleague of mine, working with the youth in our church, facilitated an exercise that helped them clarify what each group wanted from the opposite gender in a relationship. To the surprise of most of those in the room and particularly the teenage girls, what the males and females stated were nearly complete opposites. When asked to see the issue from the other gender's perspective, each group's first attempts were very inaccurate projections of what they wanted for themselves. As the facilitator forced them to think not about what they wanted or viewed but what the other side might want, one could see etched on those teenage faces the almost painful process of leaving their comfortable individual and group positions to see the other's point of view. Although it was done with very little depth, just changing at the idea level required work on each gender's part. This is the complicating factor in all diversity work. Like getting in shape or learning in any new area, it can be painful and anxiety-provoking and no results are guaranteed. Also, experience in diversity work has taught this writer that the greater the *perceived* differences among people, the more anxiety is generated at the group level.

Those examples were designed to assist in thinking about what goes into diversity conceptually, but it is also necessary to define some of the practical aspects of what diversity is and is not as defined in the context of this paper. Diversity is not having a black woman as president. Diversity is having an organization with a climate that a black woman just starting in the company could feel supported in her aspirations to one day be president. Diversity is not rushing out to hire Spanish-speaking counselors to provide badly needed services for Spanish-speaking clients. Diversity is having a relationship with Hispanic and Latino staff and community so that there are many pathways to input to the service organization's leadership the need for people to provide the services in whatever language meets that community's needs. Diversity is not filling the proper quota of "minorities" interviewed for the new trainee program. Diversity is having relationships with institutions that supply a broad range of highly qualified applicants that reflect all the clients of the company and the population surrounding the location of that company. Diversity is not one group asking "What do you want from me?" Diversity is understanding one's own reaction to other groups and one's own understanding of his or her group identities and how important they are personally. Diversity is not making sure that a particular jury has the right amount of black women, Latina women, and Asians on it to be fair to the defendant. Rather, diversity is having a jury selection process that ensures a widely representative pool of jurors that accurately reflects the total population of a given jurisdiction.

There are those who at this point might ask what diversity has to do with the focus on organizations? It is my contention that the position of many organizations with respect to diversity issues is analogous to the position of the juvenile justice arena with respect to society at large. Adolescents are viewed by society at large and by many parents as a very difficult group and the rewards for working with troubled adolescents are often difficult to see. So when adolescent behavior gets too difficult to be handled in normal arenas (home, school), it falls upon the courts to do something. Diversity issues, like juveniles in society, present a real and constant challenge, but are a standard feature of our world today. Although diversity issues (like teenagers) are really inescapable, it is my observation that human beings often choose not to deal with such issues up close, but choose to isolate themselves as much as possible and live, socialize, and worship in groups of people who look, think, act, spend, and vote like they do.

However, there are some areas of life that simply require a diverse world to function. These institutions and settings tend to be large and organized. They include most major corporations, educational institutions, governmental operations, and major commercial enterprises—in short, places where many of us must work or otherwise take care of our business. Because these settings cannot be avoided, diversity issues often end up being played out in these organizations. An example of the potential impact of diversity issues can be noted from observing the jury process in the O. J. Simpson trial. As this presentation was being formulated, a former juror had accused the police of being biased against the African-American members of the jury and favoring the white jurors. Under these conditions, the potential for stalling, if not halting, not just this trial, but the entire Los Angeles jury trial process, is enormous.[1] Ironically, based on this writer's experience with significant organizational diversity issues, any stopgap, quick-fix measures designed to patch up this or any like situation would be doomed to failure because diversity issues are never matters of a quick fix, but would be viewed as more a matter of the quality of leadership and the differentiation of that leadership.

Fundamentally then, it is the writer's belief that diversity and differentiation meet at leadership and that a leader who is not able or willing to work on his or her own process of differentiation of self cannot effectively lead a system into a diversity effort; that is, a process whereby a company or institution purposefully decides to change its structure by broadening the range of discussion around differences, opening the system to new ways of responding to difference and expanding the pool of talent used to solve issues. It has already been highlighted how any efforts to get human beings to focus on their differences and what they mean creates a certain level of anxiety. Organizational movement or change in this arena requires what Friedman (1985) has long referred to as a "non-anxious presence." A nonanxious presence in the face of diversity issues with a large organization does not just happen. This author believes that in the context of organizational change the leader who is seen as a calming influence must have done some work on differentiation at the family of origin level and have made some effort to look at his/her own group identity. To view some of these same issues from a Bowen theoretical perspective, one might ask, "Given the societal forces operating at this time, what level of differentiation would be required of a police chief, a head district attorney or a trial judge in a situation like the O. J. Simpson trial in order for the majority of those participating and watching to view the proceedings as fair, orderly and in the best interests of all concerned?"

Two decades of consultation with organizations around these issues have shown that sound diversity efforts in organizations always require the involvement of organizational leaders and individual acts of courage and leadership from various persons within the organization along the way. In order for companies that only a few decades ago were composed of 95 to 100 percent white male managers to change to 50 to 60 percent white male managers and include women and persons of color, major cultural change has to occur. That change can be shocking, highly anxiety-provoking, and reactive, or it can be anticipated, somewhat uncomfortable, and well thought out. For the latter, and in this writer's experience extremely rare, process to occur, both Bowen theory and diversity concepts would imply that the leadership has to commit to a long-term process of steering a course through rough waters based on principles consistent with strongly held values. When the leadership can do this, then the demeanor of the leader passes down infectiously through the ranks. It is my observation that a negative societal process operates today which targets the very groups diversity efforts attempt to include in much the same way society targets adolescents and isolates and demeans that group. This shifts the focus away from the deficiencies in the leadership to the problems in the "other" groups, and it is this process by far which appears to domi-

[1]As this paper was undergoing final editing, the July 30, 1995 edition of *Parade Magazine* published an article indicating that many Americans favor the elimination of citizen juries and the substitution of professional or judicial jurors. This could be viewed as a quick-fix measure designed to manage the societal reaction to juries which have become increasingly ethnically and racially diverse.

nates diversity activity and our national political scene.[2]

An essential tenet of this paper then is that there is no categorical difference between the kind of effort needed to differentiate oneself from one's family of origin and the kind of effort needed to distinguish oneself in confronting the "forces of togetherness" within any organization of which one is a part and that systems thinking is just as rare in organizational environments as it is in families. Furthermore, it is the writer's contention that within an organization, it is very difficult for any human being to be seen or to see others solely or even primarily as an individual. Unless an individual has clearly distinguished himself by behaviors that clearly identify him as being able to see and respond to differences in a positive way, one who risks leaving the comfort zone of one's individual idea box or reference group's position, he is more likely to be seen as a member of a group or groups that have important meanings within that organization (man, woman, black, white, top management, line worker, sales person) and, therefore, interact with others in ways that may be outside of his conscious awareness.[3] To become conscious of how this process operates in each of us requires leaving our comfort zones and making steps to bridge the cutoff between the self that is known and comfortable with the parts of the self that are unfamiliar.

This writer also believes it is a related but separate learning to also look at fundamental human cultural, racial, and gender identities and begin to understand how the cutoff process works in that area as well. This movement toward self-examination followed by adjustment appears to be required by any organism dedicated to the survival of its kind, but it takes on enormous weight when it is understood by the venturing-out member of a community that such steps risk rejection from the home group. (This is essentially the story of Jonathan Livingston Seagull.) Thus, from this writer's perspective, the cost of distinguishing oneself in diversity matters within an organization often turns out to be very close to the cost of differentiation of self with one's family of origin and, though the long term rewards for self and group may be great, most choose not to pay the price.

REFERENCES

Bach, Richard. 1970. *Jonathan Livingston Seagull.* New York: Avon.

Bowen, Murray. 1978. *Family Therapy in Clinical Practice.* New York: Jason Aronson.

Cross, Elsie. 1985. Issues of Diversity. *Sunrise Seminars*, 2.

Friedman, Edwin. 1985. *Generation to Generation.* New York: Guilford Press.

Kerr, Michael E. and Murray Bowen. 1988. *Family Evaluation.* New York: W. W. Norton & Co.

Kirkham, K. 1993. "Managing in a Diverse Workforce: From Incident to 'Ism.'" *The Diversity Factor*, 1 (3):22-26.

---

[2]A good example of this process was the Clarence Thomas/Anita Hill Senate hearing which did little to illuminate the facts of Judge Thomas's judicial qualifications, but which did cast heavy personal aspersions on the characters of both Mr. Thomas and Ms. Hill.

[3]The diversity notion of the distinguished individual is very close to Bowen's idea of the "differentiated self" except that the differentiated self is a product of work on the self in the context of the togetherness forces in the family of origin and the "distinguished self" is a function of work in the context of an organization's togetherness forces. This writer would view both kinds of individuals as "works in progress."

ORGANIZATIONAL DYNAMICS AND THE CLERGY

V. Sue Zabel, PhD

The model presented in this paper was developed from research with clergy about their self-defeating behaviors (Zabel 1994). The behaviors they described in their interviews resulted from complex interactions in their personal and professional milieus. Emphasis on individual manifestations was inadequate. A systemic comprehension of the web of interrelationships among family of origin, nuclear family, work environment, and societal culture is essential. Bowen theory can help describe dynamics of individual and group functioning and augment other concepts from the social sciences.

Background

Research about deficiencies in clergy focuses mostly on individual failure and conceals or ignores systemic issues. Earlier literature about parish problems focused on the clergy's role in helping others. Current research identifies numerous instances of dysfunctional behavior. Burnout threatens the effectiveness of many helping professionals, including clergy (Olsen and Grosch 1991, Rediger 1982, White 1986). Stress is a perennial issue for clergy, although recent researchers questioned whether it is greater than that of the general population (Hulme 1985, Rassieur 1982, Rediger 1982, Sanford 1982, Warlick 1982, Malony 1988, Rayburn et al. 1986). Sexual misconduct claims vast amounts of denominational leaders' time and attention (Fortune 1989, Peterson 1992, Rassieur 1976). Clergy who are adult children of alcoholics often display signs of codependency (Apthorp 1988, Torres 1989, Wilson 1989, Woititz 1987).

Few studies investigate the dynamics of the systems that help sustain these behaviors. A limited number of studies address the ways in which difficulties in individuals' family background and psychological make-up recur in their behavior at work (Burton and Weinrich 1990; Friedman 1985; Kets de Vries and Miller 1984; Levinson 1984; McGoldrick et al. 1989; Nucchterlein 1991; White 1986; Woititz 1987). A very few relate clergy's background with their dysfunctional behaviors in congregational interactions (Apthorp 1988, Friedman 1985, Krueger 1988, Maeder 1989, Torres 1989, White 1986).

While clergy are often stereotypically seen as models of exemplary behavior, an initial investigation of recent research identified behavior that suggests recurrent self-defeating patterns (Maeder 1989). Blackmon and Hart (1990) summarize "at least five areas of 'emotional hazard' that all pastors must face in their ministry: personal relationships, depression, stress and burnout, sexuality, and assertiveness" (36).

Previous research concluded that self-defeating activities are expressed in diverse ways and emerge from multiple factors. Absent, however, is an analysis of the interrelationships among these factors. Cudney and Hardy (1991) focused primarily on the individual and provided valuable insight into the ways systems in the outer world interact with a person's inner world. They suggested an adapted behavior modification program to effect change and eliminate self-defeating behaviors. Results of subsequent research using their methods were discouraging (Banks et al. 1979; Berry et al. 1982; Galliford 1982; King 1982; Musick 1982; Parks 1976). However, Winkle, Davis, and Caruso (1982) integrated Cudney's (1975) theory with a family systems approach and reported improved outcomes.

Curtis (1989) extensively reviewed significant clinical and academic research about self-defeating behaviors including: psychotic distortions of reality, depression, sabotage of success at work and in relationships, and neglect of physical health. Curtis suggested that her model of self-defeating behavior, integrating multiple linkages, correlations, and causes, should apply to groups as well as individuals.

Berglas and Baumeister (1993) define self-defeating behavior as

> any deliberate or intentional behavior that has clear, definitely or probably negative effects on the self or on the self's projects. Thus, the behavior must be intentional, although harm to self did not have to be the intended or primary goal of the action (3).

Unaccounted for in each of these studies are the dynamics that help initiate and maintain self-defeating behaviors. Additionally, there is a paucity of research about how church-related organizations may systemically collude to maintain self-defeating behavior in clergy, particularly the contradictions between what the church purports and what it practices.

Methodology

Critical science forms the philosophical foundation and investigative method for this study. Critical science research offers a useful, participative approach for understanding and affecting the complex dynamics in organizations (Alvesson and Willmott 1992, Bradshaw-Camball 1990, Steffy and Grimes 1986).

Comstock's (1982) method of critical research is used. Thirteen clergy volunteered for the project. The researcher sought to develop an understanding of the participants' experience with self-defeating behavior through extended individual interviews and collective discourse as they assessed and revised the researcher's interpretations from both individual interviews and group dialogue. A review of the literature was an iterative process that began with several careful readings of the transcript material and a review of the relevant literature in the field. As themes emerged from the analysis and categorization of transcript material, relevant literature relating to the topic was reviewed.

The participants came together for an educational event in January 1993. Participants were asked to reflect upon and discuss their understanding of the meaning of the material and its applicability in their own lives and ministries. The participants' observations and reflections affected the design of the researcher's model, the organization of the self-defeating behavior continuum, and concluding recommendations.

Self-Defeating Behavior in Clergy

The clergy in this study were able to define and describe examples of self-defeating behavior in themselves. After sharing their individual definitions of self-defeating behavior, the participants arrived at the following common definition:

> Self-defeating behaviors are those in which the course of action and its results are contrary to one's ultimate purpose or aim. These behaviors may be conscious or unconscious and harmful to self or others. They undermine the self's sense of well-being, wholeness, and spirituality, as well as one's ability to flourish personally or professionally. (Zabel 1994, 32)

Depending on the observer's perspective, the self-defeating behaviors reported by clergy in this study could be configured in an infinite number of ways. The participants helped identify the descriptive categories and agreed that typical self-defeating behaviors may be summarized on two continua: beneficial to undesirable and too little to too much.

Beneficial to undesirable continua include:

- low/positive self-esteem
- hiding, impostor/realistic
- role-appropriate public presentation
- not truthful/appropriate honesty
- procrastination and tardiness/timeliness
- inappropriate/appropriate sexual behavior.

Too little to too much continua include:

- overspending/hoarding
- undereating/overeating
- passive/aggressive
- no boundaries/rigid boundaries
- deny wants and needs/indulgence
- overfunction/underfunction
- overwork/underwork
- perfectionism/fear of failure
- dependent/counterdependent.

In contrast to previous research, these continua along with the examples described by participants emphasize the dynamics surrounding the development and maintenance of self-defeating behaviors, the outcomes, and how the individuals and those around them are affected by the behaviors.

Bowen Family Systems Theory

Family systems theory provides a helpful framework to understand the dynamics of the self-defeating behavior of the clergy and their relation to the complex organizational dynamics of the church. Systems theorists have maintained that research cannot assess individuals' behavior apart from their social context (Friedman 1985, Graham 1992, Kerr and Bowen 1988, Lee 1990, Wexler 1983). Bowen theory advanced the researcher's understanding of the multiple, complex dynamics described by the clergy participants in this study.

According to Kerr and Bowen (1988), "Family systems theory emphasizes the function an individual's behavior has in the broader context of the relationship process." (49) Individuals' behavior must be considered in the context of their relationships to other people and groups.

Bowen theory provides a lens through which the complex interplay of variables and organizational dynamics can be better understood (Bowen 1977, Fox 1994, Gilbert 1992, Kerr 1977, Rogers 1986, Sagar and Wiseman 1982, Smith 1989). The application of Bowen theory extends to church organizations (Friedman 1985; Henry et al. 1991; Kuhn 1977). The focus is on the process at work among the various factors contributing to the development of behavior, what is happening between people in a relationship system, and the function of an individual's behavior in the context of their extended social environments. In addition, participants in this study frequently associated some form of fear or anxiety with the occurrence of self-defeating behaviors. In Bowen theory, triangling is used as a way to alleviate anxiety, frequently with self-defeating outcomes. Much of the self-defeating behavior described by clergy in this study exhibited the over- and underfunctioning behavior described by Bowen. Participants often received messages from the church that reinforced togetherness forces rather than differentiation.

Systemic, Interactive Model

The self-defeating behaviors of clergy in this study were not the result of linear, cause and effect relationships among the various contributing factors. A systems view acknowledges that the minister exists in a web of interconnected relationships that shape his or her functioning. A three-dimensional, systemic, interactive, and dynamic process is more descriptive. Key components include culture, family of origin, nuclear family, work setting, denomination, and individual behavior.

Each element interrelates with the others and, as such, exhibit the dynamics of systems theory within each element as well as in the relationships among them. In addition, beliefs and belief systems function within each of the elements of the triangles.

Any three components of the model can form a triangle. Anxiety and patterns of behavior generated at any point in the triangle transmit further anxiety to other points and express themselves in relationships. A web of interlocking triangles exists throughout the extended relational systems of the work setting. These patterns sustain themselves over time because of the functional positions of the various people and groups involved.

According to Bowen theory, anxiety can be expressed by the system at any point in the triangle. Self-defeating behaviors may arise as an individual or other parts of the system attempt to reduce or bind the anxiety that exists between any two parts of the system by triangling a third. Individuals exhibit triangling in work environments. Triangling may also be manifest between groups of people within a work system as they attempt to cope with the anxiety present somewhere in the system, or triangling may appear between work systems.

Culture refers to historically transmitted patterns of meaning exhibited in social structural, and psychological processes (Geertz 1973). These social relations include economic, political, and ideological contexts. Culture includes the deeper levels of basic learned assumptions and beliefs shared by members of an organization (Schein 1985). There may be several cultures present among different groups within the organization, depending upon their histories and interests.

Cultural assumptions and shared rules of conduct provide an essential survival mechanism for deciphering and categorizing the daily mass of stimuli. Inability to cope with the potential overload increases anxiety. Anxiety can also occur "around the internal problems of social survival—whether or not one is included in the group and how one manages the balance between commitment to the group and to oneself." (Schein 1985, 180) One's experiences in childhood and family of origin underlie this basic anxiety.

An individual's family of origin refers to the family in which he or she grew up. The nuclear family is the one in which he or she currently lives. There is considerable variation in the composition and structure of each. In Bowen theory, both family of origin and nuclear family are emotional units. The thoughts, feelings, beliefs, and behavior of each member contribute to and reflect the functioning of the whole family. This interactive dynamic extends to systems outside the family as well. Thus, what occurs in the work environment affects family functioning and vice versa.

Work settings range from small work groups to multinational corporations, each with infinite variables. Work settings, including congregations, display many of the same dynamics, such as triangling, myths, projections, taboos, heroes, and scapegoats, found in family systems (Friedman 1985, White 1986).

The denominational affiliation of the congregation or clergy person significantly shapes their functioning. Each denomination posits a set of beliefs (though there may be substantial variation among congregations and individual members) and employs a distinctive polity (governance and relational principles and structures). In addition to individual representatives or officers of the denomination, the denominational body itself forms a system interacting with other elements in the model.

Organizational patterns and history may collude to perpetuate triangling and its concomitant counterproductive behavior and decision-making. Thus, the commitments, beliefs, and values espoused by organizations are often contradicted by their actions.

Examples of Triangling

Culture/Family/Work Setting. One participant who serves a rural parish poignantly described the way anxiety generated in the changing culture of a struggling community is transmitted between families and the congregation.

One congregation is mixed up in a small town that's dying, in a system that no longer works for them—the family farm system, where mom and dad work the family farm and raise their kids there, mom and dad retire and move into town, the kids have their kids and run the family farm, and they all went to church on Sunday and filled the church. . . . There is no longer a grocery store or gas station, but there are two bars. In the midst of this depressing situation, some folks are using alcohol as a way of dealing with life and continuing to screw up their families. The church is a threat to that.

Complicating this deteriorating scenario is the fact that the older generation is no longer financially maintaining the community church as it did in the past. Many retirees are moving out of the community or fearfully hoarding their savings in anticipation of some impending future crisis. The financial support of the church falls to younger families who are now paying the mortgage and raising families on farmer's wages. Further anxiety is generated and transmitted by the denominational body that is experiencing declining membership and dwindling contributions. It is worried about its own future. As a result, denominational anxiety is escalating. In a self-defeating reaction, the denomination increases the pressure on these troubled congregations and their pastors to grow in membership and financially support the denomination. Many clergy report that the spiritual nurture which is central to their personal vocation and congregational mission is thereby neglected.

Culture/Family of Origin/Denomination. One participant described an example of mutual reinforcement of culture, family of origin, and denomination. He entered marriage and ordained ministry not knowing he could make choices that were different from what the family expected. He grew up in the 1950s when one ideal cultural image was togetherness. Like several other participants who grew up in that era, he described his family of origin as doing everything together. "It didn't matter if you were married or had children of your own or starting a new family, we did things as a family." A denominational leader wrote a song that emphasizes the value of togetherness:

> Don't you know, can't you see? All the world is family. You've become my neighborhood. God said, 'It is good.'

Family business was to be kept within the family and not shared with outsiders. Additionally, the participant's experience of his father was a combination of love and fear. The father was the unquestioned authority and disciplinarian. This view is often projected onto denominational leaders—an image that is often promoted and invoked by denominational policies, structures, and practices. Another person agreed that this kind of loyalty and affiliation is consistent with the denominational norms associated with ministry. Congregations are frequently likened to a family. Behavior and mottoes emphasize that the church sticks together. Evidence of disunity and dissension are often denied. Overfunctioning is rewarded. Those who work inordinately long hours, who pick up undesirable tasks or complete those neglected by others, who uncomplainingly attempt to meet everyone's expectations are lauded as models of service and ministry. Differentiated behavior is often discouraged. Obedience to the group (whose norms and behavior are sometimes justified as God's will), conformity to publicly-stated beliefs, and silence about discontent over denominational policy and practices are indications of faithfulness to many denominational leaders.

One denominational leader takes great care not to perpetuate in denominational practices the kind of anxiety, humiliation, and shame he experienced as a child growing up poor. Despite feeling loved and valued by his family, he recalls the "feelings of nothingness and insignificance" that were created within the cultural environment

> Nothingness came from, in those days, going into the bank and not having money, you were nothing. We were always reminded, one way or another, that the poorhouse was always an option. We got put off the farm when I was in the seventh grade.

In reaction to these kinds of experiences, he avoids embarrassing clergy and attempts to help them maintain their dignity: "Some of the deepest rage is when the denominational leader will embarrass that person in public. Such humiliation eats away at one's soul. When your dignity is violated, a person who is honest, who is realistic is going to feel deep resentment."

The anxiety that began in an earlier societal and family context can influence the person's later contributions to society, further illustrating the culture/family/denomination triangle. For example, this participant said, "Growing out of my time in the depression years, I have the need to have some influence on how society moves. I have found the church to be a place where that can be expressed." A direct connection was his work as a chaplain in the state legislature. He personally identified with the less fortunate. "That fed a part of me that helped resolve some of those childhood feelings of being disenfranchised, of being nothing in society." He sought to be a "voice of the voiceless ones."

Culture/Denomination/Congregation or Work Setting. Working excessively long hours is a common self-defeating behavior identified by the participants. Overwork has the multiple benefits of satisfying cultural myths that hard work leads to success, a denominational ideal that total commitment requires self-sacrifice, and congregational expectations that a competent pastor is continuously available. Several participants observed that workaholics, particularly if they demonstrate administrative capabilities, are revered and often make it to the top. Several also reported that one of the limited rewards available to clergy is a committee assignment (which is voluntary) that entails increased responsibilities. A reward for good work is more work. Feeding clergy anxiety is uncertainty about work-related rewards. One person observed,

> I don't think a lot is rewarded, which I think is what leads people to have all this midlife second-guessing of their commitment. And then the despair that results when they find out they don't have any other options. . . . I think people are having a tougher and tougher time finding the intrinsic rewards of it.

Declining denominational and congregational resources have resulted in declines in upward mobility, pay cuts, and lateral moves. Adding to the anxiety is a diminution in status. As one participant put it,

> the status of the clergy is diminishing in society as well as in the local church. The role of the minister in the society at large has really changed while the attitudes of the population in general have changed about religion. Before church attendance plummeted as badly as it has, I think ministers were regarded as people who had legitimate roles as the conscience of society. And they could speak out and be heard—in government, in the newspaper, in media. Nowadays, the clergy still feel the drive to be the moral voice, but the only people who listen to them are their own parishioners, even if them.

Individual/Family of Origin/Congregation or Work Setting. Overfunctioning is a self-defeating behavior that functions to bind anxiety in the family or work system. One participant described the interrelationship of overfunctioning in her family of origin and her present work setting. She described the multigenerational struggle:

> I think of my mother's low self-esteem. That actually was a source of tension between us. . . . But I have a long history of proving I'm worthwhile. . . . My father had a big thing about what other people thought about you. Doing good, doing right, being respectful, and all that. I was too worried

> about what other people thought and not about what I thought.

Like many in the study, she attempted to prove her worth and gain acceptance from others through her many outstanding achievements.

> One of the things I did as an oldest child, and accepting the explicit norms in our family, is take after my dad. I always was a leader in school and pretty popular. I probably didn't believe *inside* that I was all that great, but I certainly achieved things. . . . I did well in high school and college—won all kinds of awards in college. . . . But I think there's still something inside that says "not OK."

Like several other participants in this study, this clergywoman overprepared in her professional work. Despite the personal toll, others in the work system often perceive overfunctioning behavior as an asset and they view overfunctioners as responsible and reliable.

Similarly, more than one participant correlated eating behaviors and excess body weight with family of origin and congregational dynamics. One participant consistently used the word eat to describe the habitual ways she copes with anxiety-producing situations. "I go home and eat. I wake up in the middle of the night with it just kind of eating at me." Members of one person's congregation sabotaged her diet. Even though she had announced her attendance at Weight Watchers, one member gave her a can of honey-coated cashew nuts. She said, "I was aware that on some level that my very size makes me far more comfortable to people, especially young women in relation to their husbands. I know I am perceived as a non-sexual being, and therefore, I'm less threatening."

One participant connected childhood sexual abuse with inappropriate sexual behavior as an adult. The fundamental self-defeating dynamic that persisted into adulthood was the lack of clear boundaries. "I was sexually abused when I was about twelve or thirteen by a man who worked for my grandfather. As I've learned about that, the notion of a clear boundary wasn't something that I had a clear experience of internally." A major issue as a pastor was how to say "no." For him, the core issue is, "If I say 'no,' no one will love me or accept me." Sexual involvement with parishioners became proof of his acceptability.

One participant resolved difficulties dealing with congregational expectations and a tendency toward overfunctioning by leaving parish ministry. Such a response might be construed as an emotional cutoff. Another participant described a recurring pattern of detachment, of cutoff, from painful situations, including the relationship with a former spouse and an intractable colleague.

Religious beliefs are a significant contributor to the development and maintenance of many of the triangles described here. Beliefs ground our deeply held assumptions about ourselves and others. Beliefs may be the source or amplifier of the anxiety. They may also rationalize self-defeating behaviors that help keep anxiety circulating.

Recommendations for Change

Fundamental recommendations for change emphasize efforts to support differentiation, detriangling, shared power and participation, and continuous improvement. The following suggestions were developed by the clergy participants and researcher. While they focus specifically on seminaries, denominations, congregations, and clergy, they may be useful to other organizations and individuals seeking to reduce self-defeating behaviors.

Differentiation is an underlying assumption of the systemic, interactive model presented in this paper. Individual and systemic change in church-related organizations requires increased autonomy and inner directed behavior. Changes in one's level of differentiation are difficult and take time, but they are not impossible. Any change, however small, that strengthens the individual's sense of self can make significant differences in a person's functioning especially in relationships. The analysis of the self-defeating behaviors of the participants in this study strongly suggests that increased differentiation, while concurrently remaining in connection with others, albeit difficult to accomplish, is the single most effective approach to reducing these behaviors.

Detriangling is the most important method of improving differentiation. Detriangling implies an ability to see systems, processes, and relationship dynamics at work among individuals and groups. A systems approach tends to reduce emotional reactivity and increase emotional neutrality about relationship processes.

Seeing the multiple perspectives in relationship processes, suspending blame, and avoiding predispositions about what should be facilitate detriangling. Detriangling places responsibility for relationships with the persons or groups involved. It promotes self-agency, thoughtful decision making, and accountability.

Lack of differentiation and triangling cultivate power differentials among individuals and groups. As has been noted, conflict, stress, or anxiety in one part of the system is often expressed in more vulnerable, less powerful parts. Occupants of these positions often internalize responsibility, shame, guilt, or blame for the situation.

Individuals, seminaries, and church-related groups must change the current power arrangements to reduce self-defeating behavior in clergy. Persons and groups in disadvantaged power differentials can instigate the change process on their own behalf by protesting their status and taking whatever steps that are available to them. Differentiated, nonreactive leaders realize that ultimately all are diminished by dysfunctional systems of interlocking triangles. Sharing power in organizations promotes detriangling and accountability.

As a result of their insights, the participants in this study urged efforts toward transforming seminaries and the church. Many characteristics of seminaries and church-related institutions daunt those interested in transformation: fixed or slowly adapting missions, extraordinarily diverse and voluntary constituencies, limited resources, absence of coordinated decision making, and resistance to imposed change. However, examples of transformation in church-related systems do exist (Beres and Musser 1989).

Pervasive change cannot be accomplished by individuals alone. Systemic transformation necessitates large-scale change that may take years to develop and accomplish. Participative approaches are consistent with most church-related organizations' stated commitments to inclusiveness and involvement of members. The quality leadership movement institutes participation at every level in its relentless pursuit of quality and continuous improvement. Quality leadership fosters teamwork and partnerships. It works to decrease barriers, rivalries, and distrust. Leaders of continually improving, potentially transforming organizations practice the differentiated qualities alluded to above (Block 1993; Scholtes 1991; Senge 1990; Wheatley 1992). They develop conceptual and communication skills, align their behavior with their values, listen, and appreciate others' contributions. Those influenced by them are better able to think for themselves and make wise choices.

Enduring change in individuals and organizations is complex and most often slow. One does not have to wait for direction from the top to initiate change in the systems in which one lives and works. Individuals can begin to create the kind of organization they desire by beginning in a small way right where they are. The only person one can actually change is oneself. However, if one believes that organizations are a web of interconnected relationships, then change in one part of the system eventually affects functioning in other parts.

REFERENCES

Alvesson, M. and Willmott, H. 1992. "On the Idea of Emancipation in Management and Organization Studies." *Academy of Management Review* 17: 432-64.

Apthorp, S. 1988. "The Blind Leading the Blind." *Christian Century* 9 Nov., 1010-1013.

Banks, J., Grimmer, J., Hardy, R. E., Hiatt, D., and Lowe, J. 1979. "Self-Defeating Behavior Workshops: Systems Approach for Hard-to-Serve Veterans." *Personnel and Guidance Journal* 57 (6): 313-315.

Berry, J., Demgen, M., Hardy, R. E., and Wickland, C. 1982. "Implementing the Eliminating Self-Defeating Behavior Theory in Group Home Treatment." *Personnel and Guidance Journal* 60 (9): 571-573.

Beres, M. E., and Musser, S. J. 1989. "Avenues and Impediments to Transformation: Lessons From a Case of Bottom-up Change." In *Corporate Transformation: Revitalizing Organizations for a Competitive World*, ed. R. H. Kilmann and T. J. Covin, 152-182. San Francisco, CA: Jossey-Bass.

Berglas, S., and Baumeister, R. F. 1993. *Your Own Worst Enemy: Understanding the Paradox of Self-Defeating Behavior*. New York: Basic Books.

Blackmon, R. A., and Hart, A. D. 1990. "Personal Growth for Clergy." In *Clergy Assessment and Career Development*, ed. R. A. Hunt, J. E. Hinkle, Jr., and H. N. Malony, 36-42. Nashville, TN: Abingdon.

Block, P. 1993. *Stewardship: Choosing Service Over Self-Interest*. San Francisco, CA: Berrett-Koehler.

Bowen, M. 1977. "Family Systems Theory and Society." In *Georgetown Family Symposia*, Vol. II (1973-1974), ed. J. P. Lorio and L. McClenahan, 182-212. Washington, DC: Georgetown University Family Center.

Bradshaw-Camball, P. 1990. "Organizational Development and the Radical Humanist Paradigm: Exploring the Implications." *Best Papers, Proceedings of the Academy of Management*, 253-257.

Burton, A. L., and Weinrich, C.A. 1990. "So Great a Cloud of Witnesses: The Use of Family Systems Process in Forming Pastoral Identity and Facilitating Pastoral Functioning." *Journal of Pastoral Care* 44 (4): 331-341.

Comstock, D. E. 1982. "A Method for Critical Research". In *Knowledge and Values in Social and Educational Research*, ed. E. Bredo and W. Feinberg, 370-390. Philadelphia, PA: Temple University Press.

Cudney, M. R. 1975. *Eliminating Self-Defeating Behaviors*. Kalamazoo, MI: Life Giving Enterprises.

Cudney, M. R., and Hardy, R. E. 1991. *Self-Defeating Behavior: Free Yourself From the Habits, Compulsions, Feelings, and Attitudes that Hold You Back*. San Francisco, CA: Harper.

Curtis, R. C. (Ed.). 1989. *Self-Defeating Behaviors: Experimental Research, Clinical Im-*

pressions, and Practical Implications. New York: Plenum Press.

Fortune, M. M. 1989. *Is Nothing Sacred? When Sex Invades the Pastoral Relationship*. San Francisco: Harper & Row.

Fox, L. A. 1994. Bowen Family Systems Theory: A Theoretical Framework for Organizational Change Agents. *Journal of American Health Information Management Association*, 65 (4): 49-53.

Friedman, E. H. 1985. *Generation to Generation: Family Process in Church and Synagogue*. New York: Guilford Press.

Galliford, J. E. 1982. *Eliminating Self-Defeating Behavior: The Effects of ESDB Bibliotherapy Compared to ESDB Group Therapy on Weight Control in Women*. PhD Diss., Brigham Young University.

Geertz, C. 1973. *The Interpretation of Cultures*. New York, NY: Basic Books.

Gilbert, R. M. 1992. *Extraordinary Relationships: A New Way of Thinking About Human Interactions*. Minneapolis: Chronimed Publishing.

Graham, L. K. 1992. *Care of Persons, Care of Worlds: A Psychosystems Approach to Pastoral Care and Counseling*. Nashville: Abingdon.

Henry, D., Chertok, F., Keys, C., and Jegerski, J. 1991. "Organizational and Family Systems Factors in Stress Among Ministers." *American Journal of Community Psychology*, 19: 931-952.

Hule, W. E. 1985. *Managing Stress in Ministry*. San Francisco: Harper & Row.

Kerr, M. E. 1977. "Application of Family Systems Theory to a Work System". In *Georgetown Family Symposia*, Vol. II (1973-1974). J. P. Lorio and L. McClenahan, eds. Washington, DC: Georgetown University Family Center.

Kerr, Michael E. and Bowen, Murray. 1988. *Family Evaluation: An Approach Based on Bowen Theory*. New York: Norton.

Kets de Vries, M. F. R., and Miller, D. 1984. *The Neurotic Organization*. San Francisco, CA: Jossey-Bass.

King, R. L. 1982. *Changes in Self-Concept and Behavior of College Students Enrolled in Elimination of Self-Defeating Behavior Workshops*. PhD diss., University of Michigan.

Krueger, D. 1988. "Do We Avoid the Subject?" *The United Methodist Reporter* (Minnesota edition), 25 November, 1.

Kuhn, J. S. 1977. "Interlocking Triangles: Church-Family Issues." In *Georgetown Family Symposia*, Vol. II (1973-1974). J. P. Lorio and L. McClenahan, eds. Washington, DC: Georgetown University Family Center.

Lee, C. 1990. "Spouses and Families of Clergy." In *Clergy Assessment and Career Development*, ed. R. A. Hunt, J. E. Hinkle, Jr., and H. N. Malony, 36-42. Nashville: Abingdon.

Levinson, H. 1984. "Reciprocation: The Relationship Between Man and Organization." In *The Irrational Executive: Psychoanalytic Explorations in Management*, ed. M. F. R. Kets de Vries, 264-285. New York: International Universities Press. (Originally published 1965 in *Administrative Science Quarterly* 9, 370-390).

Malony, H. N. 1988. "Men and Women in the Clergy: Stresses, Strains, and Resources. *Pastoral Psychology* 36: 164-168.

Maeder, T. 1989. "Wounded Healers." *The Atlantic Monthly*, January, 37-47.

McGoldrick, M., Anderson, C. M., and Walsh, F. 1989. *Women in Families: A Framework for family Therapy*. New York, NY: Norton.

Musick. R. J. 1982. *Assessment of the Eliminating Self-Defeating Behavior Program: As a Treatment of Depression in Marital Dyads*. PhD Diss., Brigham Young University.

Nuechterlein, A. M. 1991. "Re-recreating Family of Origin Relationships in Work Relationships." *Journal of Pastoral Care* 45(1): 49-59.

Olsen, D. C., and Grosch, W. M. 1991. "Clergy Burnout: A Self Psychology and Systems Perspective." *The Journal of Pastoral Care* 45: 297-304.

Parks, C. R. 1976. "Factors Affecting Performance in Workshops for Elimination of Self-Defeating Behaviors." PhD diss., Brigham Young University.

Peterson, M. R. 1992. *At Personal Risk: Boundary Violations in Professional-Client Relationships*. New York, NY: W. W. Norton.

Rassieur, C. L. 1976. *The Problem Clergymen Don't Talk About.* Philadelphia, PA: Westminster Press.

Rassieur, C. L. 1982. *Stress Management for Ministers.* Philadelphia, PA: Westminster Press.

Rayburn, C. A, Richmond, L. J., and Rogers, L. 1986. "Men, Women, and Religion: Stress Within Leadership Roles." *Journal of Clinical Psychology* 42: 540-546.

Rediger, G. L. 1982. *Coping with Clergy Burnout.* Valley Forge, PA: Judson Press.

Rogers, V. 1986. *Family Systems Theory in the Workplace.* Ann Arbor, MI: Women in the Workplace Symposium. ERIC, ED 271 664.

Sagar, Ruth R., and Wiseman, K. K. 1982. *Understanding Organizations: Applications of Family Systems Theory.* Washington, DC: Georgetown University Family Center.

Sanford, J. A. 1982. *Ministry Burnout.* New York, NY: Paulist Press.

Schein, E. H. 1985. *Organizational Culture and Leadership: A Dynamic View.* San Francisco, CA: Jossey-Bass.

Scholtes, P. R. 1991. *The Team Handbook: How to Use Teams to Improve Quality.* Madison, WI: Joiner Associates.

Senge, P. 1990. *The Fifth Discipline: The Art and Practice of the Learning Organization.* New York: Doubleday.

Smith, K. K. 1989. "The Movement of Conflict in Organizations: The Joint Dynamics of Splitting and Triangulation." *Administrative Science Quarterly* 34: 1-20.

Steffy, B. D. and Grimes, A. J. 1986. "A Critical Theory of Organization Science." *Academy of Management Review* 11: 322-336.

Torres, R. 1989. *Adult Children of Alcoholics in the Consecrated Life and the Response of Religious Communities to their ACOA Members.* Master's thesis, Marquette University.

Warlick, H. C., Jr. 1982. *How to Be a Minister and a Human Being.* Valley Forge, PA: Judson Press.

Wexler, P. 1983. *Critical Social Psychology.* Boston, MA: Routledge & Kegan Paul.

Wheatley, M. J. 1992. *Leadership and the New Science: Learning About Organization From an Orderly Universe.* San Francisco, CA: Berrett-Koehler.

White, W. L. 1986. *Incest in the Organizational Family: The Ecology of Burnout in Closed Systems.* Bloomington, IL: Lighthouse Training Institute.

Wilson, S. D. 1989. "Evangelical Christian Adult Children of Alcoholics: A Preliminary Study." *Journal of Psychology and Theology* 17: 263-273.

Winkle, C. W., Davis, W. C., and Caruso, M. F. 1982. "Applying Self-Defeating Behavior Principles to Family Therapy." *American Mental Health Counselors Association Journal* 4 (1): 70-77.

Woititz, J. G. 1987. *Home Away From Home: The Art of Self Sabotage.* Pompano Beach, FL: Health Communications.

Zabel, V. S. 1994. *Self-Defeating Behavior in Clergy, the Systemic Dynamics that Maintain Them, and the Implications for Seminary Education.* Ph.D. Diss., University of Minnesota.

THE CONTEMPORARY ORGANIZATION

Robert Cahill, MBA

"In this day and age, if you're not confused, you're not thinking clearly. Let go of your certainty." This observation and advice was freely offered by Margaret Wheatley, consultant and author of the widely-acclaimed book, *Leadership and the New Science*. It resonates with my current experience in organizations.

When business and economic historians write the story of our times one hundred years from now, they will probably concentrate on a few broad themes: how the hierarchies that once dominated the industrial age gave way to more entrepreneurial systems that are able to master the rapidly changing complexity of an information age; how the old image of the worker as a machine was eclipsed by the "thinking employee" and how problem-solving strategies shifted from experts working on the system to everyone working on the system.

Corporations and governments today are beginning an historic transformation into uncharted waters. People in organizations face the challenge of adapting to change and managing change and the need to foster different ways of thinking. The power of communication has magnified our exposure and therefore our awareness of how fast things are changing.

The Challenge of Adapting to Change and Managing Change

Change is an intensely personal experience. Today, reactions to change cover an incredibly broad spectrum. In workshop after workshop, I hear expressions of fear, anxiety, pain, uncertainty, and disbelief permeating the workplace. And yet, in these same settings, voices rise to express excitement, enthusiasm, and high expectations too. I think Stephen Covey is accurate when he offers that "we tend to see the world as we are, not as it is."

It may be helpful to distinguish between transitional change and transformational change, because there is a subtle, yet profound, difference. Transitional change involves moving from a known state "A" to a known state "B." For the most part, job promotions and reorganizations fall into this category. Over time, people have become fairly familiar with changes of this type. Transformational change, on the other hand, involves moving from a known state "A" to an unknown state "X." Many of today's corporate organizational redesign and realignment initiatives and government reinvention efforts fall in this category. It is this unknown landscape that provokes such uncertainty and excitement.

Successfully leading and coaching others to navigate these uncharted waters is the key leadership challenge facing organizations of every size today. In essence, we are entering a world where the past may no longer be a very good predictor of the future. As such, it is important to view change as a process, not as a linear series of transactions. Simply stated, the problem for most executives is that managing change is unlike any other task they have ever encountered. The usual mechanistic model, the legacy of Frederick Taylor and scientific management, fails to take into account that organizations are living systems. Modeled after the system of mass manufacturing pioneered during the early 1900s, the premise was simple: break complex jobs into a myriad of simple rote tasks that the worker can then repeat with machine-like efficiency.

But with change, the challenge is to manage the dynamic, not the pieces. It is essential to connect and balance all the pieces, not attend to each piece in isolation.

Seven Dynamics of Change

Ken Blanchard's "Seven Dynamics of Change" from his video series entitled "Managing the Journey" provides an excellent framework to foster a dialogue about some of the normal and necessary aspects associated with any change. All change produces loss and fear of the unknown. Until this is acknowledged people have great difficulty moving forward. These seven dynamics are listed below, including some strategies management can deploy to better guide the change process.

(1) People will feel awkward, ill at ease, self-conscious.
Strategy: Don't be surprised or dismayed by this initial reaction or response. Clearly communicate at the earliest possible stage what you know about the given change, and the compelling need for such change. Tell people to expect it. The goal is not to frighten employees, but to arouse the emotional energy of an entire organization.

"Start with reality. Get all the facts out. Give people the rationale for change, laying it out in the clearest, most dramatic terms." — Jack Welch, General Electric

(2) People will think first what they have to give up.
Strategy: Don't oversell the benefits of the change, especially at first. Legitimize losses and allow people time to mourn. All change produces loss. Grief is normal and necessary. Be alert, because grief often comes disguised as low morale.

(3) People will feel alone, even if everyone is going through the change.
Strategy: Structure actions that create involvement; don't expect them to happen on their own. Encourage sharing of ideas and networking. Increase the flow of information. During times of change, all perceptions are distorted. Things that didn't used to matter get microscopic attention and analysis.

(4) People can handle only so much change.
Strategy: Set short-term priorities or run the risk of overwhelming people with too much uncertainty.

(5) People are at different levels of readiness for change.
Strategy: Appreciate that some people are natural risk takers and others take longer to feel secure. And you can't always predict who will fall into what category.

(6) People will be concerned they don't have enough resources.
Strategy: Encourage and foster creative problem-solving. To this end, the sets of problem-solving tools associated with total quality management are very helpful.

(7) If you take the pressure off, people will revert back to their old behavior.
Strategy: Changing individual and corporate patterns of behavior is extremely complex. The past, or "old way," however uncomfortable, was at least a known quantity. It is an essential act of leadership to be clear that the change is moving forward, that there is no turning back. Wherever possible, take steps to minimize, not intensify, anxiety.

People support most what they help create. The effectiveness of a decision is not the decision itself, but the quality of the decision multiplied by the acceptance of the decision.

The Changing Employer/Employee Relationship and Related Leadership Implications

The compact between companies and their workers is changing dramatically. Under the old psychological contract, there was an implicit agreement that in return for years of service, loyalty, and good performance, employees could count on future employment. With layoffs, downsizing, and restructuring, the old contract has been broken, probably forever. This reality has caused employers and employees to rethink traditional roles and responsibilities. Everyone who holds a job is taking part in defining the new relationship between the individual and the organization.

In essence, workers today are beginning to understand the principle that the only true job security comes from satisfied customers. Companies would be well served to treat their employees as volunteers and employees would be best served to act as owners of their own employability. To manage volunteers requires a very clear mission and a willingness to provide job enrichment and continual training and education beyond each employee's own specialty, on task force teams or special assignments.

"Companies can't promise lifetime employment, but by constant training and education we may be able to guarantee lifetime employability." Jack Welch, General Electric

The design principles of the recently created Boeing Center For Leadership & Learning do a superb job of capturing this new approach.

Core Design Principles from the Boeing Center For Leadership & Learning

The Boeing Company believes each individual is ultimately responsible for his or her own development and learning. The company relies on each employee to learn through experience, and holds each accountable for improvements in learning, leading, working together, transferring best practices and performance as individuals and organizations. In support of these company expectations, the Boeing Center for Leadership & Learning has been created and designed to provide challenging learning experiences that generate curiosity, excitement and commitment to apply and transfer learning.

The Center will seek to create learning experiences that consider real work projects, customer focus, learning as teams, equal learning environments for all levels, mixed levels, just-in-time learning, and providing a practice field where it is all right to be a beginner. Learning is greatly enhanced when people prepare themselves for the learning experience, challenge their own limits, share, experiment, and reflect on their own learning.

This new approach also has profound implications for leadership. One of the most difficult challenges of our day for leaders is that they cannot readily admit that things are "out of control" and that they/we do not really know what to do about it. To compound matters, there exists an apparent unwillingness to violate the cultural norms that hold that leaders must possess solutions for all our problems. Moreover, many people in leadership positions act as if they are afraid that if they admit their confusion, they will make their followers anxious and confused.

The key to competitive advantage in the nineties and beyond, says Warren Bennis, "will be the capacity of top leadership to create the social architecture capable of generating intellectual capital. I mean an organizational environment that will be not only fast, focused, flexible, and friendly, but also fun. By intellectual capital, I mean know-how, expertise, brainpower, innovation, ideas. All the good CEOs tell me that their major challenge is, "How do I release the brainpower of the people in my company?"

"Leaders are people who do the right things; managers are people who do things right. There is a profound difference. When you think about doing the right things, your mind immediately goes toward thinking about the future, thinking about dreams, missions, strategic intent, purpose. But when you think about doing things right, you think about control mechanisms. You think about "how to." Leaders ask the 'what' and 'why' questions, not the 'how' question."

Successful companies are hard at work finding effective mechanisms to engage the creativity of everyone in the organization. The goal is to create an environment where employees are empowered to challenge, innovate and (re)create their process(es), relationships, products and services to delight their customers and themselves.

We need the ability to organize employees in innovative and flexible ways, and in doing so, to release their discretionary energy and enthusiasm. Managers coaching, seeking ideas, actively listening, and liberating the leadership at all levels of the organization will become the new norm. These changes lead to developing new organizational models that are more process-based and customer-centered. For example, Ford Motor Company wants "to provide an ownership experience so good that the customer will reward us by buying another Ford vehicle."

As Stephen Covey (1989)asserts, "Accomplishing tasks through people is a different paradigm than building people through the accomplishment of tasks. With both, you get things done. With the second, you get them done with far greater creativity, synergy, and effectiveness, and, in the process, you build the capacity to do more in the future as well."

Organizations tend to underestimate the shift in mindset and behavior needed to bridge this transformation. All the command/control actions encouraged before are no longer appropriate in this new setting.

Finally, I'd like to identify two additional emerging trends that could significantly influence future employer/employee relationships and expectations. First, there are signs of employees investing their loyalty with individual people instead of organizations. This could present a phenomenon whose impact cannot be fully predicted.

Second, as *Fortune Magazine* reported in a recent cover story, today's organization is rapidly being transformed from a structure built out of jobs into a field of work needing to be done. There still is and always will be enormous amounts of work to do, but it may not be contained in the familiar envelopes we call jobs. Organizations, like individuals, will have trouble shifting their expectations and habits to fit the new "post-job" world. Note that even the most creative work design begs the question of how unready most organizations are to manage effectively this workforce of temps, part-timers, consultants, and contract workers.

In such a situation, people would no longer take their cues from a job description or supervisor, but from the changing demands of the project. Today, 35 million people—more than 25% of the nation's work force—are employed in "contingent jobs." Typically, they are temporary employees who don't receive full benefits and only work when companies need them. The rise of the contingent worker began long before the recession of 1990-91 accelerated the process. By 1992, the latest year for which figures are available, 13.6% of federal income tax returns reported Schedule C income — nonfarm sole proprietorships — up from 7.8% in 1970.

The Need to Foster Different Ways of Thinking

One important source for learning how to think is formal schooling. Our educational training grounds us in many of the concepts we use to order and understand the world. By the time the average person finishes college, he or she will have taken over 2,600 exams, tests, and quizzes? And, for the most part, they are all geared toward teaching people the *one right answer*. Thus, the "right answer" approach becomes deeply ingrained in our thinking. This may be fine for some mathematical problems where there is in fact only one right answer. The difficulty is that most of life doesn't present itself this way. Life is ambiguous and filled with paradox. There are many "right answers"—all depending on what you are looking for. But if you think there is only one "right answer," you are likely to stop looking as soon as you find one, or get frustrated if you don't find what you think is the "right answer."

"The significant problems we face cannot be solved at the same level of thinking we were at when we created them." —Einstein

In successful organizations, management is not asking, "How can we do that faster, better, or at lower cost?" Instead, they ask first, "Why do we do that at all?" Answers are best when considered in light of the following context: What is your business? What is your mission? Is it still the right mission? Is it still worth doing? If you were not already doing this, would you do it right now?

Conclusion

Many organizations are encumbered with policies, processes, and organizational structures that they wouldn't have if they were starting over today. Today, organizations are working to discover viable models and practices that address the new realities of a complex, changing marketplace. More and more organizations are willing to experiment with new approaches. The common refrain, "Nothing I've used in the past seems to work anymore," may only be a modest exaggeration.

In most organizations, public and private, manufacturing and service, understanding of the magnitude of today's change is still in embryonic stages. In increasing numbers, however, organizations are recognizing that today's change is not about "fixing it."

"If you take smart people and put them in a stupid process, then they become stupid too. But first they become frustrated and cynical. You can't hire your way out of trouble; you've got to design your way out of trouble." Michael Hammer

Suggested Readings

Adams, John D. 1984. *Transforming Work.* Virginia: Miles River Press.

Adams, John D. 1986. *Transforming Leadership.* Virginia: Miles River Press.

Adizes, Ichak. 1988. *Corporate Lifecycles.* New Jersey: Prentice Hall.

Beer, Stafford. 1975. *Platformfor Change.* New York: John Wiley & Sons.

Bennis, Warren and Burt Nanus. 1985. *Leaders.* New York: Harper & Row.

Block, Peter. 1988. *The Empowered Manager.* San Francisco: Jossey-Bass.

Covey, Stephen R. 1989. *The 7 Habits of Highly Effective People.* New York: Simon & Schuster.

DePree, Max. 1989. *Leadership is an Art.* New York: Dell Publishing.

Doyle, Michael and David Straus. 1982. *How To Make Meetings Work.* New York: Jove Books.

Greenleaf, Robert K. 1977. *Servant Leadership.* New Jersey: Paulist Press.

Harvey, Jerry B. 1988. *The Abilene Paradox.* Lexington Books.

Kearns, David and David Nadler. 1992. *Prophets in the Dark.* New York: HarperCollins.

Osborne, David and Ted Gaebler. *Reinventing Government.* Maine: Addison-Wesley.

Owen, Harrison. 1992. *Leadership Is.* Maryland: Abbott Publishing.

Peters, Thomas and Robert Waterman. 1982. *In Search of Excellence.* New York: Harper & Row.

Schein, Edgar H. 1985. *Organizational Culture and Leadership.* San Francisco: Jossey-Bass.

Senge, Peter. 1990. *The Fifth Discipline.* New York: Doubleday.

Tichy, Noel M. and Stratford Sherman. 1994. *Control Your Destiny Or Someone Else Will.* New York: Harper Business

Zuckerman, Marilyn R. and Lewis J. Hatala. 1992. *Incredibly American.* Wisconsin: Quality Press.

7

NONHUMAN SOCIAL SYSTEMS

NONHUMAN SOCIAL SYSTEMS

Introduction

In developing his theory about the functioning of humans and human social systems, Dr. Bowen drew upon his knowledge of other life forms. The three papers in this section reflect this cornerstone of Bowen family systems theory.

In "Leadership in Nonhuman Social Systems: The Chimpanzees of Gombe," Kathleen B. Kerr, member of the faculty of the Georgetown Family Center, explores the question of whether the basis for variability in the chimpanzee is the same as in the human. More particularly, are the counterbalancing forces of individuality and togetherness observed in the human species observed in the chimpanzee?

In "Lessons from Nature on Leadership," Stephanie J. Ferrera, member of the faculty of the Center for Family Consultation in Evanston, Illinois and editorial consultant to *Family Systems*, explores the question of whether humans, like many other species, are instinctually hierarchical animals. She examines biological views of social hierarchies in Nature, social hierarchies as emotional systems, and Dr. Bowen's model of the high-functioning organization as a collection of individuals, characterized by responsibility for self, open communication, flexible structure, motivation fueled by autonomy, and a unity of vision defined by individuals.

In "A Natural Systems View of Hierarchy," Dr. Roberta M. Gilbert, a member of the faculty of the Georgetown Family Center and author of *Extraordinary Relationships, a New Way of Thinking about Human Interactions* examines hierarchy as a way natural systems are organized. She describes and summarizes work on hierarchies in nonhuman species, provides examples of human hierarchies such as the Roman Catholic Church and military organizations, and examines hierarchy and Bowen family systems theory.

In his interview with Kathleen Wiseman, Dr. Bowen discussed some of the ways he has drawn upon the functioning of other life forms. One way is in the use of models from other parts of Nature. Another relates to the instantaneous dictates of the feeling system in decisions about who lives and who dies. A third area relates to the evolution in functioning of the human brain.

Models from Nonhuman Life Forms

I would say every time there is a discrepancy between the animal model and the human, I would go back to look for another animal model. And this had to do with forms of life that were absolutely necessary for each other. You can apply that to the human. There are people that are necessary for the life and the livelihood of the one next to him. If the one next to him doesn't function, they die. Anyway that's a complex thing. A symbiosis is where one form of life is essential to the other. Where one cannot exist without the other. Okay, you say one person is going to try to improve his functioning. He does that by working on himself, but he damn well better be interested in that other guy.

Reciprocal Functioning

If one person is able to improve the functioning of self, you're going to sacrifice somebody to it. You can't save them all. It was absolutely true then and is now. It had to do with a herd of reindeer who had their young while the herd was migrating. The mother would stop to give birth to the young and if the young can't walk and keep up with her, the wolves would get him. If the mother stays behind to fight off the wolves, then the wolves would get her and the baby too. So she makes an instantaneous decision either stay with the babe and sacrifice herself or sacrifice the baby to the wolves, which is the same for the human condition too. Same thing applies to heroes and other people who do a heroic thing and come out okay. . . . Jumping into the water to rescue somebody and failing is part of the instantaneous dictates of the feeling system.

Feeling, Intellect, and the Human Brain

Personally, I think there are two centers in the brain and I'm trying to locate them now more than I did then. One, at the center of the brain deals with feelings, intuition, guess work, all the kinds of forces that go into animals migrating. This is a force within them. This is on the feeling side and that was developed long before the intellect was developed. This is a part of animals without a brain. Along came the human and he slowly developed an ability to think, which is separate from feeling, that's my view, nobody else's. So I would say that the human brain has developed the ability to feel and to know.

I tried to develop a theory which puts the emphasis on the intellectual aspect, which is separate from the other. That is a newly added function of the brain. And I attempted to say that the intellect can observe the automatic brain as it makes decisions, if the human — and I'd say that all humans have the ability to do this, but they don't use this ability — and I attempted to separate the two. And this is where the major emphasis in the theory took place. By using the intellect one could see and understand the automatic.

LEADERSHIP IN NONHUMAN SOCIAL SYSTEMS: THE CHIMPANZEES OF GOMBE

Kathleen B. Kerr, MSN, MA

My study of chimpanzees began with an interest in the great apes. I researched their behavior in hopes of being more objective about things I had difficulty seeing clearly in the human. Over time my focus narrowed to the variability in functioning of the three great apes (chimpanzee, gorilla and orangutan) that appeared similar to the variability in the human observed by Bowen. I questioned whether one could attribute such variability in the great apes to differences in the individuality-togetherness balance, that is to the level of differentiation of self, as transmitted over the generations. Said another way, is the basis for variability in functioning in the great apes the same as that Bowen postulated for the human? Are the counterbalancing forces of togetherness and individuality peculiar to the human or are they common to all life? Are they observable in the life forms closest to the human on the phylogenetic tree? I studied chimpanzees because of the longitudinal research on them in natural settings and because evidence demonstrates that of the great apes they diverged most recently from the human evolutionary line. Humans are not chimpanzees and chimpanzees are not humans but they are our closest evolutionary relative. Of the longitudinal studies, I focused on the research at Gombe because of Goodall's research interest in variability in what she called personality and its connection with early childhood experience in the family.

I intended in this paper to look at variability in how the chimpanzee study community at Gombe National Park, where Goodall and her associates have done their research, functioned under different alpha males. However, I was unable to do that as too many other factors muddied the waters. At the study sites at Gombe and Mahale (the location of Japanese longitudinal research) researchers have provisioned the chimpanzees to draw them to observational areas. Aggregation of the chimpanzees at the feeding and observation areas increases their social contact and the aggression between them. Researchers changed the provisioning method at Gombe several times to attempt to deal with these artifacts. Unfortunately these changes themselves may have played a role in the emergence of "pathological" behaviors such as cannibalism and murder and in the split of the study community (Wrangham 1974). Along with the artifact introduced by the provisioning, increased density of the chimpanzees is probably affecting their behavior. Over time the park has become an island in the midst of agricultural development, thereby isolating the chimpanzee population and removing the escape valve of roaming (Goodall 1990a). Studies have established that increased density and lack of an escape area affect functioning in animal groups and increase social pathology (Calhoun 1962, Kerr 1978). Consequently it would be inaccurate to compare the emotional climate of the study community under different alpha males as if it were primarily a product of the changing alpha male leadership. The provisioning methods, the increasing density of the group, as well as other ecological variables such as food supply, need to be taken into account.

So, this paper addresses leadership in the chimpanzee community of Gombe. It concentrates on leadership among the males as it is more observable. Male chimpanzees are more social than females, spending large amounts of time in each other's company. Thus the machinations of their relationships are more overt. Similar processes go on with the females but less frequently as females spend most of their time in the presence of their dependent offspring, not with other adults. Also, perhaps even more than for males, the relative status of two females is determined by who is present when they have an aggressive exchange. The presence of a female's siblings or offspring, and their age or sex, greatly effect the outcome of the interaction. However females at Gombe can be ranked as high (with an alpha emerging from this group), middle, and low. The apparent advantage of high rank for a female is increased ability to appropriate desirable food. Thirty-two percent of all aggressive interactions between females took place in the context of feeding (Goodall 1986). For females, a good food supply is linked to reproductive fitness. It is not known whether higher ranking female chimpanzees are more successful mothers. Two aspects of leadership observed among male chimpanzees in these communities, dominance hierarchy and leadership, will be discussed.

Dominance Hierarchy

This is a hierarchy achieved and maintained by dominance of one group member over another. It is measured by superiority in aggressive encounters, order of access to food, mates, resting sites and other objects promoting survivorship and reproductive fitness. Dominance is situation-dependent, varying with which chimpanzees are present during an interaction and the composition of the long term and short term coalitions. However, broad patterns of dominance in relationships exist and are most reliably determined by which chimpanzees pant-grunt to whom. The pant-grunt is a submissive vocalization emitted by the subordinate chimpanzee in an interaction, especially during meetings after time apart. An example of a broad pattern of dominance is the rare intimidation of the community's alpha male by other males, even in coalitions, despite his inability to control all situations.

Benefits of a Dominance Hierarchy

A dominance hierarchy is one of two mechanisms whereby species apportion scarce resources (Wilson 1975). The other is territoriality. Most species evidence dominance hierarchy and/or territoriality. Ecological conditions can influence the expression of these mechanisms. Chimpanzees demonstrate both systems. Between communities, they manage resources by each community holding and defending a territory. Within communities, they manage aggression with dominance hierarchies. The evidence that the dominance hierarchy controls aggression is the escalation in levels of fighting during times of instability of the alpha male position. For example, in 1976 after the alpha lost his clear-cut status there was one attack by an adult male (on any victim) per 103.5 hours of follows of adult males. A follow is a period of observation of a chimpanzee, away from the provisioning area, where the observer follows him wherever he goes. In 1978, when the alpha had regained his position, and dominance relationships were stable the rate dropped to one attack per 261.5 hours. The observed attack rate between males was 2.5 times higher during an unstable dominance hierarchy than in a period of stable dominance relationships. When the dominance hierarchy is stable aggression rates are low, each individual knows his place, and threats frequently take the place of attacks (Goodall 1986).

Chimpanzees mate under three different conditions. A male may take a female away to the edge of the community territory on a consortship and thus monopolize her fertile period. A dominant male may possess a fertile female within the social group and control access to her. Males may mate with the female as she copulates promiscuously with many males, taking their chances on paternity through sperm competition. Comparing the success rates of these three different approaches, Tutin (1980) found that half of fourteen pregnancies between 1966 and 1975 (with a good date on the estrous period of female) occurred during consortships. However, when Goodall (1986) analyzed nineteen conceptions at Gombe occurring from 1976 to 1983, she found that seven took place in consortships, ten in the group setting, and two while the female was staying in a neighboring group. Tutin (1975) found that when Figan was alpha he used the position to monopolize a number of females at their most fertile times. He kept proximity to the female and interrupted others copulating with her. However, Bygott (1974) reports such overt intimidation in sexual contexts to be extremely rare. Some males opt out of competing for fertile females through the dominance hierarchy. They focus instead on being more affiliative with females, grooming them and staying with them when they are not fertile. Later, when the female is fertile, she often chooses to mate with her faithful friend.

At Mahale, Hasegawa and Hiraiwa-Hasegawa (1990) found that five of the six pregnancies in M group (with an identified mating pattern at the time of conception) occurred in the group. Male rank did not correlate with copulation rate, but the alpha male mated with the most fertile females (i.e., parous, resident, ovulating) at an exceptionally high rate. The alphas frequent possessiveness of females near ovulation suggested that his status conferred especially high reproductive success.

The above findings are conflicting and based on matings, not on hard evidence of paternity. Technology now makes determination of paternity possible through genetic typing, recently done for a portion of the Gombe community. Morin et al (1994, Morell 1994) found that the two identifiable fathers were not alpha males. Rather, they were young males on the way up the dominance hierarchy. As more such hard evidence of paternity becomes available it will be interesting to see which males have fathered the most offspring.

Most of the food eaten by chimpanzees is dispersed. So individual chimpanzees space themselves out while feeding. Bygott (1974) found it impossible to determine whether any individuals had access to more food than others. Wrangham (1977) observed competition for food or feeding sites only once per twenty observation hours. Meat is the most prized food among the chimpanzees at Gombe. When a killing occurs chimpanzees distribute the meat by age, who made the kill, and priority of possession of the carcass, rather than dominance rank (Teleki 1973). Dominance rank appears to have little connection with access to food or even preferred food for the chimpanzees of Gombe.

Bygott (1974) found no evidence of any possible selective advantage to being high-ranking. He thought the ability to form clear dominant-subordinate relationships with many individuals (rather than to dominate as many as possible) important as a stress-reducing short-term adaptation. These relationships enable individuals to associate with other group members for purposes of reproduction, defense of range, and sharing of food resources. Goodall (1986) speculates that the chimpanzee, among few creatures, is prepared to expend energy and run risks in seeking high status, not only for material advantages, but for psychological benefits as well.

Characteristics of Dominant Males

Goodall (1986, 1990b) and Bygott (1974) present a number of characteristics of dominant males. Males tend to reach their highest rank in the hierarchy when *age twenty to twenty-six*. Dominant males are *physically fit, aggressive,* and *skilled at fighting*. Dominant males are often *intelligent,* permitting them to be *opportunistic*. For example, despite the general availability of discarded kerosene cans, only one male incorporated them into his charging displays. This technique scared the others into according him dominance. Similarly, another dominant male began his displays in trees above other chimpanzees, and performed them at unexpected times when the others were resting. Dropping into their midst from above at an unusual time increased the effectiveness of his displays. Successful dominant males are *courageous* and *bold* in their aggressive interactions with others. They are also *persistent* and *determined to get their own way*. They appear to *hate being dominated,* and so are *very strongly motivated to dominate their fellows*. The one exception to this pattern appeared to rise to alpha status due to his huge size, irritable temperament, and the small number of adult males in the group at the time. Dominants are *intolerant of disputes among their subordinates*. They have *dominant, highly social mothers*. Offspring acquire the same rank as their mothers, called *dependent rank*. Bygott (1974) assumes the mothers support of their offspring in interactions with others increases the offspring's dominance and thereby their dependent rank. Goodall (1986) gives examples of two males' lack of motivation to improve their rank seeming to correlate with their mothers' shyness and solitariness.

Despite sharing some common attributes, alpha males vary in a number of characteristics. They vary in the frequency and intensity of their aggressive behavior. For example, they exhibit different ratios of display to attack. A display is a form of threat, while an attack actually attempts physical harm. Alpha males differ in their ability to maintain alpha status, including their ability to develop coalitions and to withstand the coalitions of others. They vary also in their course after they lose alpha status. Some quickly plummet to the low ranks. Others gradually lose status as they age. Some remain high in rank until death (Goodall 1986).

Coalitions and Adult Male Relationships

Perhaps the most crucial factor in attaining and preserving high rank is the male's ability to form coalitions with other males. These coalitions can be opportunistic, often composed of senior males against a young challenger.

They can also be stable, long term, mutually supportive, and characterized by a high degree of association. In stable coalitions when a male is in trouble, the other is usually there to help. Typically if one displays the other joins in. Even if the ally doesn't display, his presence seems to provide moral support. Also the association of the allies itself inhibits aggression from other males.

Male chimpanzee relationships are characterized by enduring social bonds, often with siblings. Four of the five alpha males at Gombe since 1961 had a supportive relationship with a known or suspected sibling. The one exception held the alpha position the shortest time, 20 months (Riss and Busse, 1977). Sometimes a male's ally is not a sibling. Then, the association is usually between a high or middle ranking male and a subordinate companion, who is either older or disabled in some way and therefore nonthreatening (Bygott 1974). Interestingly Kawanaka (1990) studied the companions of two succeeding alpha males at Mahale. He found the alphas' partners were usually males declining in dominance rank. The male at Mahale who maintained the most intimate relationships with the two successive alphas was small and outranked by junior males. The highest position in the dominance hierarchy he ever occupied was fifth.

Leadership

Goodall (1986) and Bygott (1974) define leadership as traveling in front of a moving party. Goodall notes, however, that the front one may not be regulating the group's speed and direction of travel. A leader is a chimpanzee who more than others affects the travel patterns of his companions. For example, between 1961 and 1965, one male brought seventy-five per cent of the newcomers to the provisioning and observation area at Gombe. Because of the fluid nature of relationships in a chimpanzee community there is no single overall leader. This is a position neither achieved, nor maintained, by aggressive interactions.

Bygott (1974) and Goodall (1986) both describe characteristics of leaders. They are *not overly aggressive* yet are *self-confident*, and *when thwarted determined to get their own way*. Leaders are *calm, tolerant*, and *quick to reach out and reassure nervous or fearful subordinates*. Their *quiet approach and grooming often relaxes aroused high-ranking males*. Bygott found leadership more correlated with age than dominance, with leaders *more often being the senior member of the party*.

Bygott (1974) found no one individual invariably leading, but the most frequent leaders were *mid-ranking males*, and one young high-ranking male. This young male could initiate group travel by setting off with a brisk and purposeful walk. Nishida, (1970) looking at leadership at Mahale, found it associated with dominance. However, dominance more often correlated with age at Mahale. The literature review didn't reveal any conjecture about the benefits of leadership for the individual or the group.

Summary

1. It is not possible to compare the Gombe study community under different alpha males. The provisioning of the chimpanzees, the gradual isolation of Gombe National Park (that changed the density levels of the chimpanzees and the availability of escape), plus other possible ecological changes, make time periods under different alpha males incomparable.

2. Male chimpanzees are more social than females, who spend most of their time alone with their dependent offspring. Consequently, this paper looks at leadership among males, where there is more interaction to observe. Similar, less frequent processes occur among females and are affected more by the presence of kin during aggressive interactions.

3. Dominance hierarchies function to control aggression. Levels of fighting escalate during times of instability of the alpha male position.

4. Evidence about reproductive advantage conveyed by the alpha male position is conflicting. Researchers found monopolization of fertile females by one alpha male. Findings on where the most conceptions occur conflict, suggesting both consortships and the group situation. All this research is based on observation of matings rather than genetic paternity. Genotyping of the study group at Gombe established paternity for only two individuals. Both fathers were young males on their way up the dominance hierarchy.

5. There is little direct competition for food and it is difficult to determine whether any individual has access to more food than others. When a killing occurs, the meat, a prized food, is distributed by age, who made the kill, and priority of possession of the carcass, rather than by dominance rank.

6. Bygott suggests the ability to form clear dominant-subordinate relationships with many individuals (rather than to dominate as many as possible) is an important stress-reducing short-term adaptation. These relationships enable individuals to associate with other group members for purposes of reproduction, defense of range, and sharing of food resources.

7. Goodall speculates the psychological benefits of dominance may motivate chimpanzees to seek high rank.

8. Goodall and Bygott present a number of characteristics of dominant males: young adult age, physical fitness, aggressiveness, skill at fighting, intelligence, opportunism, courage, boldness, persistence, determination to get their own way, hating to be dominated, intensely strong motivation to dominate their fellows, intolerance of disputes among their subordinates, and high dependent rank conferred by dominant, highly social mothers.

9. Alpha males vary in their frequency and intensity of aggressive behavior, ability to maintain alpha position, build coalitions, and withstand others coalitions, and their course in the dominance ranks after losing alpha position.

10. Perhaps the most crucial factor in attaining and preserving high rank is the males' ability to form coalitions with other males. These coalitions can be opportunistic or stable. Stable coalitions are long term, mutually supportive, and characterized by a high degree of association.

11. Male chimpanzee relationships are characterized by enduring social bonds, often with siblings. Four of the five alpha males at Gombe since 1961 had a supportive relationship with a known or suspected sibling. The one exception held the alpha position the shortest time. When a male's ally is not a sibling the association is usually between a high or middle ranking male and a subordinate companion who is either older or disabled in some way, and therefore nonthreatening.

12. Goodall and Bygott define leadership as traveling in front of a moving party. A leader is a chimpanzee who more than others affects the travel patterns of his companions. This is a position not achieved, or maintained, by agressive interactions.

13. Leaders are not overly aggressive yet are self-confident, determined to get their own way when thwarted, calm, tolerant, quick to reach out and reassure nervous or fearful subordinates, senior to others in the party, generally males of middle rank, and quiet when approaching and grooming others (thereby often relaxing aroused high-ranking males).

14. The characteristics of dominant males and leaders are not the same.

Discussion

The major findings about leadership among the male chimpanzees of Gombe raise interesting points when held up against Bowen family systems theory. Both types of leadership, dominance and leading the group in travel, appear to be products of the emotional system (as described by Bowen) and to have aspects of togetherness and individuality. This is consistent with Bowen theory that postulates both forces existing in nature in varying proportions in different individuals and groups. The variation in the functioning of alpha males both during and after the time they hold alpha status is consistent with the concept of the scale of differentiation. The differences in the characteristics of dominant males and leaders raise an interesting question. Are both or one or the other correlated with higher level of differentiation of self?

Both types of leadership appear to be useful for individuals and the group. However most analysis in the field of animal behavior has been at the level of the individual and specifically informed by sociobiological theory. Sociobiology uses reproductive fitness of the individual as a criterion of success.

Leadership can be looked at as group phenomenon and as affected by the ecological context of the group. For example, dominance hierarchies function to control aggression. Bowen theory focuses on the anxiety level of the group and the leader as important variables for understanding what unfolds between them.

The dominance hierarchy is always there in the chimpanzee community. The tone of the dominance interactions varies from quiet to excitedly exaggerated. The frequency of aggressive interactions over dominance also varies. Some equate dominance hierarchies in non-human primates with hierarchies in general. It seems that administrative hierarchies function with a variable level of dominance status jockeying, depending on the level of differentiation of the organization, and the individuals leading and comprising it.

Dominance and differentiation of self are not equivalent. In this vein Bygott's hypothesis seems important. He speculates that the ability to form clear dominant-subordinate relationships with many individuals, rather than to dominate as many as possible, is important as a stress-reducing short-term adaptation. This ability to carve out a clear spot in the dominance hierarchy, provided the spot is not too compromised, might correlate with level of differentiation better than dominance rank. Goodall's speculation that chimpanzees may be motivated to seek high rank by the psychological benefits of dominance is important. Do the alpha males vary in their dependence on being the top chimpanzee for a feeling of psychological well-being? Do some alpha males emerge naturally and others claw their way to the top? A careful study of the five alpha males in the history of research at Gombe might elucidate some of these points.

Relationships are very important in achieving and maintaining dominance. The descriptions of coalitions and their machinations could have been written by Bowen as he developed the concept of the triangle. Family relationships with siblings, or for females with offspring, are very important in the outcomes of aggressive interactions. Family relationships among chimpanzees persist until death or emigration and form a natural support network for each individual. Relationships with nonfamily members can also bolster functioning. High or mid ranking males without sibling allies often have coalitions with older or disabled low ranking males. As described these sound like reciprocal one up/one down relationships that elevate the functioning of the higher ranking male of the pair and provide protection to the lower ranking male.

In summary, there are a number of interesting illustrations of Bowen family systems theory reported in the literature about leadership among the Gombe chimpanzees. It is an assumption of Bowen theory that the basic processes operating in the human are not discontinuous with those operating in other life forms including the chimpanzee.

REFERENCES

Bygott, J. David. 1974. "Agonistic Behaviour and Dominance Among Wild Chimpanzees." A paper presented at the Burg Wartenstein Symposium No. 62, entitled *The Behavior of Great Apes*, July 20-28.

Calhoun, John B. 1962. "Population Density and Social Pathology." *Scientific American*, 206: 46-58.

Goodall, Jane. 1986. *The Chimpanzees of Gombe*. Cambridge, Massachusetts: The Belknap Press of Harvard University Press.

———. 1990a. "Area Status Report: Tanzania." In *Understanding Chimpanzees*. Paul G. Heltne and Linda A. Marquardt, eds. Cambridge, Massachusetts: Harvard University Press.

———. 1990b. *Through a Window*. Boston: Houghton Mifflin Company.

Hasegawa, Toshikazu and Hiraiwa-Hasegawa, Mariko. 1990. "Sperm Competition and Mating Behavior." In *The Chimpanzees of the Mahale Mountains*, 115-132. Toshisada Nishida, ed. Tokyo: University of Tokyo Press.

Kerr, Kathleen B. 1978. "Density and Social Pathology: In Mice and Man." In Georgetown *Family Symposia*, 77-97. Ruth Riley Sagar, ed. Washington, DC: Georgetown University.

Kawanaka. Kenji. 1990. "Alpha Males' Interactions and Social Skills." In *The Chimpanzees of the Mahale Mountains*, 171-187. Toshisada Nishida, ed. Tokyo: University of Tokyo Press.

Morell, Virginia. 1994. "Decoding Chimp Genes and Lives." *Science*, 265: 1172-1173.

Morin, Phillip A.; James J. Moore, Ranajit Chakraborty, Li Jin, Jane Goodall, David S. Woodruff. 1994. "Kin Selection, Social Structure, Gene Flow, and the Evolution of Chimpanzees." *Science*, 265: 1193-1201.

Nishida, Toshisada. 1970. "Social Behaviour and Relationships Among Wild Chimpanzees of the Mahale Mountains." *Primates*, 11: 47-87.

Riss, David C. and Busse, Curt D. 1977. "Fifty-Day Observation of a Free-Ranging Adult Male Chimpanzee." *Folia Primatologia*, 28: 283-297.

Tutin, Caroline E. G. 1975. Mating Patterns and Reproductive Strategies in a Community of Wild Chimpanzees. *Behavioral Ecology and Sociobiology*, 6:29-38.

Tutin, Caroline E. G. 1980. "Reproductive Behaviour of Wild Chimpanzees in the Gombe National Park, Tanzania." *Journal of Reproduction & Fertility*, 28: 43-57.

Teleki, Geza. 1973. *The Predatory Behavior of Wild Chimpanzees*. Lewisburg: Bucknell University Press.

Wilson, Edward O. 1975. *Sociobiology*. Cambridge, Massachusetts: The Belknap Press of Harvard University Press.

Wrangham, Richard. 1974. "Artificial Feeding of Chimpanzees and Baboons in Their Natural Habitat." *Animal Behavior*, 22:83-93.

Wrangham, Richard. 1977. "Feeding Behaviour of Chimpanzees in Gombe National Park, Tanzania." In *Primate Ecology*. Timothy H. Clutton-Brock. ed. New York: Academic Press.

LESSONS FROM NATURE ON LEADERSHIP

Stephanie J. Ferrera, MSW

A leader is one who directs, commands or guides a group, one who goes first and shows the way. Leaders are thought of as individuals who stand apart from the crowd, possess a greater vision or sense of direction than others, and have strong influence on others. From an individual perspective, central questions about leadership are: What qualities make an individual a leader? What does an effective leader do? What is his or her leadership style?

From a systems perspective, the focus is less on the person of the leader and more on the functional state of the system and the functional position of the leader within the system. Looking at an organization as an emotional system, we can describe its functional states, past and present, on continua ranging from calm to anxious, from orderly to chaotic, from stable to unstable. The central questions are: What kind of leadership is the organization producing? How is it selecting its leaders? How is it supporting or undermining its leaders? The quality of leadership and the way the organization selects and responds to leaders are measures of emotional process in the organization and indicators of whether it is headed in a progressive or regressive direction.

This paper is based on three premises. The first is that humans are animals and can take many "lessons from nature," from other species of animals, in understanding social behavior and leadership. Second, hierarchical modes of organization are widespread, if not universal, in the animal world. John T. Bonner states that all social animals form peck orders (Bonner 1993). Following from these two premises, the third is that humans are instinctually hierarchical creatures. Much human intelligence and energy is devoted to pursuing social status, to creating ever more elaborate status symbols, and to monitoring the signals, be they subtle or blatant, through which rank is maintained or altered.

Biological Views of Social Hierarchies

Edward O. Wilson, Robert Sapolsky, Robert Trivers, Frans de Waal, Sandra Vehrencamp and Barbara Smuts are biologists who have described different types of hierarchies and the conditions under which they evolve. Wilson defines the social hierarchy, also called the dominance order, as the set of sustained aggressive-submissive relations among an organized group of animals sharing a territory (1975). The hierarchy serves the important function of enabling a group to share a territory with minimal hostility and conflict. The stable hierarchy is advantageous to varying degrees to all group members. The group benefits from the leadership and protection provided by the dominant and from relative harmony and order. High-ranking members clearly benefit by having superior access to resources and they routinely displace subordinates from food, mates and nesting sites. Subordinates have a more marginal existence yet, as Wilson points out, there are "compensations" in being subordinate. These include the safety of being part of a group, the attachment to close kin within the group, and the chance for future upward mobility. Pressures on subordinate members give them an impetus to move up in the hierarchy or to move out. The behavioral ontogenies of species seem designed to give each loser a second chance, and in some of the more social forms the subordinate need only wait its turn to rise in the hierarchy. The most frequent recourse, from insects to monkeys, is emigration (Wilson 1975).

The hierarchy is established in the initial period of group formation. Through threats and fights, the members discover the relative strength of each. Wilson states:

> When a group is newly constituted, such as a group of hens or rhesus monkeys thrown together in an enclosure, the initial dominance orders tend to be established on the basis of size, strength and aggression. But later the more personal and experiential factors assert themselves as well. (1975, 143)

In species with greater brain size and more flexible behavior, dominance chains are more complex and numerous factors, beyond size, strength and aggression, enter into the determination of rank. These determinants include the status of one's parents, maternal influence, coalitions and protectorates. Robert Sapolsky describes the social reality for baboons in the Serengeti:

> A dominance hierarchy exists with markedly different degrees of access to all sorts of resources: food, a safe place when predators are near, a shady spot during the day's heat, someone to groom them or mate with them. What goes into attaining a high rank and then maintaining it? Among female baboons, rank is inherited; you get a rank one below that of your mother or, if one exists, your older sister. Among males, rank changes over time. The high-ranking male is typically of prime age, in good health, with an impressive array of muscles and a terrifying set of canines. But dominance among the males is not merely a matter of being good at fighting. These are far more sophisticated animals than that, and much of what they do falls into the realm of what must be described as psychologically stressing each other—intimidating someone with just the start of a threatening gesture until he gives up, forming a cooperative partnership with another male, . . . harassing another male's sexual relationships with a female—no overt fighting or threatening, just relentlessly shadowing the guy until you so wear him down that he gives up the consortship. (1994, 259-60)

When the group is in a stable, peaceful state, there is little visible aggression and order is maintained with subtle "status" cues such as postures, gestures and acoustical and chemical signals. However, under the calm surface, there is potential for violence which can be triggered in various ways including the arrival of an outsider who threatens the group, signs of aging or weakness in leaders, or a challenge to a leader by a lower-ranking member.

Types of Hierarchy. Wilson delineates three forms of hierarchy: despotic, linear and circular. In despotism, one individual rules over all others and there are no rank distinctions between the subordinates. Absolute despotisms are relatively rare in nature. Insect colonies are one example. In primitive colonies, one female, the queen, dominates all other adults through physical coercion. In more advanced colonies, the queen dominates without overt aggression through use of pheromones which inhibit the development and reproductive functioning of immature colony members.

Linear hierarchies are more common. Here, there are multiple ranks in a more or less linear sequence: an alpha individual dominates all others, beta dominates all but alpha, and so on down the line. The pecking order of chickens is a well-known example. The paper wasp is another. Adult female paper wasps gather to found nests, and after an initial period of intense struggle, a linear hierarchy emerges. One indicator of rank is the size of ovaries; experiments have shown that a female paper wasp's ovaries will grow or shrink as she rises or falls in rank order. Another indicator is egg production; the dominant female lays most of the eggs and eats more of other females' eggs than subordinates (Wilson 1975; Trivers 1985).

The third type of hierarchy contains circular or triangular elements which make group social life more complex and unpredictable, and in Wilson's view, make these systems less stable and efficient than linear orders (1975). A key feature of the circular hierarchy is the reliance of dominant individuals on the support of others to maintain high rank. One member alone cannot maintain dominance, at least not for long. Cooperation is essential to success, and relationships operate more as two-way streets of give-and-take, and less as one-way streets of dominants taking, subordinates giving.

The work of Frans de Waal with chimpanzees is rich with descriptions of the cooperative strategies which mark the more sophisticated society. The Arnhem Zoo colony was dominated for many years by the coalition between Nikkie, a young, strong male, and Yeroen, an older, more experienced male. When the two occasionally fought, the crack in their united front was evident and a third male, Luit, would quickly seize the opportunity to challenge. Luit would stir up the group by terrorizing females and making bold displays toward Nikkie and Yeroen. With this threat, the two leaders would quickly reconcile, Nikkie would display to Luit, and Luit would retreat back to his subordinate position. Other colony members, especially Mama, the female leader, played their parts in mediating disputes and cementing relations between Nikkie and Yeroen, thus keeping the coalition in place and the colony at peace (de Waal 1989).

A Continuum of Social Hierarchies. How have different forms of hierarchy evolved? Sandra Vehrencamp addresses this question in her model for the evolution of despotic versus egalitarian societies (Vehrencamp 1983). Vehrencamp is interested in delineating conditions in group living which would promote individuals interacting in despotic modes as opposed to conditions which would promote egalitarian interaction. She defines an egalitarian society as one in which benefits are divided roughly equally or in proportion to the risk or effort taken, and a despotic society as one in which benefits accrue disproportionately to a few individuals at the expense of others. She uses the term "bias" to describe the degree to which groups operate for the benefit of the dominants. In despotic or strongly biased groups, dominants are able to coerce subordinates so that dominants accrue most of the benefits and control most of the resources. In egalitarian or slightly biased groups, there is still a hierarchy but the difference between top and bottom ranking members is much reduced.

Vehrencamp looked at a broad range of animals including birds, social canids and felids, mongooses, and social anthropods. A similar picture emerged across diverse taxa. Within each taxa, some species have evolved with more despotically organized societies and other species have evolved with more egalitarian societies. The common feature of despotic societies is that nonbreeding auxiliaries, helpers-at-the-nest or -den, who are usually offspring or relatives of the breeding pair, are retained in their natal territories to help feed and protect the breeders' offspring, even though they are physiologically capable of breeding on their own. The common feature of the egalitarian societies is that communal territories or nests are occupied by groups of breeding adults who share in the care of offspring.

What are the conditions which determine the degree of bias within groups? Vehrencamp sees a combination of ecological factors and kinship as the answer. The ecological factors are: (1) the cost of dispersing and (2) the relative benefit of group living vs. solitary living. The cost of dispersing is related to the availability of alternative habitats and the risks of entering a new group (probably as a subordinate). The benefits of group living include reduced risk of predation, improved foraging success and greater reproductive efficiency. The kinship factor, or degree of relatedness among group members, has a large impact on the degree of bias. When the degree of genetic relatedness is high, a high degree of bias becomes possible, especially when dispersal options for subordinates are poor. Parents may dominate offspring to stay in the parental unit and help raise siblings, and offspring will do so to the extent that this strategy maximizes the overall reproductive success of the family unit.

To summarize Vehrencamp's point, many variables affect the benefits of staying in the group and the options for leaving the group. The balance between the two is what establishes the limits of biasing or the degree to which the group functions as despotic or egalitarian.

In a comment on Vehrencamp's work, Barbara Smuts (1993) has framed the despotic/egalitarian continuum in terms of individuality and togetherness. She observes that human societies, historically and in the present, cover the spectrum from highly despotic to more egalitarian. In more despotic societies, the options for individuation are limited. These are "togetherness" societies insofar as members are forced to serve the interests of those who dominate. These societies function based on the imposition of a certain way of being by certain individuals on others. The constraints on individuals to pursue their own interests are related to their having few options to leave. In more egalitarian societies, dominants, in order to reap the rewards of group living, must allow increasing individuation for other members. Therefore, the society operates as a cooperative unit based on all individuals asserting their self-interest and gaining something back from the process of group interaction. The constraint on dominant individuals in promoting their interests at the expense of others is related to the options others have to leave and form a new group.

Social Hierarchies as Emotional Systems

Biologists have identified all of the features that constitute an emotional field. They have seen the functional interrelatedness among group members, the regular, predictable patterns of interaction, the degree to which signaling and responsiveness among group members influences the behavior of each, and they have seen that this signal-response system almost always results in animals organizing themselves in hierarchical modes. However, they have not conceptualized the group as an emotional unit or emotional system.

The conceptualization of a group as an *emotional system* is an original contribution of Murray Bowen (1978). The organism which Bowen studied, the human family, is arguably the organism best suited for such a discovery. To all appearances, the family is a collective of separate individuals, bound together by the ties of blood and marriage, yet each of its members guided by a unique, individual personality, motivation and sense of direction. What Bowen was able to see, first through observation of himself and the extent to which his own thoughts and feelings were affected by contact with family and colleagues, and later through long-term, structured research (1978), was that these seemingly autonomous individuals were in fact so profoundly responsive to one another and so strongly influenced by the emotional field of family relationships that they were, functionally, an emotional system. The behavior of each person could be understood far better when seen in the context of the system than it could be by seeing that person as a separate individual.

In looking at social behavior, Bowen introduced a variable which is related to all the variables described in the biological literature but is different. Simply put, this variable is *anxiety*. Bowen defined anxiety as *emotional reactivity to a real or perceived threat* (Kerr and Bowen 1988). In his study of human families, Bowen observed significant differences among families in their level of anxiety or emotional reactivity as they dealt with life's stresses. He saw the level of anxiety as related to the number and severity of stressors the family was dealing with, and also to the family's *level of differentiation*. The level of differentiation is a product of the way the family balances the force for *togetherness* with the force for *individuality* (Bowen 1978, Kerr and Bowen 1988). Better differentiated families are those in which togetherness is not overly intense, and there is room for the members to develop and operate as relatively autonomous individuals. The result is a relatively calm family that is able to deal realistically and effectively with stressors. In poorly differentiated families, the togetherness pressures are more intense, leaving less room for members to function as separate individuals. The result is a more anxious family that has greater difficulty dealing with stressors.

This author proposes that looking at social hierarchies from the perspective of Bowen theory adds greatly to our understanding of hierarchical behavior in humans and other animals. Bowen theory would view the hierarchy as an emotional system. The variables which govern emotional systems—level of anxiety and level of differentiation—interplay with the variables defined by biologists to determine whether the hierarchy will be more or less "biased," more or less stable, more or less orderly, more or less beneficial to its members. In looking at the hierarchy as an emotional system, one focuses on the emotional process among the members, the level of intensity of that process, and the degree to which that process influences the shaping of the hierarchy. A continuum of social hierarchies as emotional systems would place the highly anxious group at one end, and the relatively calm group at the other. Following is an attempt to contrast the two polarities and to suggest how the interplay of variables might work in each.

The Highly Anxious Social Hierarchy. At this end of the continuum, the social hierarchy functions like a highly anxious family. In a climate of intense togetherness, people's behavior is guided less by thoughtfulness and more by reactivity among group members. Struggles for dominance can be fierce. Leaders have difficulty maintaining their position. Leadership by popularity and accommodation is one approach. Leadership by coercive control is another. When leaders employ despotic, coercive tactics, subordinate members, in turn, become extremely submissive to survive within the status quo or take high risks to challenge it. The level of anxiety is expected to increase when opportunities for subordinate members to leave the group are few or nonexistent. As those at the top are overtaken and replaced by new dominants, the periodic voids of leadership cause attendant confusion. During the periods of instability, individuals and subgroups vie for the upper hand, often producing a forceful leader. The group seeks a hierarchical leader who will take control and produce order quickly. The reactive group puts pressure on leaders for quick solutions, but at the same time opposes any initiative taken by the leaders. It becomes increasingly difficult to lead. The group goes through cycles of despotism when tyrannical leaders are in place, and chaos when no leaders are in place.

In a despotic system, rigidity and stratification work against stability and cohesiveness. Severe emotional cutoff and projection process mark the relationships between dominant and subordinate members. The emotional climate is one of mistrust, fear and vigilance. Even when resources are adequate or plentiful, people behave, like Sapolsky's baboons, as though there is not enough to go around. There is little opportunity for individuals at widely different social strata to associate, come to know one another as human beings, and find common interests. Although dominant members enjoy disproportionate control and consumption of resources, their position is one of uneasy and uncertain privilege purchased at a price of having to police and control others.

The analyses of both Vehrencamp and Smuts point to dominant members as having greater influence than subordinates in determining the level of bias in the hierarchy. As long as dominants maintain control through aggressive, coercive tactics, and as long as subordinates have no exit, do subordinates have any choice but to submit or risk injury or death by opposing? Historically and in the present, many human societies have reached extreme levels of despotism or bias, and it appears that dominant members and their allies have, indeed, played the greater part in creating and perpetuating such systems. The reciprocal behaviors of subordinates, and their role in maintaining the system, are less obvious and merit further study.

From the perspective of the emotional system, dominance and subordinance are viewed as reciprocal, mutually reinforcing modes of relating. The process is two-sided though the two sides do not in all cases have equal influence on the outcome. Just as dominants force subordinates to be subordinate, so also do subordinates force dominants to be dominant. When the hierarchy is viewed as an emotional system, the question, "Who has the upper hand?" becomes more complex. If dominance is defined as the ability to evoke a response from others and influence their behavior, then it is often the "weakest" or poorest functioning members of the group who are dominant. Every parent knows the ability of children to dominate. The least mature members can become the focal point of a group or whole society, forcing the group to be responsible for them. Immature, poor functioning members, whether they be high or low in social rank, have considerable ability to bias a group, consuming a disproportionate share of the resources and exerting pressure on others to serve their interests.

As the dysfunctional extremes of the hierarchical process begin to outweigh the functional side, the adaptive benefits are lost. Presumably, the social hierarchy has evolved in nature because it functions so effectively to achieve order and stability and to reduce overt conflict. However, the buildup of stress and emotional reactivity in a group can push that group beyond its adaptive capacities. The unit has then become an anxiety-driven, anxiety-producing organism. Enlightened leadership is greatly needed, but the group's ability to produce and support such leadership is poor.

The Calm Social Hierarchy. At the optimum end of the spectrum, the hierarchy behaves like a well-functioning family in its better moments. This group "knows" that the territory is big enough for all and behaves in a way that encourages each member to claim his or her niche as both a contributor and a beneficiary. The system is flexible. Thoughtfulness predominates over automatic emotional reactivity. The emotional climate is one of relative freedom for individuals within an orderly context. There is room for each member to take charge of resources, roles, tasks and decisions based on his or her individual needs, strengths and competencies. The group functions in ways to combine the best features of hierarchy—stability, order and harmony—with the best features of egalitarian society—cooperation and mutual benefits.

Rank order exists but is linked to the diverse levels of responsibility and contribution among the members rather than to their ability to dominate others. The distance between high and low ranking is not great. Relationships among members are based more on mutual respect and exchange of benefits and less on rank order. Roberta Gilbert views equality as a natural outgrowth of relationships among calm, well-differentiated people:

> In a high-level relationship, equality does not have to be worked at, it is just there. That equality is not based on tallying up individual assets; rather, it is a relationship stance, a posture assumed by the individuals. Each accepts the other as no more and no less talented, responsible, or free than him-

> or herself. Respect for the other, so often pointed to as essential for relationship success, is based on the equal posture. (1992, 103)

People do not work at equality *per se*; people work at high-level relationships and equality follows. Central to this work is the toning down of automatic behaviors on both the dominant and subordinate sides. People work at monitoring and containing both the impulse to dictate to others and the impulse to lean on others for direction.

In the flexible, egalitarian system, there is room for numerous leaders. The quality of relationships is such that ideas are communicated openly, creative thinking is stimulated by this exchange of ideas, and energy is freed for productive work. Leadership is determined not by dominance struggles but by the willingness of individuals to come forward and take responsibility for areas of group functioning or take initiative in developing new endeavors. "Followership" is determined not by coercion but by interest in and cooperation with goals, plans and projects within the group.

Bowen's Model for High-Functioning Organizations: A Collection of Individuals

Murray Bowen developed a concept or model for high-functioning organizations based on his knowledge of emotional process. The broad spectrum of human social functioning and social hierarchies presented in this paper provides a context for looking at Bowen's model. This context allows us to appreciate how unusual this kind of organization is and to understand what it takes to create and maintain it.

Dr. Bowen believed that an organization would do best when it functioned as a collection of individuals. He distinguished between a collection of individuals and a group. In a group, emotional process is always operating to greater or lesser degree. Groups are vulnerable to disruption or disintegration because emotional process will always do somebody in, or if it gets intense enough, will do in the whole operation. A collection of individuals, in contrast to a group, is relatively free of emotional process and interaction works to support individual functioning, to spur each person to go further than he or she could go alone (Papero 1993 and 1994).

An organization operating as a collection of individuals has the characteristics of a calm hierarchy functioning at an optimum level. It retains the benefits of a hierarchy while minimizing the costs. It takes dominance out of the dominance order. Order is achieved without people behaving in dominant or subordinate modes. It is difficult for people to sustain this way of relating, and can only be done with consistent effort and considerable self-awareness, and perhaps only under reasonably favorable conditions.

The Georgetown Family Center, founded by Dr. Bowen, has made an effort to operate as a collection of individuals. Dr. Bowen arrived at Georgetown University Department of Psychiatry in 1959 and started the family program. The Family Center moved off-campus in 1975, and Bowen headed it until his death in 1990.

He brought his knowledge of emotional systems to his position as director and focused primarily on differentiation of self in his own functioning as leader. In "Toward the Differentiation of Self in Administrative Systems," published in 1974, he wrote:

> At Georgetown I have utilized knowledge and experience from research, theory and the practice of family therapy in my effort to function on the best possible level of differentiation. The Georgetown Family Faculty and . . . training programs have grown slowly around me since 1959. This is the kind of an administrative system that is most vulnerable to becoming involved in all kinds of emotional alliances and intense emotional processes that would make it more like a family. A good percentage of such organizations do not continue for many months or years before there are major splits and disruptions in the central organization . . . . It has been a fascinating challenge to me to find a way toward a reasonable level of differentiation among professional colleagues, who are far more important to me than most employees would be in other situations. . . .The goal is to be as much of a "self" as is possible for me, and to permit the others as much latitude as possible toward developing their selfs. . . .

Several years later Dr. Bowen observes that he found himself focusing on problems in the staff and offering solutions with the result that the staff became increasingly dependent on him.

> It was then that I discovered I was being overresponsible for the staff in some areas, and that I was in fact being irresponsible in my own functioning in other areas. My effort went into clarification of my responsibility as head of the research, and functioning responsibly there, without assuming responsibility for others. Very quickly I learned that if there was an emotional issue in the organization, I was playing a part in it, and if I could modify the part I was playing, the others would do the same. (1978, 462-463)

Since Dr. Bowen's death, his successor, Michael Kerr, and the faculty and staff of the Family Center have continued the effort to operate as a collection of individuals. In conversations with this writer, Daniel Papero, Director of Training at the Family Center, has described how this effort has played out, including its strengths and pitfalls. From these conversations, some basic principles emerge. The intention here is not to focus on the details of the Georgetown Family Center, which are specific and somewhat idiosyncratic to that organization, but to abstract from the experience of the Family Center some general principles which may be useful to organizations interested in pursuing an individuality-based way of operating.

Responsibility for self. This is the wellspring from which all else flows. The organization will run only if each member accepts responsibility for dealing with whatever problems or opportunities he or she sees. Part of this is taking responsibility for defining one's own interests and tasks; a more difficult part is taking responsibility for one's own emotional functioning. In Dr. Bowen's example, he recognized that his emotional functioning, in the form of overresponsibility, was promoting dependence on the part of the staff, and his response was to shift focus from the staff to his own job. In Papero's words:

What sustains the organization, and what is always its potential Achilles' heel, is that the atmosphere can only be maintained by everyone doing their best to respect boundaries, to work on responsibility for self, and to work on autonomy. The Achilles' heel is the tremendous pressure to let it slip and let someone else carry the load. That is a daily struggle.

Open communication. Dr. Papero gives this description of communication at the Family Center: "Meetings are held and a lot is discussed. It appears that no decision is ever made and yet things happen. In that interactional sequence, there is something tremendously motivating. You learn so much from other people." When the collection of individuals is working well, it appears that communication operates as a cross-fertilization of ideas and information that stimulates further ideas. Open communication keeps people informed of one another's interests and work, leading to opportunities for collaboration among those with common interests.

Open communication is work. It is sustained only as long as people define their own thinking and find a way of saying it that allows others to hear, and only as long as others listen. A danger is people's tendency to bury disagreements or gloss over them. Dr. Bowen had a simple rule; he didn't care what you thought, but he wanted you to say it so it didn't go underground.

Flexible structure. The organization has a director and other defined leaders, but these individuals do not order others to do anything. People see what needs to be done and do it. At the same time, there is a wide latitude of choice in what people do. The orderly but free atmosphere encourages individuals to pursue their interests, initiate projects, and contribute to projects initiated by others. The pitfall here is that, when anxiety increases, people will look to the leader to be a hierarchical leader and tell them what to do.

Motivation fueled by autonomy. The level of motivation and energy is similar to that of people who work for themselves. The benefits and the pitfalls are also similar. In a collection of individuals, people make their own decisions and carry their own consequences.

A unity of vision defined by individuals. The Family Center recently worked on a mission statement. Each person, from the new secretary just out of college to the senior staff who had been there for years, sat down privately and put down his or her view of the mission. When the statements came in, there was variation yet consistency. The basic principles were the same for everybody. There was a kind of unity of vision, and within that, each person spelled out his or her own mission.

All of these principles are based on the ability and willingness of people to monitor and modify emotional process. Emotional process is ever-present in humans, including those who attempt to function as a collection of individuals. Automatic reactivity leads to submerging differences in togetherness—"We must all pull together"—or the opposite, reacting emotionally to differences and breaking contact. The great challenge is to express differences and, at the same time, stay in fundamental contact with one another. This is the essence of differentiation of self. The collection of individuals calls on its participants to have knowledge of emotional process, the ability to observe it in the organization, the ability to see it within self, and the commitment to manage it as responsibly as possible.

REFERENCES

Bonner, John T. 1993. *Life Cycles.* Princeton, NJ: Princeton University Press.

Bowen, Murray. 1974. "Toward the Differentiation of Self in Administrative Systems." *Georgetown Family Symposia Volume I.* J. Lorio and Louise McClenathan, eds. Georgetown University Medical Center.

———. 1978. *Family Therapy in Clinical Practice.* New York: Jason Aronson.

de Waal, Frans. 1989. *Peacemaking among Primates.* Cambridge, MA: Harvard University Press.

Gilbert, Roberta. 1992. *Extraordinary Relationships.* Minneapolis, MN: Chronimed.

Kerr, Michael E. and Murray Bowen. 1988. *Family Evaluation.* New York: W. W. Norton.

Papero, Daniel, with Stephanie Ferrera. 1993 and 1994. Interviews on Leadership. Chicago: Center for Family Consultation.

Sapolsky, Robert. 1994. *Why Zebras Don't Get Ulcers.* New York: W. H. Freeman.

Smuts, Barbara. 1993. Comment made at conference June 19-20, 1993: *Marriage: Differentiation and Togetherness.* Georgetown Family Center, Washington, DC.

Trivers, Robert. 1985. *Social Evolution.* Menlo Park, CA: Benjamin/Cummings.

Vehrencamp, Sandra. 1983. "A Model for the Evolution of Despotic versus Egalitarian Societies." *Animal Behavior,* 31:667-682.

Wilson, Edward O. 1975. *Sociobiology.* (Abridged edition). Cambridge, Massachusetts: The Belknap Press of Harvard University Press.

A NATURAL SYSTEMS VIEW OF HIERARCHY

Roberta M. Gilbert, MD

Hierarchy, a body of entities arranged in a graded series, is observed in many different species. It is an emotional or instinctual organizational pattern of groups. Some of the descriptions of hierarchical behavior—the relationship behaviors between individuals that lead to a hierarchical group formation—in different species were focused on by Price and Sloman (1987).

Lorenz described *ritual agonistic behavior* (RAB) as a form of signaling between two individuals to create, readjust, or reinforce asymmetry of behavior resulting in an agreed-upon winner and loser. There is a need for recognized winners and losers in a group since a symmetrical behavioral relationship has a potential for escalating conflict and thus, the instability of the group. These "asymmetrical relationships" in a matrix form a social hierarchy (Price and Sloman 1987).

Dawkins refers to the yielding (submissive, subordinate) component of "RAB" as a "yielding subroutine." "Hardware" for this behavior has been located in the "reptilian" brain by MacLean who, by ablating various portions of the brain, pinpointed areas that control specific functions (Price and Sloman 1987).

Schjelderup-Ebbe's pecking order in birds is well known (Price and Sloman 1987). It is a hierarchical arrangement where there is one bird that no others peck that can peck any of the others. The second bird in the hierarchy is pecked by only that one, does not peck the top one, but can peck all the others, and so on down the line.

DeWaal has described hierarchy and the behaviors by which it is identified in studies of chimpanzees at the Arnhem Zoo. He classified and compared 15 behavioral variables stemming from agonistic and competitive interactions. These included nine agonistic variables such as the "rapid oh-oh," nonvocal bluff, kissing, and grooming. He also studied two behaviors not considered agonistic which he thought could be considered evidence of a pecking order or hierarchy in the group. He called these "self evident indisputable rights" such as "competition-space" (approach-retreat, or avoidance) and "competition-social" (refraining from contact with a partner because another chimp takes up contact with that individual) (deWaal 1980).

DeWaal also studied phenomena related to hierarchical reciprocity in three different primate species—chimpanzees, rhesus monkeys, and stumptail monkeys. He watched for interactions of revenge and found a complex picture characterized by different types and degrees of hierarchical behavior in different species. While the monkeys could be relied upon not to take revenge upon an individual of higher rank after an "agonistic intervention" (an aggressive behavior), chimpanzees had subtle and sometimes complex ways of retaliating against their superiors. There was, for example, "a democratic tendency in chimpanzee society." Individuals of lower status seem to try to influence the configuration at the top of the hierarchy. Middle-ranking individuals direct a disproportionate amount of their interventions at conflicts among individuals positioned above them. In this class, there was considerable female involvement in status struggles among dominant males. In social interactions such as grooming, the monkeys showed more asymmetry in these behaviors, and thus, a more rigid hierarchical society than did the chimpanzees who tended to reciprocate more in grooming (deWaal 1988).

Hierarchy in the Human Species

Examples of human hierarchies are plentiful. Some of the more prominent include churches and military services. They are well-known human organizations built according to clear and explicit hierarchical lines. Other groups, such as the Mafia, have been cited as examples of hierarchical organizations.

Religious organizations often have a leader at the top with other high level leaders ranking just below him. Local organizations with their own leaders and hierarchical arrangements are under the top leaders. In a military situation such as combat, where direction must be decided upon quickly, there may not be time for the rational discussion needed for consensus that may be brought into play at other times. Orders are given, rank is "pulled." Hierarchy among humans is a way to organize complex groups, whether implicitly or explicitly. Like triangles, it may more easily be seen at times of higher anxiety in the group.

Bowen described a relationship posture called "the dysfunctional spouse" or "the adaptive posture," later referred to as overfunctioning/underfunctioning reciprocity where the underfunctioning person "gives up self" to the overfunctioner in the reciprocal relationship. "This is the result when a significant amount of undifferentiation is absorbed in the adaptive posture of one spouse. The dominant one assumes more and more responsibility for the twosome." (Bowen 1978, 378) This relationship posture may be homologous to Lorenz's ritual asymmetrical behavior, with the yielding subroutine of Dawkins strikingly similar to underfunctioning as described by Bowen.

If the emotional unit being considered is an organization rather than a family, it is not difficult to see how a series of these posturings (overfunctioning/underfunctioning reciprocities) can form a hierarchy. In this way, theoretically, the individual at the bottom of the hierarchy would be contributing self to each individual of higher rank in the system. The second individual from the bottom in rank would contribute self to everyone except the lowest one, but would be gaining some self from that one, and so on, up to the top. The individuals at the top of the hierarchy would be considered to be gaining the most self. The individuals at the bottom would be donating or giving up the most. Bowen described the adaptive, or underfunctioning position as being at risk for physical or other symptoms.

The one in a more dominant position does better, all things considered.

The Cost and Benefit of Hierarchy

What price is paid for hierarchy? Price and Sloman suggest that when two individuals engage in a fight for dominance, the losing animal shows signs of depression that reassure the winner that further fighting or discouragement are not necessary and that the individual is incapable of making a comeback. Schjelderup-Ebbe commented that

> hens lead a more or less worry free existence according to their position on the peck order." [A low-ranking hen was] very nervous because of the number of pecks she received. I had the impression that she tired herself out in a constant attempt to avoid punishment and to get enough food. [The high-ranking hen] who was never bothered by anybody, seemed to feel very well. . . . it is possible to trace the order of despotism in the appearance of the birds. Those which are despots over many thrive, become stout, look contented: those in the middle rank are usually normal; those which have nearly all the others over them are thin, restless, and often pine away. In the case of magpies and other birds which live in the same manner, we can correctly conclude which birds stand high on the pecking list and which low from the brightness of the plumage and the appearance of cleanliness. Those which stand low have rumpled, disordered plumage, often with dirt hanging to it, while the birds that have good social conditions have bright, sleek, beautiful and clean plumage. The birds which are dirty have little opportunity to clean themselves and keep themselves in order, partly because they are often chased immediately if they stand still, and partly because so much of their energy is used in obtaining food. (Price and Sloman 1987)

Sapolsky's work with olive baboons also pointed out the stressful nature of life at lower levels of the social primate hierarchy by measuring adrenocortical hormonal activity over time in individuals at different positions on the hierarchy . He was able to see striking differences in the levels of stress the animals lived with by the chronic differences in levels of adrenocortical hormones. (Sapolsky 1992)

Bowen described the effects of underfunctioning, or the "adaptive" posture thus:

> The one who functions for long periods in the adaptive position gradually loses the ability to function and make decisions for self. At that point, it requires no more than a moderate increase in stress to trigger the adaptive one into dysfunction, which can be physical illness, emotional illness, or social illness, such as drinking, acting out, and irresponsible behavior. These illnesses tend to become chronic, and they are hard to reverse. (Bowen 1978, 378)

This description by Bowen of a human relationship phenomenon would seem to be identical to descriptions of individuals at various levels on hierarchies of other species.

If hierarchy is so readily observed among species, it must be assumed that it is a useful part of the evolution of all life. What is the function of hierarchy ? Hierarchy seems to be a stabilizing force in other natural systems with the function of avoiding conflict in the group. No doubt hierarchical systems function for human organizations in the same way they do in groups of other species. As the underfunctioning individuals show more symptoms they convey less threat to the overfunctioners, so conflict becomes unnecessary and in this way the group becomes more stable, but at a price to some of the individuals.

Like other products of the evolution of emotional systems such as triangles, conflict or distance, hierarchy can be considered neither good nor bad. Since humans are products of evolution, they perpetuate emotional patterns of their evolutionary heritage. Individuals further up the hierarchical organization apparently are better off physiologically and seem to gain their advantage at the expense of those further down. And yet, even for those on the lower rungs, the benefits of being a part of the group may yet compensate for physiologic and other consequences of status. That is, it may be better to survive with symptoms than not to stay in the group, which could mean not surviving.

If hierarchy is a result of emotional programming—the automatic group interaction behavior we share with other species—then, as with other automatic patterns, we might expect that when anxiety rises, hierarchical behavior would be more in evidence. When the group is in relative calm, hierarchical behavior would be less in evidence and individuals could treat each other more as equals, rank being less important and apparent.

Differentiation as a Guide

The concept of differentiation provides a way of thinking about the relationships of individuals in a system that goes beyond automaticity. Differentiation of self, in "broad terms similar to an emotional maturity scale" (Bowen 1978, 472) yet different in some respects, defines the basic aspects of human existence largely in relationship terms. The concept provides a way for any individual to think about managing self in a hierarchy, whether at the top or the bottom. For example, when the leaders of an organization are acting out of a more differentiated position, one might expect them, by thoughtful focus on self, to display an open and facilitative posture to all members of the group, regardless of status. Status would be less emphasized by these leaders than qualities needed by the group, such as the creative and self-management potential of every member. A leader using differentiation as a guide would keep the goals of the organization in focus without sacrificing the creativity of any individual member. Such a leader would encourage participation of the best in all its members and find ways to deal with less mature aspects of individuals and the group as they arose.

Likewise members of lower ranks, acting with differentiation as a guide would seek to define self to all levels when necessary and appropriate, regardless of position. Further, when hierarchical behavior becomes more prominent at times of increasing anxiety in an organization, it can be seen for what it is, a manifestation of anxiety, and managed accordingly rather than allowing hierarchy by itself to determine the group member's destiny.

Consideration of the patterned reactions and interactions among individuals in an emotional system can provide guidelines for people as they seek to survive current upheavals of organizations going through downsizing and re-engineering. If hierarchy is a part of the evolutionary programming of the human, then attempts to reorganize organizations with the goal of doing away with hierarchy are probably destined for only limited success. In highly differentiated groups such a reorganization effort may modify hierarchical behaviors, but it would be expected that a covert, or implicit hierarchy will in fact appear, in spite of best attempts to legislate it away. As is a rare relationship that is relatively free of the over/underfunctioning reciprocity, it is probably a rare organization that is relatively free of hierarchical behavior and organization.

Presumably hierarchy would not exist in groups where every member was functioning at the theoretical and nonexistent "100" on the scale of differentiation. The separation of selfs would be so complete that there would be no need for the donating and lending that takes place at all levels below 100. Such a group would function as a collection of individuals. Different functions necessary to the survival of the group could be divided among its members without carrying any particular status. In this group it would be difficult for an observer to tell "leader" from "followers." Hierarchy would be a foreign concept although accomplishment could be recognized and valued.

REFERENCES

Bowen, Murray. 1978. *Family Therapy in Clinical Practice.* New York: Jason Aronson.

deWaal, Frans and Jan A. R. A. M. van Hooff. 1980. *Folia Primatologia.* 34:900-110

deWaal, Frans and Lesleigh Luttrell. 1988. "Three Primate Species: Symmetrical Relationship Characteristics or Cognition?" *Ethology and Sociobiology* 9:101-118.

Price, J. S. and L. Sloman. 1987. "Depression as Yielding Behavior: An Animal Model Based on Schjelderup-Ebbe's Pecking Order." *Ethology and Sociobiology* 8: 85S-98S.

Sapolsky, Robert. 1992. *Stress, the Aging Brain and the Mechanisms of Neuron Death.* Cambridge, Massachusetts: MIT Press.